Praise for *THE EFFORTLESS EXPERIENCE*

"Driving down customer effort results in pushing up brand loyalty, right along with sales."

—DANIEL F. BALISTIERRI,

vice president, Global Service & Experience, MasterCard

"Almost effortless reading, the pragmatic approach of the authors is just what we need to help us grapple with this global opportunity."

—DAVID THOMPSON,

managing director, Fusion Contact Centre Services

THE
EFFORTLESS
EXPERIENCE

The EFFORTLESS EXPERIENCE

CONQUERING THE NEW BATTLEGROUND FOR CUSTOMER LOYALTY

Matthew Dixon, Nick Toman, and Rick DeLisi

PORTFOLIO / PENGUIN

PORTFOLIO / PENGUIN
Published by the Penguin Group
Penguin Group (USA), 375 Hudson Street,
New York, New York 10014, USA

USA | Canada | UK | Ireland | Australia | New Zealand | India | South Africa | China

Penguin Books Ltd, Registered Offices: 80 Strand, London WC2R 0RL, England
For more information about the Penguin Group, visit penguin.com

LIBRARY OF CONGRESS CATALOGING IN PUBLICATION DATA
Dixon, Matthew, 1972–
    The effortless experience : conquering the new battleground for customer loyalty /
Matthew Dixon, Nick Toman, and Rick DeLisi.
        pages   cm
    Includes bibliographical references and index.
    ISBN 978-1-59184-581-2
    1. Customer ralations.   2. Customer loyalty.   I. Toman, Nick.
II. DeLisi, Rick.   III. Title
    HF5415.5.D576   2013
    658.8'12—dc23   2013017449

Printed in the United States of America

10 9 8 7 6 5 4 3 2

Book design by Elyse Strongin

To the members of CEB around the world, who challenge us every day
to deliver insights worthy of their time and attention

CONTENTS

FOREWORD

On July 16, 2012, Shaea Labus, a Zappos customer service representative, took a call from a customer named Lisa. Their conversation started with shoes and broadened out to other areas of life: movies and favorite foods and more. They talked and talked and talked some more. At one point, Shaea took a bathroom break and came back to the phone; helpful colleagues brought her food. In total, their conversation lasted nine hours and thirty-seven minutes. "Sometimes people just need to call and talk," explained another Zappos rep.[1]

In a North Carolina Nordstrom, a security guard spotted a woman crawling around on the floor, frantically looking for something. She'd lost the diamond from her engagement ring. The guard and two other employees joined the search, and after a long, fruitless combing of the area, they finally discovered the diamond buried deep inside the bag of a vacuum cleaner.[2]

One clear evening at the Four Seasons in Kapalua, Maui, a bartender overheard a honeymooning couple talking about how lovely the moon looked. The next morning, someone knocked on the door of their suite. To their shock, it was a NASA administrator, holding up two space suits. "Guess who's taking our space shuttle for a ride today?" he said, smiling. "Better bring a bag for the moon rocks."

Okay, I made that last one up.

The other two stories are true, though. And you've probably heard many more like them. We live in a golden age of customer service, an era when many customer service leaders say explicitly that their goal is to "delight the customer." (Parenthetically, "delight the customer" is a truly odd-sounding phrase to have caught on in our sober business world. Should we also aspire to "mesmerize our employees" and "titillate our vendors"?)

The idea, of course, is that customer service operations should aspire to provide superlative service—service that is so good, so over-the-top that it's surprising and memorable. Delightful.

It's a worthy goal. But what if it's dead wrong?

What if, in fact, these viral stories of delightful service have served as a siren song for customer service leaders, luring them away from a more sensible and effective mission?

There are times when stories stick too well—when they are so compelling that they distort our thinking. Take, for instance, the phenomenon of people being "discovered" on YouTube. A few years ago, Neal Schon, the lead guitarist of the band Journey, came across a video of a Filipino named Arnel Pineda, who was singing Journey cover songs. Pineda was so mind-bogglingly good that he was invited to be Journey's new lead singer. Another YouTube discovery involved a young Canadian singer named Justin Bieber. (Somehow I suspect you've heard that one.)

These YouTube tales have everything we crave in a story: likable heroes who make it big. The drama of unexpected discovery. The emotion of a rags-to-riches tale. But we must be careful not to confuse a great story with a great strategy. The fact that Justin Bieber was discovered online does not mean that a budding young rapper should blow his savings producing YouTube videos. That's lottery-ticket logic. (*Someone has to win, why not me?*)

Similarly, the fact that the public loves sticky customer service stories does not mean that customer service leaders should gear up their departments to deliver them. It's not so much that delivering these stories is improbable, in the way that becoming a YouTube sensation is improbable. Certainly any customer service rep could be trained to stay on the phone for nine hours. ("What's your five-digit zip code? Thank you, Ms. Barkley. Now, let's start with your childhood.")

Rather, it's that "delighting customers" is an inspirational but potentially misguided goal. Most companies are nothing like Nordstrom or Zappos, which bet their brands on service. Do we really need our credit card companies or utilities trying to "delight" us? (Personally, I'd settle for not having to repeat aloud the very same account number that I just punched into the phone eight seconds prior.)

Maybe customer service should be less about offense—bending over backwards to please customers—and more about *defense,* in the sense of preventing frustration and delay. What if the Holy Grail of service isn't customer delight but customer *relief*—the simple relaxing of the shoulders that comes from having your problem handled quickly and smoothly?

In the pages ahead, you'll follow a business detective story, in which cherished truths about customer service are systematically investigated—and frequently debunked. *The Effortless Experience* is what every business book should be like: stuffed with practical advice, well supported by research, and written in a way that will keep you eagerly flipping the pages.

Along the way, you'll find out the solution to the mega-mystery—should customer service departments aim for delight or relief?—and also encounter lots of fascinating mini-mysteries like these:

- What irritates customers more, being transferred or being forced to repeat information?
- What happened when Linksys stopped offering customer service via e-mail? Did costs go up or down? Did people switch to phone or self-service?
- And what's the fatal flaw with the seemingly smart metric, used by hundreds of companies, that tracks "first call resolution" (that is, the number of customers whose issues were resolved successfully during the first phone call)?

Turn the page to find the answers. And if you find yourself *delighted* by what you read and you want to discuss it with someone, don't forget there are Zappos reps standing by to take your call . . .

—DAN HEATH,
Co-author of *Decisive, Switch,* and *Made to Stick*

THE
EFFORTLESS
EXPERIENCE

INTRODUCTION:

BLINDED BY DELIGHT

Have you ever heard the story of Joshie the giraffe?

Joshie is the property of a little boy who, during a family trip to a Ritz-Carlton in Amelia Island, Florida, accidentally left him behind in his room when the family was checking out. As you can imagine, Joshie's owner was borderline apoplectic when he realized he'd gone missing, and so his parents did what any sane parent would do. They told their son that Joshie wasn't "missing," per se; he was just taking an extended vacation. Just a small ruse to get the boy to go to sleep.

As it turns out, they weren't exaggerating. Joshie, you see, was in very good hands.

Upon finding him, the housecleaning staff at the Ritz-Carlton brought him to the hotel's Loss Prevention Team, who called the family to tell them that they'd found Joshie in the hotel laundry and thought they might want him back. Needless to say, the little boy's parents were thrilled to find out that his beloved stuffed animal had been located.

But instead of doing what most companies would do and just mailing Joshie back to his owner, the team at the Ritz-Carlton went the extra mile.

The loss prevention manager instructed his team to document Joshie's "extended stay" at the hotel. They created a photo album with pictures of the giraffe lounging by the pool, getting a massage (with the requisite slices of cucumber over his eyes), relaxing on the beach, making new (stuffed animal) friends, and heading out in a golf cart to play eighteen holes. Not only that, but Joshie and his photo album were shipped to the family in a box full of free Ritz-Carlton swag.

It's a heartwarming story and really epitomizes what it means to receive extraordinary customer service—service that *delights*. But if you're a business person, you know what this really is: a story about building lifetime customer loyalty.

Business people know that the *truest* test of a company's ability to delight is when things go wrong—when a problem or issue arises and the customer needs the company's help to fix it. Customer service is the crucible of the customer experience—the place where all of the company's claims, its mission and its values, are tested. And it's been a long-held belief in business that when your customer is most in need of help and you deliver an "above and beyond" service experience, you are effectively building a moat around your customer relationship, one that keeps your customers close and your competitors at bay.

It's for this reason that managers celebrate these rare moments of customer delight when they happen. Companies plaster the thank-you notes and e-mails from grateful customers on the walls of their service center (almost always called "The Wall of Fame"). They recognize employees at the annual company meeting for going the extra mile. These stories of selfless service become the stuff of legend in company hallways, the new bar to which all employees are asked to aspire. Not only that, but companies spend millions on training and consulting engagements to help their frontline staff more effectively and consistently deliver these "moments of wow" to customers.

Stories like the one about Joshie the giraffe force a kind of deep introspection for senior service leaders. There probably wasn't a company executive anywhere in the world who, upon hearing the Joshie story for the first time, didn't immediately furrow her brow and wonder aloud, "How can *we* deliver that kind of experience to our customers? How do I get *my* people to go above and beyond like that? Why can't *our* company be known for that kind of delightful service?"

The questions we ask ourselves aren't about *whether* we should delight our customers, but rather *how* to delight them. We know that serving customers this way is *best*—we feel it deep in our bones.

There's just one problem.

While delighting customers with above-and-beyond service feels right and seems to make a great deal of sense at an intuitive level, the reality is that for virtually every company out there, the Joshie story is in fact a perfect example of what *not* to base your service strategy on.

While most companies have for decades been pouring time, energy, and resources into the singular pursuit of creating and replicating the delightful experience for their customers, they've ironically missed the very thing customers *are actually looking for*—a closer-in, more attainable, replicable, and affordable goal that's been sitting right in front of them all this time: *the effortless experience*. This book is the road map for building that experience.

1

THE NEW BATTLEGROUND FOR CUSTOMER LOYALTY

We don't know exactly what you do for a living. The topic of customer experience management is so broad, so encompassing, that this book will be read by any number of professionals—heads of customer service, marketers, contact center supervisors, web site designers, consultants, small business owners, and even CEOs.

But while we don't know what hat you wear from nine to five, we do know what you do the rest of the time: Like all of us, you're a customer. You go grocery shopping, you take the dog to the vet, and you go on vacations. You choose what cable operator to use, where to take your car to get the oil changed, where to get your shirts laundered. You make dozens—maybe hundreds—of decisions in a week about what products and services to buy and from whom to buy them. Some of these decisions you don't even think about, such as when you flip on the TV or fill up your gas tank, but others are significant and time-consuming—for example, when you buy a new car or laptop, or when you pick a contractor for a major home improvement.

So, thinking with your customer "hat" on, consider the following two questions: First, what companies do you do business with or buy from *specifically* because of the exceptional customer service they provide? Second, what companies have you *stopped* buying from and refused to do business with because of the awful service you've experienced?

We're willing to bet that you found the second question a lot easier to answer than the first. Consider those companies that you buy from strictly because of their great service, because they go "above and beyond." You might be able to think of one or two—a special restaurant or resort, for instance—but that's a rarity for most. But the other question—naming those you've stopped buying from—is much easier to answer, isn't it? You could probably fill up a list a mile long with companies you've stopped doing business with because of the bad service you've experienced: the cable company that makes you take a day off from work because they can't do better than an all-day service window, the dry cleaner that ruined your favorite suit and refuses to reimburse you, the airline that lost your bags en route to a long-awaited vacation, the contractor who never showed up to finish the punch list, the bank that took five phone calls to resolve your issue.

Why is that? Why are customers much quicker to punish companies for bad service than to reward them for good service?

It's this mystery that lies at the heart of this book.

Killing Them with Kindness

In many ways, it's no surprise that many senior leaders see customer service as a great opportunity to differentiate their companies in the market.

Commoditization, not just of products but of brand promises, is one of the unavoidable hard truths of doing business in the twenty-first century. The time from launch to peak of market acceptance to everyone else ripping off your great new idea and calling it their own is shrinking down to almost nothing. As soon as you have something that you think sets you apart, your competitors launch an identical product or service or make a similar claim. It's no surprise that customers can't tell the difference between companies they do business with. According to a recent study by our company, CEB, customers see only about 20 percent of corporate brands as *truly* differentiated (see figure 1.1). All others look more or less like flavors of the same thing, with very little difference from one to the next.

With so little opportunity to stand apart with their products or even their brands, many companies have turned to *customer service*—not just the routine delivery of everyday service, but specifically the *issue resolution* experience normally delivered over the phone or on the web—to help them differentiate themselves in a world of sameness. Pick up any trade rag written for the customer service or contact center industry and

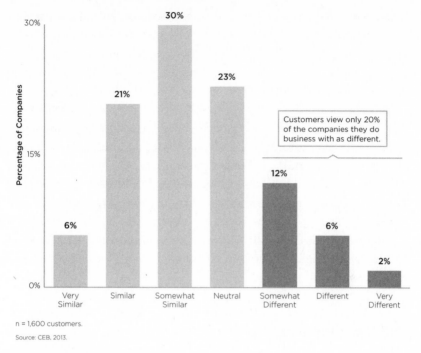

n = 1,600 customers.

Source: CEB, 2013.

Figure 1.1 Customer Views on Company Uniqueness

it's clear those guys got the memo. One magazine proclaims that "Loyalty is now driven primarily by a company's interactions with its customers."[1] Another declares that "Customer loyalty is an ongoing relationship and the key is, of course, excellent customer support."[2]

But does this strategy even make sense? Should companies try to create differentiation and build customer loyalty by delivering superior service?

Before we answer this, let's back up for a moment and define what we mean by "loyalty." For the purposes of this book—and in particular the data we'll discuss in this chapter—we will cast the widest net possible by defining loyalty in terms of three specific behaviors: *repurchase* (customers continue to buy from your company), *share of wallet* (customers buy more from you over time), and *advocacy* (customers say good things about your company to family, friends, coworkers, even to strangers).

As you can see from how we're defining it, loyalty is much more than what we call "retention" or "locking in" customers so they can't or won't start buying from your competitors. In other words, it's not just getting them to stay with you because they *have* to, but rather because they *want* to. Plus, they don't keep you at arm's length; they actually increase spend with you over time and tell others that you are a company worth buying from. That's *real* loyalty.

This concept isn't just for business-to-consumer (B2C) companies. Business-to-business (B2B) organizations are also looking for the same thing from their customers. Of course, getting to loyalty can be more challenging in the B2B context because it has to be achieved twice, not just with your actual business customers (i.e., the decision makers who sign the contract) but also with end users (i.e., the people who use the product or service). The story we're about to tell will be one that is consistent across both B2C and B2B operating environments, though we'll be sure to highlight any important differences in the data—and our recommendations—throughout.

The Big Questions

Over the past several years we've conducted hundreds of conversations with customer service leaders around the world in every imaginable industry and have found that the conversation on customer loyalty comes down to three fundamental questions:

1. To what extent does customer service matter in driving customer loyalty? It seems like everyone believes that customer service plays a major role, but how exactly?

2. What are the things customer service can do to drive customer loyalty? Most companies are working to create some form of "extraordinary service"—attempting to build better relationships with customers, believing that will make them more loyal. But as any service leader will tell you, that's incredibly hard to achieve on any kind of consistent basis.

3. How can customer service improve loyalty, while also reducing operating costs? Any idea that sounds great on paper but costs millions is very unlikely to get the green light in the current "do more with less" environment. Even when you can make a rock-solid business case, the average company is still incredibly conservative when it comes to new expenditures. We're all looking for smart ways to allocate our limited budgets.

Our Methodology in Brief

We constructed a quantitative research model to answer these pressing questions. We wanted to know—directly from actual customers— exactly which elements of the interaction with customer service have the biggest effect on making people more (or less) loyal.

At the heart of our work was a widespread study of customer service interactions. Our company manages the world's largest network of customer service organizations (the Customer Contact Leadership Council)—more than 400 companies around the world are members. These companies gave us unprecedented customer access to conduct our research.

In the first of these surveys, over 97,000 customers—all of whom had a recent service interaction over the web or through calling a contact center and were able to remember the details clearly—were asked to answer a series of questions about their recent service interactions: What *really* happened when they contacted the company? How well did it actually solve their problem? Generally speaking, these questions fell into three categories: (1) questions about the customer's experience with the service rep they interacted with; (2) questions about the amount of energy or number of steps, generally speaking, the customer had to put into the service interaction (what we've dubbed "customer effort"); and (3) questions about the company's ability to deliver a delightful experience to the customer. Let's cover each of these categories briefly.

•   •   •

PARTIAL LIST OF VARIABLES TESTED		
Experience with the Rep	**Customer Effort**	**Moments of "Wow"**
• Rep confidence	• Number of transfers	• Willingness of service to go "above and beyond"
• Rep understanding of customer	• Repeating information	
• Rep listening ability	• First contact resolution	• Applying knowledge about customer
• Personalization of service	• Number of contacts to resolve	• Exceeding customer expectations
• Rep knowledge of how to resolve issue	• Perceived additional effort to resolve	• Teaching the customer
• Rep concern	• Ease of contacting service	• Offering alternatives
• Rep tailoring to customer state of mind	• Channel switching	• Perceived value of alternatives offered
• Rep accent	• Time to resolve	
• Rep setting of expectations		
• Certainty of follow-through		

First, in terms of the interaction with the service representative, we were looking to understand how customer service reps (also known as "agents" or "associates" or "CSRs") handled the issue. For instance, in the customer's estimation, was the rep confident? Was she a good listener? Did she have the knowledge required to address the customer's issue? Did she show a clear understanding of the customer's issue? Did she demonstrate ownership of the issue, or did she pass the buck to somebody else?

Second, in the area of customer effort, we asked about things such as whether the customer had to contact the company repeatedly to get his issue resolved, whether he was transferred to another department or rep, whether he had to repeat himself, his perception of how hard it was to get his problem fixed, how easy it was to contact the company, whether he had to switch channels at any point (e.g., starting on the web, but then having to resort to the phone), the total time it took to get the problem fixed, and so on.

Lastly, we wanted to get a sense of whether the company did any of the "little things" that we tend to think delight customers. Did the company go above and beyond to resolve the customer's issue? Did the company demonstrate any depth of knowledge about the customer and his history with them? Did the company teach the customer something new about their product or service? And, generally speaking, did the company exceed the customer's expectations in the course of resolving his issue?

In addition to these experience-based questions, we asked for information that we would later use as control variables in our analysis. These included each respondent's age, sex, income, the type of issue they were calling about (simple or complex, service or sales), their personality type, and their mood prior to contact. We also collected data on additional control variables, including the perceived switching costs of leaving the company, exposure to company advertising, and perceived product quality, price, and value.

From a company perspective, we collected data from companies whose service organizations provide service only, as well as those that provide service and sales. We included both in-house and outsourced service organizations, onshore, near-shore, and offshore. We also had representation from companies large and small and from every major industry and geographic market imaginable.

By controlling for these variables, we were able to isolate the elements of loyalty that are specific to customer service—even where there are variations between different types of companies—so that the results really do represent the *universal* truths that we found, the things that are foundationally true for *all* companies.

At the end of the survey, we asked customers to assess both their satisfaction with the experience and their loyalty to the company based on the service interaction in question. Specifically, we asked how likely they would be to keep buying from the company, buy more over time, and advocate on the company's behalf.

The survey categories described above are just a simple construct for explaining what we studied. Naturally, we could have segmented things differently, but what matters most is that this was an exhaustive study of the customer's service experience, covering not just the facts about the customer (who they are and what they wanted help with), but what they went through to get their issue resolved and how they felt about the experience. From a service standpoint, this allowed us to cast a very broad net in order to understand which of the variables we tested had the biggest impact on that individual customer's loyalty to the company in question. In other words, of all the things in a service interaction that *could* make customers loyal to companies, which ones actually *do*?

An important disclosure before we reveal the results and their implications: We intentionally limited this study to service transactions and their impact on customer loyalty. Obviously, customer loyalty is a product of *all* the interactions a customer has with a company—its brand and reputation, their friends' and family's perceptions of the company, the value and quality of the products, and of course customer service, among other things. This allowed us to understand, in great detail, the impact that each service interaction can have on total customer loyalty. Moreover, it allowed us to understand what specific actions business leaders can take to maximize customer loyalty resulting specifically from service interactions.

Through all of this research, we ended up with a few *million* data points, which were then boiled down to what turned out to be four simple but profound findings.

The Conventional Wisdom

Before we show you what we found, let's pause for a moment to consider the conventional wisdom out there. We asked dozens of companies around the world to describe their strategy to achieve customer loyalty within customer service, and by far the preponderant answer was that most organizations try to provide a level of satisfaction that *exceeds the customer's expectations.*

Companies strongly believe customer satisfaction leads directly to loyalty—by a margin of 83 percent to 12 percent (with 5 percent unsure). Not surprisingly then, an overwhelming percentage of the companies we surveyed (89 percent to be exact) told us they were either focusing *more* of their efforts on exceeding expectations or they're *continuing* their focus in this direction. As one vice president of customer service from a consumer electronics company told us, "Our biggest growth opportunity comes from delighting our customers. If we're not delighting customers, we're not doing our job."

What companies tell us is that they try to do this—not just because it feels good, but because they strongly believe there are significant economic gains to be made by exceeding the service expectations of their customers.

If one were to graphically depict the conventional wisdom, it would look a lot like what you see in figure 1.2. Service leaders believe that

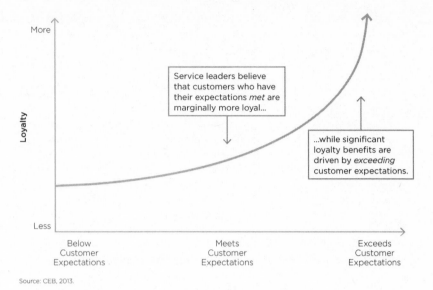

Source: CEB, 2013.

Figure 1.2 Perceived Impact of Customer Service on Loyalty

customers who simply have their expectations *met* are only marginally more loyal, while significant loyalty benefits accrue once customer expectations are *exceeded*. The belief that a tremendous loyalty payout awaits firms that exceed customer expectations is, again, firmly rooted across companies around the world.

In other words, the common belief is that when service is *below* customer expectations, loyalty is also subpar. But as satisfaction improves beyond simply meeting expectations, all the way to *exceeding* expectations, loyalty naturally rises—exponentially.

This leads us to the first of our four major findings.

FINDING #1: *A Strategy of Delight Doesn't Pay*

While leaders clearly believe in the power of exceeding customer expectations in building customer loyalty, the data tells a different story. As we analyze responses from more than 97,000 customers, what we find is that there is virtually *no difference at all* between the loyalty of those customers whose expectations are exceeded and those whose expectations are simply met (see figure 1.3). Rather than a "hockey stick effect"—where loyalty skyrockets upward—loyalty actually *plateaus* once customer expectations are met.

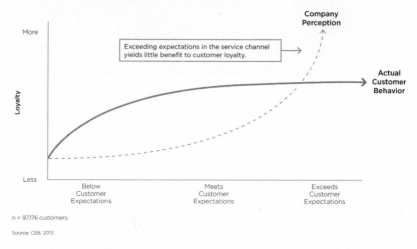

Figure 1.3 Impact of Customer Service on Loyalty: Perceived vs. Actual

There are two big takeaways here. First, companies tend to grossly *underestimate* the benefit of simply meeting customer expectations. In a world in which customer expectations are significantly inflated and seemingly on the rise all the time, what we find is that customers are in fact quite happy to simply get what was promised them. If there happens to be a problem, just resolve it quickly and easily. No more, no less. It's a surprising finding, and one that stands in stark contrast to most of what is reported in the trade press or presented by self-proclaimed customer experience gurus.

Think about what that means for how contact centers, other service organizations, even entire businesses are managed. Once you're consistently meeting the expectations of the majority of your customers, you've *already done* the most economically valuable thing you can do.

Second, companies tend to massively *overestimate* the loyalty returns from exceeding customer expectations. If your goal is to increase loyalty, it turns out that whatever additional resources, energy, or budget you need to consistently *exceed* expectations brings almost no corresponding financial return at all. Of the two takeaways here, this one is clearly the more surprising to service leaders and is seen as the more provocative counterpoint to conventional wisdom. How could it be that going above and beyond—"wowing" the customer—doesn't make the customer more loyal? The very idea itself doesn't seem to make sense, but as we analyze a massive sample of customer service interactions, this is exactly what we find.

Every company has legendary stories about some rep who did some remarkable thing to wildly exceed a customer's expectations, and as a result that customer was impressed enough to write a letter to the CEO about it, which is now displayed prominently in the contact center break room. One VP of customer service at a large U.S. bank told us the story of a rep who took several hours off the phone to make sure that loan documents that were needed for a closing were completed. She hunted down a notary and then drove the loan docs to the branch office closest to the customer so that the customer could sign them. The VP told this story so many times at their regular all-hands meetings that almost every rep could repeat it verbatim.

But as powerful and compelling as these stories are, what if you checked back with those same customers a year or two down the road to see how much *more* business they're bringing you? Because the data shows that in the aggregate, customers who are moved from a level of "below expectations" up to "meets expectations" offer about the *same* economic value as those whose expectations were exceeded

The data tells us that from a customer's perspective, when something goes wrong, the overriding sentiment is: *Help me fix it.* No need to dazzle me, please just solve the problem and let me get back to what I was doing before. It's a sobering thought for service leaders who've grown up in companies where creating moments of sheer delight and exceeding expectations are celebrated.

When we present this data to senior leaders, the immediate reaction typically resembles something like the stages of grieving. First, there is denial . . . but, eventually, there is acceptance. Think about it. What does it take to constantly delight customers who are having some problem? In practice, it means longer calls, more escalations—not to mention costly giveaways, refunds, and policy exceptions. In fact, an overwhelming majority (roughly 80 percent) of senior leaders we surveyed told us that a strategy of exceeding customer expectations means significantly higher operational costs for their business—depending on the company we asked, the estimates range from 10 percent higher to more than 20 percent. In short, delight is expensive.

What's more, delight is rare. According to the customers in our study, their expectations were exceeded a mere 16 percent of the time. An overwhelming 84 percent of the time, customer expectations were *not* exceeded (and indeed, often not even met). Delight is a tough target to hit with any regularity, and we typically miss that target. That it is so exceptional is what makes it so memorable.

However, basic competence, professional service, getting the fundamentals right . . . it turns out that these things really do matter, *maybe even more than we'd led ourselves to believe.*

"Okay," you might be thinking, "but our company has staked our entire brand on our ability to delight customers—our whole strategy is premised on going above and beyond." When we present this research to companies, we often hear this objection. What we ask, in turn, is whether they can *truly* lay claim to a "delight" strategy. For how many of these questions can your company answer with a firm "yes":

- Would customer service leaders approach the CEO or CFO to ask for *additional funds* to support their ability to delight the customer in the service channel?
- Does your company empower frontline reps to do *anything* possible to exceed customer expectations, regardless of cost?
- If your product or service doesn't live up to customer expectations, would you allow your customers to choose any replacement or alternative—*outside of the warranty period* and perhaps even *beyond the value* of the original product?
- Have you removed *all productivity measures* (such as call length, also known as handle time) from frontline staff scorecards so that they can focus all of their energy on delighting customers and delivering the highest-quality experience possible?

Sure, there are some companies that do pass this high hurdle (e.g., some of the companies cited in the foreword and introduction, such as the Ritz-Carlton hotel chain, where reportedly even a janitor has the discretionary authority to spend money to help resolve customer issues). But time and again, we find that most companies claiming a true delight strategy tend to wither under such cross-examination. And truthfully, one might ask the question of whether the real "delight brands" out there are exceeding customer expectations at all, or are they just meeting the amazingly high expectations they themselves have set over the years? When you stay at a Motel 6 property, what do you expect? A low price, a clean room, and some baseline of decently acceptable service, but nothing like what you'd get at a Ritz-Carlton. And that's perfectly fine. Expectations, after all, are relative.

We spent a lot of time exploring the underlying reason for this disconnect. How could it be that no matter what a customer's expectations going into a service interaction may be, *exceeding* those expectations doesn't create an increase in loyalty? Some deeper analysis of the data leads us to our second major finding.

FINDING #2: *Satisfaction Is Not a Predictor of Loyalty*

For students of marketing and the massive amount of work done on the customer experience, most notably Fred Reichheld's groundbreaking work on the Net Promoter Score, this next finding may come as no surprise, but time and again, we find that most senior leaders remain in the dark about the real relationship between satisfaction and loyalty, a conclusion verified by our own study of customer service interactions.

In our global survey, we found virtually no statistical relationship between how a customer rates a company on a satisfaction survey and their future customer loyalty (see figure 1.4). To be precise, we found an

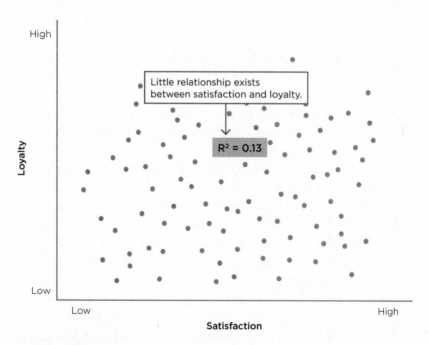

Little relationship exists between satisfaction and loyalty.

$R^2 = 0.13$

n = 97,176 customers.

Source: CEB, 2013.

Figure 1.4 The Relationship of Customer Satisfaction Compared to Loyalty

R-squared of 0.13. (For those non-statisticians out there, an R-squared of 0.0 would mean no relationship at all, and an R-squared of 1.0 would mean a perfect correlation.)

By way of comparison, researchers have shown the correlation between "getting good grades in school" and "achieving career success later in life" is 0.71. But between satisfaction and loyalty—two things that many leaders have long assumed to be strongly related (to the extent that many believe that satisfaction actually *causes* loyalty)—the relationship we found was weak at best.

Again, how's *that* possible?

When we dig into the data, we find that fully 20 percent of the customers who reported that they were satisfied by their service interaction also expressed *at the same time* that they were actually intending to leave the company and buy from somebody else. That's pretty scary. They said they were satisfied, but that didn't mean they were loyal. However, just as much of a head-scratcher, 28 percent of customers who reported that they were *dis*satisfied told us they fully intend to stay loyal.

Of course, that sounds a whole lot better, except for the troubling fact that many companies still consider customer satisfaction (CSAT) rates as the barometer for customer service success. Unfortunately, the data tells us that a strong CSAT score is not a very reliable predictor for whether customers will be loyal—whether they'll repurchase from you, buy more from you, and say good things about you to friends, family, and coworkers. Now, we're not suggesting for a second that companies shouldn't want their customers to be satisfied. It's just that when we ask a customer, "How satisfied were you with the service you just received?" their answer doesn't provide us with a strong indication of their future loyalty behaviors. Again, satisfaction and loyalty are not the same thing, and aren't even well correlated.

As one of our members said, "We are at 8.2 on the CSAT scale (1–10). To get to 8.6 or 8.8 might cost us millions of dollars, but will we get millions of dollars in return? I don't think so. We are at the top of the CSAT scale—and that is where all of our competitors are too, so we have to find a different way to set ourselves apart."

CSAT is one of those metrics that's simply taken for granted in companies. We're not suggesting it's a bad thing to measure, just that it's not nearly as predictive of future loyalty as all of us in the industry have always assumed. And this isn't just our finding. It's one that's been verified by others in the field. According to Reichheld in his book *The*

Ultimate Question, 60 to 80 percent of customers who ultimately defect had said they were *satisfied* or even *very satisfied* the last time they participated in a survey.[3] As a chief customer officer at a telecommunications company told us in a moment of frustration around CSAT, "I just don't know what it means and I don't see any point in trying to decode it. Let the rest of them try to make sense of it."

A metaphor that has helped us distinguish satisfaction and loyalty came from a director of operations at a financial services firm, who told us of his love of a good steak dinner. He explained, "I live in a small town with only one steakhouse. The steak there is fine. But the minute a new restaurant opens, you bet I'll go there. So am I satisfied? Sure. Loyal? No way."

So far we've learned that a delight strategy doesn't pay . . . and that satisfied customers by no means translate into loyal customers. But there's still one more piece of bad news.

FINDING #3: *Customer Service Interactions Tend to Drive Disloyalty, Not Loyalty*

The harsh reality of the customer service world is that we tend to do more harm than good. To be precise, according to our research, *any* customer service interaction is *four times* more likely to drive *disloyalty* than to drive loyalty (see figure 1.5).

In some respects, this feels unfair. After all, the customer service team is typically called upon only after something's gone wrong. So the job of service is to return the customer to a state of neutrality—back to where they started before the problem occurred in the first place. And that's *good* customer service. As we discussed earlier, most companies often don't even meet customer expectations, so the result is that most customers end up more disloyal to our companies than before they called. We tend to make things worse—in some cases, *much* worse.

The data also tells us that the consequences are disastrous—because those customers we make disloyal are much more likely to spread that disloyalty to other potential customers, through negative word of mouth.

If you want to fully understand customer loyalty, one question you really need to consider is: What kinds of experiences have the biggest impact (both positive *and* negative)? Not just how would a customer

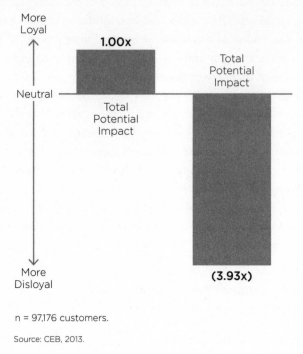

n = 97,176 customers.

Source: CEB, 2013.

Figure 1.5 Impact of Customer Service on Customer Loyalty

rate those experiences in a satisfaction survey, but which ones would cause enough of a reaction to make that person want to *tell everyone they know?*

What we find in the data is startling.

Let's start with customers' experiences with products. What we find is that 71 percent of people who have positive product experiences engage in word of mouth, but only 32 percent of customers with a negative product experience want to tell other people (see figure 1.6) about it. Now let's contrast product experiences with customer service experiences. Poor customer service experiences are much more likely to create negative word of mouth—a 65 percent likelihood, to be exact—compared to only a 25 percent likelihood that a customer will spread positive word of mouth about excellent customer service. As the data plainly shows, customers hardly ever talk about good service experiences. When it comes to customer service, the vast majority of the word of mouth that gets spread is just plain negative.

That also seems pretty unfair, but unfortunately it makes sense when

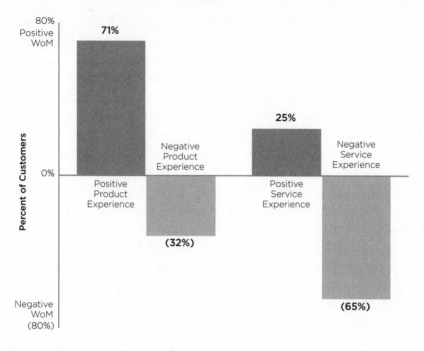

n = 97,176 customers.

Source: CEB, 2013.

Figure 1.6 Customer Word of Mouth by Experience Type

you think about what motivates people. What motivates people to say *anything* about your company?

When people have a positive product experience, word of mouth usually comes in the form of a recommendation: "Hey, I have to tell you about this cool new gadget I bought, or great new restaurant or hotel I found, or some excellent new company I discovered!" We believe there's a basic psychological explanation for this. When we discover something great, we want to tell other people as a reflection of our own wisdom. If, for instance, I recommend a great new restaurant to you and then you actually go there, you'll probably seek me out to thank me as a result. It's almost like I get the credit for it. I didn't actually cook your meal, but somehow I still get to *own* your love of that restaurant.

On the other hand, when it comes to customer service, people are much more likely to vocalize about a *negative* service experience. At a psychological level, when a person has a bad service interaction, their primary motivation in telling others is to evoke their sympathy:

"I'm the victim . . . I was disrespected . . . I'm a smart person, but that service rep treated me like an idiot!" Friends and family immediately come to your aid: "How awful for you to go through such a bad experience. You deserve better treatment than that! You poor thing."

In fact, a vice president of customer service we work with told us that on a recent business trip, he ran into a fellow guest in a hotel elevator—a person he'd never met before in his life—who immediately launched into a full-on tirade about how bad the service was in the hotel's restaurant, strongly recommending that he eat elsewhere and that they join forces in depriving the hotel restaurant of any additional business. "My first thought," he told us, "was that I should change my dinner plans. But my second thought was whether my service organization was doing anything to our customers to generate this kind of customer backlash and negative word of mouth. I then lost my appetite altogether and went back to my room."

All of this is borne out clearly when you consider the *reach* of word of mouth—in other words, the number of people who are on the receiving end when we get on our soapbox.

The data from our study show that 45 percent of the people who had something positive to say about a company told fewer than three other people (see figure 1.7). By contrast, 48 percent of people who had negative things to say reported that negative-speak to more than ten people.

And the stark reality is that the web and social media have made getting on a soapbox much easier for customers. Blogs, Twitter, Facebook, LinkedIn . . . they all enable customers to amplify their voices, to reach hundreds, thousands, even millions of your current and potential customers. Look up the Facebook page of any major company and you'll see as much: So many of the comments you'll find are about bad service—customers who feel they've been wronged by the company, venting for the entire world to see.

This isn't just bluster. There's strong evidence that negative reactions are a far more powerful "change agent" among customers—almost twice as strong, in fact.[4] Suffering through a service experience, whether it was outright rude service or, as we'll discuss in a moment, an experience with a high "hassle factor," drives customers to want to tell anyone and everyone who's willing to listen.

We almost can't help but wonder, is there even such a thing as a negative *product* experience? This is all pretty semantic—it's hard to prove through research—but think about your own experiences. If you

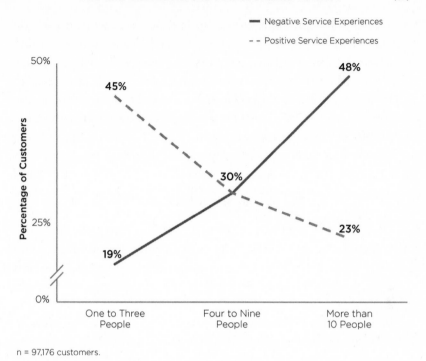

n = 97,176 customers.

Source: CEB, 2013.

Figure 1.7 Reach of Customer Word of Mouth by Experience Type

have a negative issue with a product—the Bluetooth in your new car stops working or your flight to Hawaii just got canceled or your insurance company won't cover water damage from a leaky pipe—is that a *product* problem, or does it morph into a *service* problem? Who gets the blame?

In fact, have you ever stopped to think about why we pick—or drop—the companies we do business with? Here's a simple example to illustrate: Almost all of us have that one airline we avoid at nearly all costs, maybe because they lost our bags and it took ten phone calls to track them down, or maybe because they refused to give us mileage credit for a flight we obviously flew. Whatever the reason, they delivered an awful service experience and now have incurred our wrath. Now, what makes us pick the *next* airline we give our business to? Do we pick our next carrier on the basis of which airline has the best service reputation? Probably not. We pick based on price and flight availability as long as it isn't "those guys." In other words, *we pick companies because of their products, but we often leave them because of their service failures.*

While all of this might sound a little depressing at first glance, it's actually some very valuable knowledge you should use as you rethink your strategy. By any objective measure, customer service is a huge driver of disloyalty—and the negative experiences that service tends to create get amplified in the public arena. It's clear that the role of customer service, therefore, is not to drive loyalty by delighting customers, but to *mitigate customer disloyalty.*

The question is: How, exactly, do we do that?

FINDING #4: *The Key to Mitigating Disloyalty Is Reducing Customer Effort*

When we peel apart the data to see what's driving the customer service disloyalty effect, what comes out is an incredibly clear picture—and one, frankly, that's quite different from the conventional wisdom (see figure 1.8).

What we find is that the specific things customer service does to drive disloyalty among customers are largely associated with the amount of work—or effort—customers must put forth to get their issues resolved.

In fact, *four of the five* drivers of disloyalty are about additional effort customers must put forth. Having to contact the company more than once to resolve the problem is the biggest of all, delivering a massive potential negative impact on loyalty. Because of its importance in the effort story, we'll devote an entire chapter to discussing some very specific research we've done around the whole concept of *first contact resolution* (FCR), often held up as the Holy Grail of customer service organizations. It turns out that FCR is something of a red herring. Leading companies don't stop just at FCR, but actually think more about how to help customers avoid downstream issues. As a customer, imagine how refreshing it would be to have a service rep *proactively* suggest ways to solve issues that will likely happen after you hang up the phone, helping you to avoid having to call again unnecessarily. We've dubbed this concept *next issue avoidance,* and we'll talk about it in much more detail in chapter 3.

The next biggest driver of disloyalty is "generic service"—when a customer feels like the rep is treating them like a number, making no attempt to personalize the experience whatsoever. As customers, we know the pain of this sort of treatment all too well. The disinterested

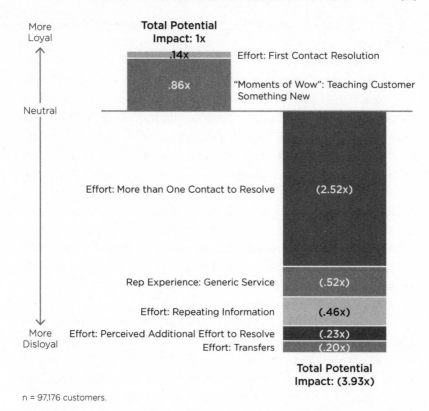

More Loyal

Total Potential Impact: 1x

.14x — Effort: First Contact Resolution

.86x — "Moments of Wow": Teaching Customer Something New

Neutral

Effort: More than One Contact to Resolve — (2.52x)

Rep Experience: Generic Service — (.52x)

Effort: Repeating Information — (.46x)

Effort: Perceived Additional Effort to Resolve — (.23x)

Effort: Transfers — (.20x)

More Disloyal

Total Potential Impact: (3.93x)

n = 97,176 customers.

Source: CEB. 2013.

Figure 1.8 Customer Service Driver of Loyalty and Disloyalty

recitation of policy. The halfhearted offers of empathy. The scripted thanks for our loyalty. It's enough to make the blood boil.

Of the five, this is the only one that's not directly based on effort per se, but rather seems to be part of a generally negative rep experience. While this appears to be inconsistent with the effort theme, it turns out that generic service itself is a major driver of repeat contacts—when customers feel they aren't being treated in a manner they can relate to (e.g., they are looking for decisive ownership and are met with a noncommittal response, or they are looking for empathy and are met with a "corporate" demeanor, or perhaps they just don't like the answer they received), they call back and "shop around" for somebody better. It happens a surprisingly high percentage of the time. More to come on this in chapter 3.

Having to repeat information also makes an appearance in the top drivers of customer disloyalty, something we think is closely related to repeat contacts (e.g., telling your story over again to a supervisor or even having to repeat your account number after just entering it using your touchpad).

Following closely behind is "perceived additional effort to resolve." Our team spent an entire year studying this notion of how to control the perception of effort and learned that this perceptual effect is in fact much more impactful than it appears on the surface. It turns out that many companies miss a huge opportunity to manage the customer's perception of the experience by focusing their resources on traditional soft skills (i.e., being nice, courteous, and professional) instead of teaching their people how to use *carefully crafted and thoughtful language* to guide the customer to an outcome that would otherwise be considered less than ideal. In other words, there are many ways to say the exact same thing to the customer, but some ways fuel disloyalty and others mitigate it. Leading contact centers are doing some truly groundbreaking work to arm their frontline staff to manage customer perception, something we will devote much of chapter 4 to exploring.

Lastly, there is the "bouncing around" story. Whether it's the rep who first answers the call but then transfers that call to another department, or the customer who tries to resolve an issue online but is forced to pick up the phone and call for service because the online options failed him (i.e., channel switching), this is about customers being turned around to get help elsewhere. While it is seemingly small compared to some of the other drivers discussed above, we actually think this is one that has the potential to change customer service as we know it. Our team devoted another full year of research, including a full-blown quantitative study, to understanding the *channel preferences* of customers. In the end, what we found has become one of the biggest shocks to the customer service establishment in decades. Not only are customer preferences shifting away from live service, but the way in which customers want to engage with companies through new self-serve channels is exactly the opposite of what most service leaders assume. Breaking the bounce-around cycle and shifting service channel investments to the emerging preferences of customers is something we will discuss in detail in chapter 2.

Here's the kicker, just to drive home the idea of effort: When we took all of these discrete drivers—everything from repeat contacts to channel switching—and compared the loyalty of those customers who had "low-effort" interactions (i.e., who experienced few, if any, of these negative scenarios) with those customers who had "high-effort" interactions (i.e., those who reported experiencing many, and perhaps all, of these scenarios), we found that *96 percent of customers who had high-effort experiences reported being disloyal, compared to only 9 percent of customers with low-effort experiences who reported being disloyal.*

Ninety-six to nine! In all our research we've never seen a finding as starkly dramatic as this.

It's a phenomenon we've been tracking now for several years using a diagnostic tool we call the Customer Effort Assessment (which we'll discuss in more detail in chapter 6). The results of that diagnostic show that low-effort companies outperform others by 31 percent when it comes to intent to repurchase and positive word of mouth. These companies also outperform their peers by 29 percent when it comes to first contact resolution in the phone channel, they outperform peers in web issue resolution by 53 percent, in web chat issue resolution by 46 percent, and in e-mail issue resolution by 67 percent. Put simply, low-effort companies deliver a vastly superior service experience and reap the loyalty benefits from doing so.

Defining the Opportunity

Let's put these findings into more human terms. What exactly does customer effort—the kind that makes a customer more disloyal—actually look like in real life?

Put your customer hat on and think about your recent service experiences—a great one and a horrible one. Write down the qualities of the good versus the bad one. Look at the difference—what did you put on the horrible one? Were you on hold for a long time? Did you get passed around? Were you told, "No, sorry, that's against our policy?" Is it possible that the issue is *still* unresolved? How did that experience make you feel? Now put your business hat on. In your job—at your company—how many of these things do you put your own customers through on a regular basis?

When we look at real-world service situations, it becomes clear that even when the contact center team is trying to do a good job, and even when the interaction seems to go well, loyalty still ends up moving in the wrong direction.

Consider the following scenario:

- The customer's issue was fully resolved by a rep who went above and beyond (that sounds great, but it tests relatively neutral for increased future loyalty).

- Unfortunately, this was the second time he had to call about that issue (a huge negative).

If you were listening to this call, you would have to conclude, "We did a great job there." But since it took the customer two tries to get to that moment, and knowing the huge negative impact that repeat contacts have on the customer experience, this person is still very likely to end up *more* disloyal—meaning less of a chance he'll repurchase, less of a chance he'll spend more, and a greater chance that he'll say negative things to other people—despite the fact that the rep who eventually solved his problem went above and beyond to do so. That's a totally different reaction than you'd expect if you were just listening to that one call.

Let's consider another situation:

- Unlike the last customer, this customer's issue *was* resolved on the first call, and that creates a big positive impact, as we know from our data. In fact, it's the best thing we can possibly do to mitigate disloyalty.
- On top of this, the rep she dealt with expressed clear concern for the customer (again, that sounds good, but it turns out it's actually neutral for loyalty).
- However, she was transferred (that's a negative).
- As a result of the transfer, she had to repeat information (another negative).
- Ultimately, the person she was transferred to treated her more generically than the first rep (an even bigger negative).

Just like with the last call, if any of us were listening to this call, we would very likely think, *Hey, we resolved the customer's issue, so . . . mission accomplished. How could that possibly be bad?* But the data tells a very different story. The customer got what she ultimately needed, but at the cost of significant additional customer effort, so all things considered, this customer is likely to be *less* loyal at the end of that call. Not good.

While these sound like no-win situations, you should actually look at them as a glass half full. After all, here's all the evidence you need to see the big, glaring opportunity that's right in front of you. Instead of optimizing for satisfaction, if you're correctly optimizing for loyalty, it's obvious that what you need to focus on is finding new ways to get rid of the hassles, the hurdles, the extra customer effort that leads to disloyalty.

And here's the thing. You don't have to look very hard to find these opportunities. According to our data, these sources of customer effort happen *all the time:*

- Fifty-six percent of customers report having to reexplain their issue during the course of a service interaction.
- Fifty-nine percent of customers report moderate to high perceived additional effort to resolve their issue.
- Fifty-nine percent of customers say they were transferred during a service interaction.
- And an astounding 62 percent of customers report more than one contact to resolve their issue.

Perhaps these customer-reported measures didn't exactly match up with your own performance data. Perhaps you're looking at these numbers and thinking, *Luckily, that's not us, because we only transfer 10 percent of all calls,* or *Our FCR rate is 85 percent . . . there's no way 62 percent of our customers call back.* There are really two explanations here, which we'll cover in full detail in the coming chapters. First, most metrics used in contact centers today suffer from a kind of myopia: They take a very narrow view of things that tend to make service organizations look much better than they really are. It's sort of like judging your weight by using one of those funhouse mirrors that makes you look all stretched-out and skinny. Here's an example: Most companies measure transfer rates by relying on switch data, which is captured when calls are handed from one agent to another. But when you interview customers, it turns out they have a different definition of what constitutes a "transfer." What if the customer started on the web—maybe in a chat session—and then had to call the contact center? In the customer's mind, *that's* a transfer. If the customer started in the IVR (interactive voice response) and then bailed out to speak to a live person? Transfer. Same thing with repeat contacts, repeating information, channel switching, and so on. As the VP of service from a retail company told us, "We want to be customer-focused, but everything we do to be customer-focused is actually driven from the company (not the customer) perspective. We feel better at the end of the day, but do our customers?"

Second, and more important, it doesn't really matter that *your* data says something different. All that matters is how the *customer* sees things. If the customer felt she was transferred but your systems say otherwise, who's right? After all, there's no Disloyalty Court of Appeals where your case can be argued. Customers don't live in the contact center world. Their world operates according to a much broader and, arguably, simpler set of rules. Either you make things easy or you don't. Either you're a hassle to deal with or you aren't. Fortunately, we now understand how *they* define these things. Ultimately, we'll argue for reengineering customer service metrics to better align to this customer view of things. It's not a beauty contest—these measures will likely make you look much worse than your old ones, at first—but the important thing is that you will have reoriented your dashboard toward capturing what really matters to customers, not what matters to your superiors and business partners. And ultimately that's where loyalty, and disloyalty, come from.

Putting It All Together

The argument of this book, put in its most simple form, is that the role of customer service is to *mitigate disloyalty by reducing customer effort.*

Contrast this with the strategy most of us try to pursue—to boost loyalty during service interactions by delighting the customer. The harsh truth is that most organizations and managers struggle to try to make this strategy work. Which it doesn't. And now we know why. Our study of thousands upon thousands of customer service interactions around the world shows not only that these experiences tend to (by a wide margin) make customers disloyal more than they make customers loyal; it also suggests that it is an uphill battle trying to make customers more loyal by the end of a service interaction. But it also shows that when we do, on rare occasions, actually "wow" the customer, even then we have only a 12 percent probability of making that customer more loyal to us—and that's only if we don't do anything wrong to undermine our efforts. A strategy of delight, in other words, is like trying to win a basketball game by throwing up shots from half-court. Sure, it might work once in a while, but it certainly isn't the playbook that will make you a consistent winner.

Reducing customer effort, however, is entirely different. It speaks directly to the "natural state" of customer service interactions—making customers more disloyal. Not just that, but reducing effort is tangible. What would be defined as a "moment of wow" by one person is likely very different than what it would be for another person. It's not just that delight is a low-probability way to drive loyalty; it's so ambiguous as to be almost indefinable. On the other hand, when we look at the effort drivers—repeat contacts, transfers, channel switching—these are real things that are much more black-and-white. The customer called back or they didn't. They were transferred or they weren't. They had to repeat information or they didn't. And so on. Given its binary nature, these are things that can be measured by most organizations. In fact, chances are they are probably already being measured right now in some way, shape, or form—likely buried on a spreadsheet somewhere in the bowels of the service department.

Now, compare these strategies in terms of how your frontline staff will interpret them. When you get up in front of the service team on Monday morning and say that you want them to go out and delight your customers, how do your reps interpret that? If you haven't clearly articulated exactly what you want them to do to achieve delight (and how *could* you, since it's so variable from one customer to another?), you're playing a costly and potentially risky game. When your reps return to their cubes and start taking calls, what happens? Many won't care about delighting customers, because it sounds like generic corporate jargon—a meaningless platitude that managers say because it sounds good. Some—probably a small, unjaded percentage—may take you seriously and will leave inspired to delight customers . . . but what action will they take? Unless you're one of those very few companies (e.g., Ritz-Carlton, Nordstrom, Zappos, etc.) that have a well-documented strategy and policy of delight, most reps in most companies will interpret this guidance to mean they should take their soft skills techniques to a new extreme, to be as empathetic and friendly as possible. Others will see it as a free pass to make all kinds of policy exceptions, issuing credits and refunds and giveaways to pacify upset customers. Delight is something that can be interpreted in many (often unprofitable) ways by the frontline.

But what if you got up in front of the team and instead of asking them to delight your customers, you asked them to make things as easy as possible for your customers—and you told them to do this by focusing on a small set of actions, like avoiding situations where the customer is likely to have to call back, not transferring customers when they can handle the issue themselves, not asking customers to repeat themselves, not treating people in a generic manner, and so forth. These are things that your people *can* do something about. To quote one rep we interviewed, "For me, the light bulb went off when [our supervisor] told us to focus on making it easy. I had this 'a-ha!' moment. I always felt like you were either good at service or not—it just came naturally to certain people. But reducing effort is about doing *very* specific things with customers. It makes total sense."

Now think for a minute about the potential power of actually *measuring* customer effort. Not only can the operational drivers of effort be clearly measured, but measuring effort gets us much better predictive capability when it comes to what we're all after: customer loyalty. Remember when we talked about CSAT we found that 20 percent of customers who reported being satisfied also said they were disloyal? That's a high margin of error—something we don't see when we measure effort. In chapter 6, we're going to spend some time digging into this question of metrics and measurement and introduce a new concept that's come out of our work: the Customer Effort Score, a metric we believe should be on every customer service dashboard.

Shifting the Loyalty Curve

If you're really serious about creating the loyalty outcomes that matter most to the performance of the customer service department, and ultimately the success of your company, reducing customer effort must become the new centerpiece of your service strategy.

With customer service leaders, we often talk about the idea of "shifting the loyalty curve" (see figure 1.9). Since the dawn of time in customer service, all of our focus has been on shifting the natural distribution of customer experience scores to the right. Doing so means getting rid of the bad interactions, obviously, but more importantly, increasingly exceeding expectations with customer across the board. By doing so, the conventional wisdom goes, we can execute a wholesale shift in which more of our customers are more loyal to us.

If you've taken nothing else from the discussion in this chapter, you should at least now know that a strategy of delight doesn't work—for three reasons:

- It doesn't work because delighting customers is rare, and even when delight does occur, it doesn't make customers much more loyal than simply meeting their expectations does.
- It doesn't work because customer service interactions are four times more likely to drive disloyalty than loyalty.
- It doesn't work because optimizing toward delight doesn't focus any of our resources, investments, performance metrics, and incentives on reducing and eliminating the sources of customer effort that make customers disloyal.

Wrong Loyalty Goal: "You exceeded my expectations."
Illustrative

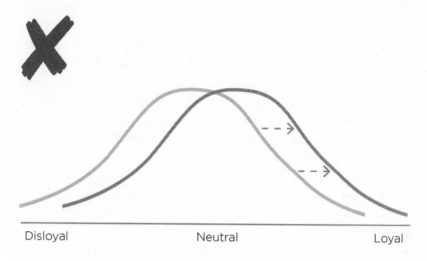

Disloyal   Neutral   Loyal

Correct Loyalty Goal: "You made it easy."
Illustrative

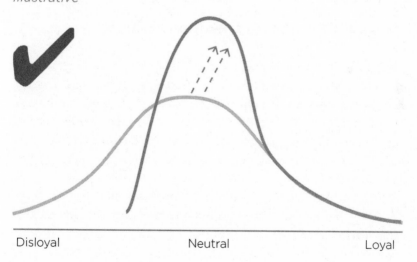

Disloyal   Neutral   Loyal

Source: CEB, 2013.

Figure 1.9 Contrasting Loyalty Goals in Customer Service (Typical vs. Recommended)

By contrast, a strategy of effort reduction is about delivering on the most basic service promise we can make to our customers: When things go wrong, we'll fix it. When you need help, we'll help you with solid service delivery. Customers really don't care to be delighted by you as much as they want to just get on with their lives, so your job is to eliminate the obstacles that prevent your customers from being able to do just that. Their call may be "very important" to you, but it's not (in the grand scheme of things) that important to them, so do what you can to let them get back to their lives quickly, efficiently, and with full confidence that their problem has been fixed. Reduce customer effort.

By focusing on the sources of customer effort, we can eliminate the bad interactions and shift the disloyal customers into the middle. Instead of getting customers to say, "You exceeded my expectations," we really ought to be trying to get customers to say, "You made that *easy*." See the difference? You need to give your customers fewer reasons to be disloyal, and the best way to make that happen is to reduce customer effort.

Of course, there's still one more (big) piece of the puzzle, isn't there? What exactly can you do to make all of this happen?

The Four Principles of Low-Effort Service

Armed with this initial data, our team embarked on a multiyear study of the various sources of customer effort—repeat contacts, channel switching, generic service, effort perception, and so on. Along the way, we conducted several additional quantitative studies to dive deeper into the real nature of customer effort, as well as hundreds of interviews with service leaders to identify innovative practices for reducing customer effort.

While we'll go into much more detail on this work in coming chapters, here's the top line—the four best practices that virtually all low-effort service organizations share:

1. Low-effort companies minimize channel switching by boosting the "stickiness" of self-service channels, thereby keeping customers from having to call in the first place. These companies recognize that customer preferences have shifted dramatically in recent years—away from live service and toward self-service. But they also recognize that what customers want isn't a whole host of bells and whistles, but a simple, intuitive, and guided self-service experience that makes it unnecessary to call the company if a customer doesn't want to call the company.

2. When customers are forced to call, low-effort companies don't just resolve the current issue for a customer; they arm their reps to head off the potential for *subsequent* calls by employing *next issue avoidance* practices. Low-effort companies understand that first contact resolution isn't the goal—it's only a step in the direction toward more holistic, event-based issue resolution.

3. Low-effort companies equip their reps to succeed on the "emotional" side of the service interaction. This isn't about being nice (i.e. what's typically taught as "soft skills" training) but rather about more advanced *experience engineering* tactics that allow reps to actively manage the customer interaction. Such tactics are rooted in the principles of human psychology and behavioral economics.

4. Finally, low-effort companies empower their frontline reps to deliver a low-effort experience by using incentive systems that value the quality of the experience over merely speed and efficiency. They've moved away from the "stopwatch" and "checklist" culture that's long permeated the service organization to instead give reps more autonomy and the opportunity to exercise a greater degree of judgment. They understand, in other words, that to *get* greater control over the quality of the experience delivered, they need to *give* greater control to the people delivering it.

These are the things low-effort companies do. Again, each is based on a unique body of quantitative and qualitative work. Throughout the remainder of this book, we'll dive into each of these principles and show you all of the data behind them. Along the way, we'll share case profiles of companies that are doing things the right way, as well as tools and templates that you can use to make similar progress in your own organization. It is very possible for you to get off to a fast start making real, measureable progress on your journey toward delivering a low-effort experience to your customers. If you do, you will ultimately make them less disloyal to your organization—the most important responsibility of any customer service operation.

The rewards for you and your company are there for the taking, and the pathway to achieving them is now more clearly marked than ever before.

KEY TAKEAWAYS

♦ *Delighting customers in the service channel doesn't pay.* Customers whose expectations are exceeded are only marginally more loyal than those whose expectations were simply met.

♦ *Customer service drives disloyalty, not loyalty.* The average service interaction is four times more likely to make a customer disloyal than to make them loyal.

♦ *The key to mitigating disloyalty is reducing customer effort.* Companies should focus on making service easier, not more delightful, by reducing the amount of work required of customers to get their issues resolved. This includes avoiding their having to repeat information, having to repeatedly contact the company, switching channels, being transferred, and being treated in a generic manner.

2

WHY YOUR CUSTOMERS DON'T WANT TO TALK TO YOU

H ere's a scenario most of us have experienced at one time or another: You arrive at the airport, see a customer service agent standing there, yet you still head straight for the self-serve kiosk to change your seat, perhaps request an upgrade, and print your boarding pass. Or how about this one: You stand in line at the bank to use the ATM, but know full well there's a teller inside the bank who's ready to help you. Most customers don't just *like* self-service, but there are endless similar examples of times we go *out of our way* to self-serve. How customers want to be served and how they want to engage with companies have changed considerably in the past decade. The problem is that most service strategies haven't followed suit, and this is hurting companies not just once, but twice, through increased operating costs, as well as decreased customer loyalty.

There are a variety of reasons why self-service has become so appealing to customers. It's efficient—the kiosk is simply faster than the ticketing agent. Social norms have shifted to the point where it's not cool to have to speak to some customer service agent when you could just as easily use your smartphone. It's almost embarrassing to be seen in line at the airport nowadays, isn't it? *Why would anyone want to get in line with all those travel rookies?*

But if you ask the average executive how customers want to interact with his company, almost without fail he will tell you his customers generally prefer to *call*. Service leaders are almost hardwired to think this way, and it's really not hard to understand why. Live phone service represents the most significant operational cost in their organizations. It's the most visible channel companies oversee—the subject of many YouTube montages and customer letters threatening to end their relationship with a company. And it's the channel most service leaders cut their teeth on as they came up through the ranks in their own careers.

This mismatch between how customers want to be served, and how companies *think* they want to be served is actually masking one of the biggest and most insidious drivers of high customer effort. It's called channel switching—when a customer initially attempts to resolve an issue through self-service, only to have to *also* pick up the phone and call—and it's plaguing the customer experience in a way few service leaders fully understand or appreciate. In fact, channel switching happens in the *majority* of service interactions—more than most companies would ever imagine. And each time a customer switches channels, it has a significant negative impact on customer loyalty.

There's no disputing that this problem ought to be in every company's spotlight, but ironically, it's not. This is in part because most companies tend to take a myopic approach to capturing the customer experience. While just about all companies are good to excellent at tracking a customer's usage of any *one* channel, few companies have systems capable of tracking the experience across *multiple* service channels. Companies tend to think of their customers as "web customers" or "phone customers," not as customers whose resolution journeys actually cross multiple channel boundaries. And so it's no wonder most companies aren't even aware that channel switching is happening.

If you ask nearly any business leader or manager what their company's biggest challenge is regarding self-service, invariably you'll hear some version of "getting our customers to *go* to self-service." Service leaders know the potential cost savings all too well. "Our call volume is too high. If we could just get more customers to use our self-service channels we'd save a ton of money . . . so how can we do that?" But what these leaders don't realize is that a sizable majority of the live phone calls they're taking every day are from customers who *already tried* to self-serve. In fact, on average, nearly 58 percent of a company's inbound call volume comes from customers who first were on the

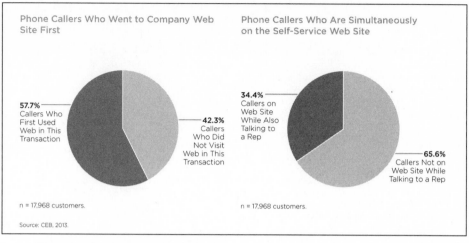

Figure 2.1 Customer Channel Switching

company's web site but, for some reason or another, *still* ended up calling the contact center. What's more, over a third of customers who are on the phone with a company's service reps at any one moment are also on that company's web site *at the same time* (see figure 2.1).

The thought that customers are using self-service *first* and *then* calling is hugely troubling for the average company. Think of it like conducting an energy audit on your house—looking at the efficiency of your insulation and doors and windows—only to find out that a huge bundle of money you're spending on heating and cooling is literally flying right out the window. It suggests that companies are incurring a drastic and entirely unnecessary expense taking phone calls from customers who never intended to call in the first place.

What about the customer experience? Just how painful is channel switching? Customers who attempt to self-serve but are forced to pick up the phone are *10 percent more disloyal* than customers who were able to resolve their issue in their channel of first choice (see figure 2.2). Each seemingly minor switch has real impact.

That massive group—the 58 percent of customers who are forced to switch from web to phone—fall into the "lose-lose" scenario: They cost companies more to serve *and* end up being less loyal as a result. As one CFO exclaimed when he saw this data, "Let me get this straight. You're saying we're *paying* for our customers to be *disloyal* to us?!?" In a manner of speaking, yes.

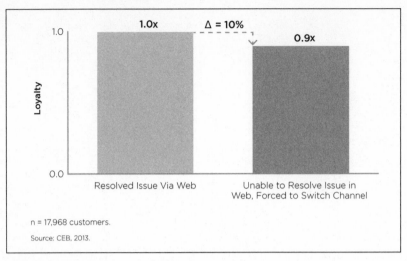

Figure 2.2 Impact of Channel Switching on Loyalty

The challenge is not in getting today's customer to *try* self-service. The challenge lies in getting today's customer to avoid channel switching from self-service to a live phone call—and in doing so, avoiding the cost and disloyalty that comes with it. Put simply, the self-service battle isn't about getting customers to *go*, it's about getting them to *stay*.

Understanding the Opportunity

To help shed more light on this shift in channel preferences and the prevalence of channel switching, we surveyed over 20,000 customers during the course of three different studies, spanning both B2C and B2B interactions. These represented all major industries and a wide variety of customers from North America, Europe, Africa, Asia, and Australia.

We asked about their experiences: Which service channels did they use—web chat, phone, online self-service, all of these? In what order did they visit those channels? Was their issue resolved or not? How easy or difficult was the interaction? We were trying to understand precisely what was happening through the entire course—literally start to finish—of these thousands of service interactions.

We also sought to understand more about channel preferences—how

| Attribute | Package E | Package F |
| Attribute | Package C | Package D |
Attribute	Package A	Package B
Method of contacting the company	Phone a live representative	On the company's Web site, reading written information (e.g., FAQs, knowledge articles or general information)
Number of attempts to resolve your issue	2	1
Time to reach a live representative	15 seconds	N/A
Customer service's operating hours	Weekdays only, normal business hours	N/A
Location of representative	In your country	N/A
Select One:	○	○

Source: CEB, 2013.

Figure 2.3 Conjoint Methodology for Testing Customers' Service Preferences

much value do customers really place in the different service channels they use? We tested a variety of service channels, like web self-service, IVR, chat, e-mail, and so on. What we really wanted to determine was the value placed on live versus self-service channels. This portion of the survey relied on a powerful statistical method known as *conjoint analysis,* which helped us distinguish customer preferences by forcing customers to make trade-offs over and over again (see figure 2.3).

Companies Love the Phone

So just how important is the web in the average company's service strategy? The preponderant answer is, "Not as important as live phone service." On average, service leaders believe that customers prefer phone service *two and a half times more* than online self-service—mainly because companies believe their customers want some sort of personal relationship with them.

So just how far into the future will it be before customer preference shifts toward self-service? The vast majority of service leaders believe this is at least several years away, if not more (see figure 2.4). So it wasn't terribly surprising that only a third of the companies we spoke with had recently taken on a self-service project of any kind. It just isn't a priority

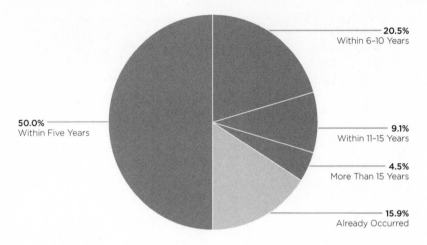

n = 44 companies.

Source: CEB, 2013.

Figure 2.4 Service Leader Perception of When Customer Preferences Will Shift Toward Web

for many companies. The thought that customers are frequently switching channels from web to phone isn't even remotely on the radar screen.

In our conversations with service leaders, we encountered several "hardwired" assumptions that colored their perception of self-service:

Assumption #1: Customers only want to self-serve for easy issues— for instance, checking balances, viewing the status of an order, or making a payment. But when issues are more complex or urgent, customers are only comfortable with live phone service.

Assumption #2: Only the millennial generation (people in their teens and twenties) has a strong desire to use self-service, and older generations simply don't. In other words, the tipping point when more people prefer self-service over live service is potentially *at least* ten years away.

Assumption #3: It costs a lot of money to really improve the self-service offering. Current service web sites are ill-equipped to help customers self-serve, and so significant capital investment, well beyond current levels, would be required to make self-service work for most customers.

As one executive vented to us, "The self-service opportunity is like the sword in the stone." The cost savings are clear, but the limitations of self-service are simply too great and the timing just not quite right. His belief is that neither he nor his customers are ready to capture that upside just yet. He is far from alone. Most service leaders express similar frustration. As a result, their strategy is to better manage the phone channel and devote relatively little attention to improving self-service.

The Tipping Point Is Already Here

Contrary to what most companies believe the three assumptions shown above are, in fact, simply not true. They are myths that need to be busted. The reality is customers *already* value the web as much as the phone, if not more. In fact, customers see just as much value in self-service as they do in phone interactions, a finding that largely holds true in both B2C and B2B interactions (see figure 2.5)*. This is nowhere near what executives expected—a 2.5-to-1 margin in favor of phone service. Phone and self-service preferences are ships passing in the night—the desire to use self-service increasing very rapidly, while the preference for picking up the phone is decreasing at the same rate. The day of that tipping point isn't ten years away; it's already here.

Some customers don't even feel like they're making a choice between calling a company or using the web to self-serve. In fact, calling is literally not even *part* of their thought process. Ask any college student which pizzeria they *called* to order a pizza for a party, and they'll probably look at you like you had three heads. "You don't call someone to order a pizza, you just go online and order it. Why would you call someone?" We are in the era of self-service first.

What about the harder issues? Recall the initial assumption—that customers only had confidence in self-service for the really simple issues like checking their balance or order status. If that were the case, you would expect customers to be indifferent about the channels they use. So we dug more deeply into our data and isolated scenarios where

---

* The difference between business-to-business and business-to-consumer preferences reflects that business customers generally value customer service interactions less than consumers. There are lower personal stakes in a typical business customer service interaction, and therefore less value assigned.

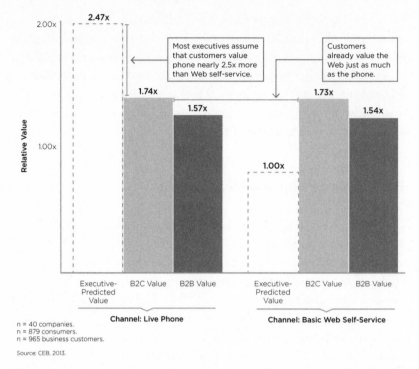

Figure 2.5 Value of Live Service versus Self-Service (Service Leader Perception versus Actual Customer Preference)

customers had these more difficult and complex issues in order to test that assumption. While preferences did swing back slightly in favor of phone service, the difference was nowhere near as pronounced as most service leaders had expected. Even in situations that are not routine, customers still consider self-service as their first option far more than most of us ever thought. Naturally there are instances when an issue is so complex, you would simply *have* to speak with a live rep, but as it turns out, those instances are pretty rare.

Consider this scenario. It's late in the evening and you notice that your child is starting to develop a slight rash and has a fever. Few would dispute that your child's health isn't high-stakes. Now, of course you could call your pediatrician or a nurse on-call. You could also visit a twenty-four-hour clinic, or even go the emergency room. But increasingly, what do most parents do in this situation? We turn to an online resource, such as WebMD. We trust these resources—and our own ability to make an informed interpretation of what these online resources are telling us—in ways that we didn't just five or ten years ago.

Customers really do trust web self-service. Many people are now just as confident self-serving as they are talking to a service rep. Self-service also places the customer in control, particularly when information that is confidential or potentially embarrassing might be exchanged. So the well-ingrained mind-set that the phone is far and away the most valued option in critical service situations is no longer true—or at least not nearly as true as we once believed.

What role does age play in service preferences? Recall the other assumption—that the preference for self-service was only strong within younger demographics. Naturally, you'd have to think that there would be *some* differences in channel preferences by age. There's little doubt that older customers have less of a predisposition toward technology, not having grown up with smartphones, PCs, and the Internet. You'd expect that fact to be reflected in the way they want to interact with companies. And while that's definitely true to some extent, it's nowhere near what any of us would have guessed (see figure 2.6). There are plenty of folks in their sixties, even their seventies, who prefer going to the web first when they have a problem or a question. The balance even among older age groups in favor of phone service is far closer to 60:40, not the 90:10 or 80:20 ratio many of us would have guessed. So even customers who are the last to adopt self-service are much further along than most of us would have imagined.

It turns out that the age of fifty-one is where preference tips from one side to the other. That's quite different from what most companies think. The comfort and confidence that baby boomers are showing in using the web for service transactions seem to be constantly increasing. Indeed, this age demographic has accounted for some of the most explosive growth in online usage. Facebook, for instance, has reported that users over sixty-five years of age represent their most significant growth segment over the past few years.

Here's a sobering thought related to just how off-base most companies are: What executives initially told us, the 2.5-to-1 margin, turns out to actually reflect the service preferences of at least one segment of customers. That segment? Customers who are seventy-seven years old and above. For most companies, that's a far cry from their target customer demographic. It's not that companies had no idea that the

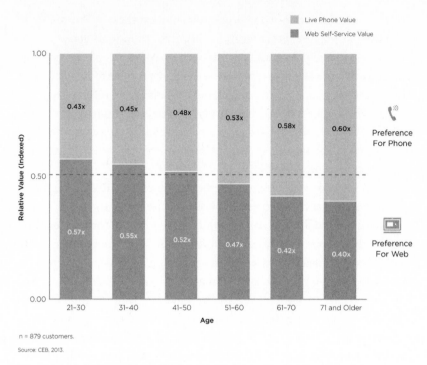

n = 879 customers.

Source: CEB, 2013.

Figure 2.6 Web Versus Phone Preference by Customer Age Decile

preference for web usage is shifting. Rather, it's that this shift is happening far more quickly than any of us could have predicted.

So Why Are Phones Still Ringing?

This shift in customer preferences is a fairly recent phenomenon. Nearly 67 percent of customers said that that even five years ago they *primarily* relied on the phone for service. Compare that to only 29 percent of customers making the same claim today. It's a remarkable shift that's caught many companies flat-footed. But if the only bad news here is that most service leaders were drastically off the mark, well, that's not so bad, right? Customers want to self-serve. The shifts most companies were expecting to see in five, ten, or even fifteen years have already occurred.

It only stands that call volume *should be* dropping like a rock. *But it hasn't.* We didn't find this to be the case for a single company in our ongoing analysis. While phone volume is decreasing, it's dropping *more like a feather than a rock.* (In fact, for most companies it's declined by only 4 to 5 percent over the past few years.) The customer remarks captured in our survey help explain what's really going on. Here are some of the more telling customer comments we received:

> "I always feel like I have to call, not that I want to call, but I have to call. It's hard to think of other companies where I always have to call. Their sites make sense to me."

> "Your web site told me to call. If I wanted to call I would have."

> "Your agents are very nice and I always have good experiences when I talk to them. I just don't always want to have to talk to them."

Take a minute and imagine yourself manning the phone lines, talking to a customer about a service issue. You come to learn that this customer was just on your web site and could have self-served, but for whatever reason they still ended up picking up the phone and calling. How would you feel about spending valuable time (theirs *and* the company's) having a live interaction with a customer who not only wanted to self-serve but actually *tried to?*

One of the first executives we shared this with had this reaction: "We think of our customers as either 'phone callers' or 'web users,' but what we're finally beginning to realize is that we actually need to think of them as *both.*" It's a simple, perhaps obvious point, but very few companies think this way about their customers.

Companies need to shift their focus from getting customers to *try* self-service to getting customers to *stay.* Ten years ago self-service was about educating customers about the existence of the company's web site and building their confidence that they could use self-service to resolve their issues. In fact, in 2005 our team wrote a study on this very topic, entitled *Achieving Breakout Use of Self-Service.* That study now feels to be ancient history. That era has already passed us by. So don't fight it. Phone lovers are a small (and shrinking) minority of customers. The channel switchers are where you'll find the win-win—a lower cost to serve for you, and lower effort for the customer. And best of all, there are still plenty of opportunities to get this right.

The Channel Stickiness Opportunity

Let's just establish right up front that some percentage of channel switching falls outside the immediate control of a service organization. Of the 58 percent of callers who reported switching from web to phone, roughly 11 percent of these are not easily mitigated (see figure 2.7). For instance, customers with issues that are simply too difficult to resolve via self-service, technical glitches in the web site, or situations where customers are prompted to place a live call. While there is some opportunity to reduce channel switching in these cases, there are easier wins to be had elsewhere.

The more controllable drivers of channel switching (47 percent in B2C settings and 37 percent in B2B) can be categorized into three groups:

1. The customer couldn't find the information they needed.
2. The customer found the information, but it was unclear.
3. The customer was simply using the web site to find the phone number to call the company.

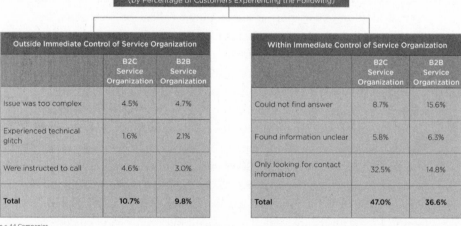

Reasons for Switching from Web to Phone (by Percentage of Customers Experiencing the Following)						
Outside Immediate Control of Service Organization				**Within Immediate Control of Service Organization**		
	B2C Service Organization	B2B Service Organization			B2C Service Organization	B2B Service Organization
Issue was too complex	4.5%	4.7%		Could not find answer	8.7%	15.6%
Experienced technical glitch	1.6%	2.1%		Found information unclear	5.8%	6.3%
Were instructed to call	4.6%	3.0%		Only looking for contact information	32.5%	14.8%
Total	**10.7%**	**9.8%**		**Total**	**47.0%**	**36.6%**

n = 44 Companies.

Source: CEB, 2013.

Figure 2.7 Channel-Switching Root Causes

Over the coming pages we'll detail several best practices that will help companies mitigate these causes of channel switching. These practices don't rely on expensive, bleeding-edge technologies. Instead, you'll find a series of near-term, low-cost, and highly actionable practices that can deliver tremendous impact. For most organizations, this is very good news.

When it comes to how information is presented on the web, *simplicity matters a lot*. Most customers who channel-switch do so because they become confused or lose confidence. It's not that the web site fails them, or that it isn't capable of answering their question. Surely that happens, but not as frequently as a customer getting lost in the language or layout of a company's service web site. Can you get *all* of the channel switchers to stick to self-service just by simplifying the web site? Probably not. But we believe getting two in ten customers to avoid channel switching is an easily attainable goal. Of course, capital investment in a slicker interface and greater functionality could put a far greater dent in this number. But "two in ten" is a worthy and realistic first step, and can be achieved primarily through simplification of the web site. And if two in ten feels somehow non-aspirational, consider this—for a company with a million annual phone calls and an average cost per call of $8, even this would result in annual cost savings of roughly $564,000 (see figure 2.8 for cost savings estimates). Added to this, those two in ten customers

Annual Call Volume

	500,000	1,000,000	5,000,000	10,000,000
$2	$ 70,500	$ 141,000	$ 705,000	$ 1,410,000
$4	$ 141,000	$ 282,000	$ 1,410,000	$ 2,820,000
$6	$ 211,500	$ 423,000	$ 2,115,000	$ 4,230,000
$8	$ 282,000	$ 564,000	$ 2,820,000	$ 5,640,000
$12	$ 423,000	$ 846,000	$ 4,230,000	$ 8,460,000

Cost Per Call (USD)[1]

[1] These figures assume 75% of customers have Web access.

Source: CEB, 2013.

Figure 2.8 Estimated Cost Savings from Getting 2 in 10 Customers to "Stick" on the Web

will end up less disloyal, because they've had a lower-effort experience. *This represents the nearest-term, easiest win-win opportunity any service organization faces.*

Before you do anything else, you should assess your own company's channel-switching opportunity. This can be done very easily by employing a simple practice we learned from the financial services company, Fidelity.

It All Starts with a Simple Question

While you *could* assess your channel-switching opportunity by combing through CRM, web site, and phone trunk data, Fidelity takes a much more straightforward route to accomplishing the same thing. Fidelity's contact center reps are armed with a simple question tree they use when a customer calls. This helps reps quickly understand which customers have channel-switched from web to phone. Customers who switched are then asked two questions to help Fidelity zero in on what caused the channel switching to occur (see figure 2.9). It's a really clever approach

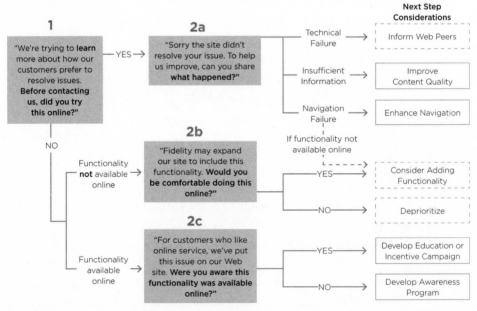

Source: Fidelity; CEB, 2013.

Figure 2.9 Fidelity's Channel-Switching Voice of the Customer Exercise

because they capture great information about channel switching, but also get valuable information on how customer preferences are evolving, plus a sense of how aware customers are of self-service options.

Here's how it works: Customers are initially asked if they tried to use self-service. Those who answer yes to this question are asked what happened—*why* did they have to call? Was it a technical issue? Was something confusing? Did they lose their way in the web site? These are the channel switchers, telling Fidelity *exactly* why they had to switch. To get this data alone makes the practice worthwhile.

However, Fidelity takes it a couple of steps further. Customers who *didn't* try to self-serve are also asked if they were aware the functionality existed (in situations where it in fact does). And in situations where the functionality doesn't yet exist for their issue, customers are instead asked if they would feel comfortable attempting to self-serve for that issue should the option become available. The whole exercise is really a market research exercise designed to help Fidelity make future self-service investments. Fidelity's reps present it to customers as a learning exercise that the company is conducting to help customers. It's not explained as a survey, nor does Fidelity use this exercise as an opportunity to push customers to the web. Positioning the questions as a way to learn from customers is the reason so many customers offer their input. Additionally, customers feel that they are truly being listened to when they speak with a Fidelity rep, versus a survey, about their online interaction.

Different groups of contact center reps are asked to conduct this live survey with customers for one week each quarter, which helps Fidelity balance costs with obtaining enough data to make informed decisions. Once reps have collected this information, it is passed along to several teams, including marketing, a group of process engineers, and their IT team. These teams triage the data and prioritize immediate opportunities to improve self-service, clarify web site language, or otherwise tweak the web site, and also amass evidence for business cases for improved web site functionality.

This simple exercise—just a few innocuous questions—has helped improve the customer experience, reduced channel switching, and lowered call volumes. In one instance, Fidelity was able to improve online PIN resets simply by adjusting the placement of links, adjusting some language on the site, and shortening the lengthy process associated with these resets. This easy fix led to a 29 percent uptick in online PIN reset completion rates, and an 8 percent reduction in call volume associated with PIN resets, which together delivered an estimated 7.25× ROI on this one project.

Many companies have had tremendous success with this sort of customer learning exercise. In fact, we often hear that they only need to collect a few days' worth of data before they start seeing patterns. As one vice president of service told us, "This exercise yielded more low-hanging fruit than our team knew what to do with. It was like a gold mine of improvement opportunities."

Using an approach like this can quickly highlight which types of channel switching are plaguing your own company and your own customers. Let's further examine those three big channel-switching categories, starting with the first—instances when customers couldn't find the information they needed.

CATEGORY #1: *Customers Couldn't Find the Information They Needed*

Most companies are unintentionally making this first category of channel switching far worse than it should be. This is because of a commonly held belief that customers want *more choices* in how they interact with a company. Companies provide a near-endless stream of choices on the web: proactive web chat, click-to-chat, knowledge bases, step-by-step guides, e-mail, click-to-call, interactive or virtual service centers, online support communities, and so on. More is always better, right? A full 80 percent of companies we surveyed reported recently adding new self-service options to existing channels, or adding new channels entirely (see figure 2.10). All of that choice is viewed by most companies as a good thing. But this turns out to be an erroneous assumption—one that unnecessarily drives up expenses and undermines loyalty. Consider for a moment that the average customer service web site has between *twenty-five and fifty* potential choices for a customer to make before even starting the resolution process (FAQs, phone options, chat options, options within options). And for most companies, this number continues to grow.

We went to fairly extensive lengths to better understand why it is that customers aren't able to find what they're looking for, particularly considering all the choices they're offered when resolving issues online. As part of this analysis, we conducted a series of focus groups with customers who had had a recent online interaction. When we asked these customers

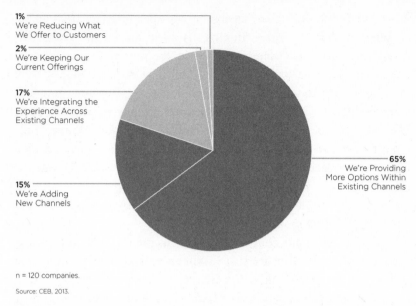

1%
We're Reducing What
We Offer to Customers

2%
We're Keeping Our
Current Offerings

17%
We're Integrating the
Experience Across
Existing Channels

15%
We're Adding
New Channels

65%
We're Providing
More Options Within
Existing Channels

n = 120 companies.

Source: CEB, 2013.

Figure 2.10 Company Response to Changing Customer Channel Preferences

to describe their experiences with companies' self-service web sites, what we heard was completely unexpected. Here are some direct quotes:

"I felt like I could have gone to multiple places on the web site to get my answer . . . and I wasn't really sure where to go first."

"It took me two minutes to read [through all of the options]— it just left me confused."

"I wasn't sure where to start."

"I felt like their web site was complex and overwhelming."

What became clear was that the variety of options to resolve an issue—all of which were presumably added in an attempt to *improve* the customer experience—were actually *detracting* from it. It's an illustration of what's known as "the paradox of choice": As more and more choices are added to any decision, it actually hampers our ability to make a good decision. A classic study done by researchers at Stanford University demonstrated this effect. A display of various flavors of jam was presented to customers, to observe how people select from an increasing number of choices. In virtually all instances, the greater the variety of flavors that were presented in the display, the fewer total number of jars were sold. When the number of varieties was reduced, sales increased.[1] In one well-documented case, the consumer products giant Procter & Gamble reduced the total number of varieties of its Head & Shoulders brand by about half, and saw sales immediately jump by over 10 percent.[2] The lesson is clear: More choices create a higher-effort decision, a bad outcome both for the customer and the company.

All of the options put in front of customers actually exacerbate the channel-switching problem.

And this wasn't just confined to our focus groups. A follow-up survey we conducted confirmed that customers will gladly trade off choice and options for a more guided experience. Customers are best served by being *directed* to the lowest-effort channel and options to resolve their issue, even if that channel would not have been their first choice (see figure 2.11).

According to our survey, low effort beats channel choice by a landslide. We found that a whopping 84 percent of customers simply want

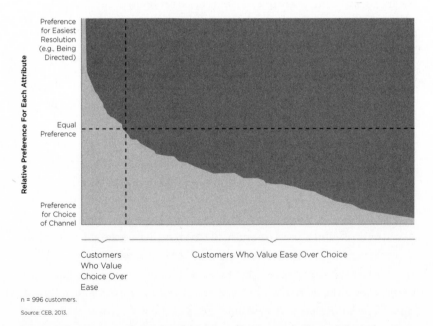

Figure 2.11 Customer Resolution Preference (Ease versus Channel Choice)

their issue resolved as quickly and easily as possible—and were willing to be directed to the best option to achieve that outcome. A much smaller portion of customers (16 percent) preferred having *a specific service option* available to them. In other words, the vast majority of customers will entertain nearly any self-service option or channel as long as they are confident it will create a faster and easier resolution experience. This notion of a "guided" experience echoed through our focus groups as well. As one participant said, "Make it simple for me—it's [the company's] job to tell me what to do. I don't want to waste my time."

Of course, while customers are willing to be guided through their interaction, this doesn't mean companies should *tell* customers what to do. People prefer to choose how they do things. Choice seems almost like a basic human right. But we've discovered that when it comes to preferences, there are two distinctly different types. We refer to this as the distinction between "big P preferences" and "small p preferences." The big P preference is the ultimate preference of customers, the one they're willing to prioritize over less important preferences—in this case the ultimate preference is "get my issue resolved." A small p preference would be something a customer *says* they prefer if you gave them a variety of choices to consider and asked them to select one.

Just to illustrate the difference, when we asked what customer service channel the participants liked best, one respondent quickly said, "My preference is chat. I like when companies offer the ability to chat online with a representative." But when we asked what he cared about most when it comes to customer service, this same participant blurted out, "Fast and easy service." So what that tells us is that a fast and easy service experience is this customer's big P, and having access to web chat is his small p. In other words, if there's a better (i.e., faster and easier) way to resolve his issue, he's fine with using something besides chat, even if he says clearly that chat is his preference.

When it comes to resolving service issues, for 84 percent of customers, all they really want is for the problem to go away. This is their big P preference. But customers still say they want *some* degree of control in how they get to that outcome—that's a small p preference.

How do we square this with the idea that these same customers also want to be directed to the best service options by the company? It turns out there's a subtle but important distinction between *telling* and *guiding* customers. Consider this scenario: Pretend you're in a new city you've never visited before. Wanting a great seafood dinner, you ask the concierge at your hotel for a recommendation. Here are three responses you might hear. Which of them sounds best to you?

- "Sure, I have the perfect place for you—in fact, let me put you in a taxi right now and send you on your way."
- "Here's a list of six different places where you can get a seafood dinner, with a bit of info on each place. Let me know if you have any questions."
- "I'm happy to help, but first can you tell me just a bit about what kind of evening you're planning? Is this for a family dinner or a business dinner? Okay, with that in mind, I can suggest two places, but the first of those two is my personal favorite."

Almost invariably, we'd all pick the third option—a recommendation that's based on the specifics of your personal situation, while still giving you some say in the matter.

With all the choices available for customers to resolve a given issue—phone, web, e-mail, chat, FAQs—how could you possibly expect anyone to make the right (lowest-effort) choice based on the issue or problem they're experiencing? Some kinds of issues are very fast and easy to resolve through web self-service. Some issues are so complex that they require a live interaction with a customer service rep in order to be resolved with the lowest effort possible. *No one channel is best for all issue types.* But the vast majority of companies simply leave it up to the customer to choose their own adventure, believing that customers prefer more choice over a lower-effort experience.

As one vice president of service at a large consumer technology company told us, "Our customers want to be able to solve their problems *their* way, so we need to offer as many options and channels as possible and let them decide what works best for them. It makes things hard for the service organization but it's the reality of service for today's empowered customer." This is fatally flawed thinking. Eighty-four percent of customers are telling us they just want to have their issue resolved—they don't really *care* to choose which channel to use, they just want the problem to go away. If you asked them which channel they prefer, perhaps they would have said they preferred to use online chat, or e-mail, or some other web offering. But if they learn for their specific problem a phone call would be faster and easier, then they're more than happy to call. So in this example, using self-service is a small p preference, but fast and easy resolution—through whatever channel is required to achieve it—is the big P preference for the vast majority of customers.

So, choice is not nearly as powerful as we might have expected. Instead, guiding customers to the pathway that will require the least amount of effort is much more likely to mitigate disloyalty and create the best experience.

There are a variety of ways to guide customers, some of them better than others. We tested four common methods:

1. Company issue–based guidance. Options are positioned to customers based on how the company categorizes issues, such as account information, billing requests, order status, or returns. These are often based on the company's point of view, most commonly aligning to different departments.

2. Channel-based guidance. Options are positioned according to the service channel or online tool the customer wants to use.

3. Peer advice–based guidance. Options are positioned according to what customers with similar requests tend to do.

4. Customer task–based guidance. Options are positioned according to customer intent or need entering a service interaction. These are positioned from the customer's point of view. For example, "If you have this issue, you should e-mail us."

Of these four methods, customers presented with *task-based guidance* selected the lowest-effort resolution path 66 percent of the time, compared to only a 20 percent success rate without any type of guidance (which is typical of what most companies offer) (see figure 2.12).

MasterCard has one of the best task-based guided resolution sites that we've seen to date. MasterCard's customer support web site is built for decision simplicity. Instead of offering an overwhelming number of choices, it offers a limited number of choices, with a couple of them presented more prominently.

Their support site operates like a "virtual concierge": Based on what

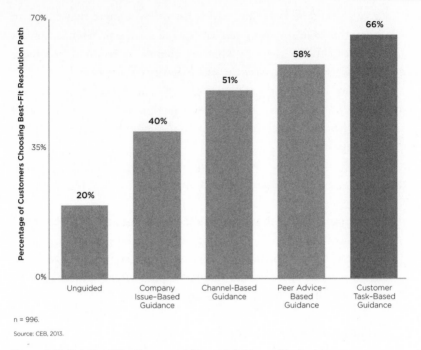

n = 996.

Source: CEB, 2013.

Figure 2.12 Relative Effectiveness of Channel Guidance Strategies

you tell it, you are then guided to the lowest-effort pathway (see figure 2.13). Customers are first asked to select the nature of their relationship with MasterCard—whether they are a cardholder, issuer, or merchant. A small set of issues, written in customer-friendly, task-oriented language, is then shown in a drop-down menu. Once a specific issue is selected, the system asks one more qualifying question to narrow down the specifics of the customer's issue, and then directs them to the channel that will create the lowest-effort experience. In some cases, that might be an option to chat with a live rep. In other cases, basic FAQs are sufficient to solve a specific problem. And sometimes, customers are urged to call to speak to a live rep. What MasterCard has learned is that *the channel selection should* not *be the issue; the customer's issue is the issue.*

Using this new interface, MasterCard has seen a marked reduction in customer effort, including a 30 percent decrease in e-mail volume. Additionally, MasterCard reports a significant shift in their mix of simple versus complex interactions handled via phone, indicating that fewer customers are actually channel switching. The net outcome is that customers

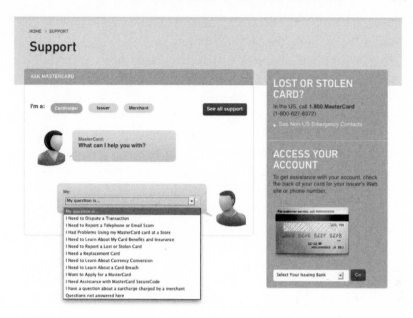

Source: MasterCard; CEB, 2013.

MasterCard Customer Support Site 1

Source: MasterCard; CEB, 2013.

Figure 2.13 MasterCard Customer Support Site 2

who need live rep attention are getting it, and the customers who wanted to self-serve are easily able to finish online.

The MasterCard example is particularly impressive since they accomplished this through a fairly basic HTML build. This isn't an interface chock-full of bells and whistles, or one that relies on intelligent search or other costly means to direct customers. It's simply an overlay that sits on top of all the features, options, and choices the company *already* offers, to help guide customers to the fastest and easiest pathway to resolve their specific issue. Reflecting back on the goal we set out for this chapter—getting two in ten customers to avoid channel switching (while not having to invest significant capital)—it's clear why the MasterCard example hits the mark.

Amazon.com takes the MasterCard approach one step further, and presents another great example of guiding customers through service interactions. What makes Amazon's approach distinct from MasterCard is that Amazon makes a recommendation directing customers to the best channel for their issue, but still leaves customers with some choice. Think back to our example of the concierge making a dinner recommendation. Amazon's approach is very similar. After selecting the order in question, customers choose their issue from a series of drop-downs similar to MasterCard's. Based on the issue the customer selects, the service options are presented to the customer along with a recommendation (see figure 2.14). If a self-service option is available, that's *always* presented to mitigate channel switching. But for more complex issues that Amazon knows are less likely to be resolved online, they recommend that the customer call, chat, or e-mail. It's a remarkably low-effort experience.

Some might argue that Amazon is actually promoting channel switching by recommending the phone or chat. But the fact that customers don't have to struggle through self-serve prior to being forced to make a phone call greatly reduces the perception of effort. It's almost like their online portal is saying, "Based on what you told us, your issue is kinda tricky. Let's have a quick phone call because that would be much easier for you and us." It's a great example of guidance with a dash of customer choice.

Amazon's recommendation approach highlights something that most service leaders already know—what the best channels are for resolving different issue types. But unlike most companies, Amazon puts it front and center for their customers. To better help companies quickly consider which issues could—and potentially *should*—be resolved through

Contact Us

Source: Amazon.com; CEB, CEB Customer Contact Leadership Council, 2013.

Figure 2.14 Amazon's Customer Support Site

self-service, we've added a tool to appendix A of this book. We call it an "issue-to-channel mapping" tool, and it's designed to help companies assess common issue types against the channel(s) best suited for resolution. A short workshop-style discussion among service leaders, managers, and tenured reps (using this tool as a road map) will surface opportunities to start guiding customers. A word of advice: Trying to figure out the *best* channel for some issues can often be a challenge. Instead, think about which channel is the *worst* for your most common issues, and ensure that customers don't inadvertently choose that option. Remember, selecting the channel shouldn't be the issue; the customer's issue is the issue.

One of the organizations that inspired this sort of channel assessment approach was Linksys (a division of Belkin). They conducted their own similar analysis, which led them to make the bold decision to kill e-mail support entirely. The company realized that e-mail resolution

AVERAGE B2B COST PER E-MAIL RESOLUTION	
Labor:	$2.19
IT/Capital:	$1.39
Overhead:	$2.63
Average Number of Contacts to Resolve:	2.53
Total Cost per "E-Mail Resolution"	$15.72

AVERAGE B2B COST PER PHONE CALL RESOLUTION	
Labor:	$1.66
IT/Capital:	$1.39
Overhead:	$2.63
Telecom:	$0.26
Average Number of Contacts to Resolve:	1.50
Total Cost per "Phone Call Resolution"	$8.91

Average number of contacts to resolve an issue is the most significant cost variable among e-mail and phone, making e-mail 76% more expensive, on average.

Source: CEB, 2013.

Figure 2.15 True Cost of Resolution in Email versus Phone Channel

was inefficient for nearly *any* issue and often required multiple e-mails to resolve. CEB data corroborates this point: On average, e-mail requires 2.14 contacts for a company to fully resolve an issue, compared to 1.55 for phone conversations (see figure 2.15). This means that for most companies *it's actually cheaper to serve customers on the phone than over e-mail.*

Linksys realized that only a very small percentage of customers preferred e-mail, and it was frequently the worst support option for customers' issues. So their team pulled the plug on e-mail and never looked back. While it's not necessarily an example of guiding customers, it is a great example of proactively removing bad choices for customers. And while they had some negative feedback from customers initially, that soon passed (mainly because customers who preferred e-mail quickly learned to use alternate support channels with success). The move was a win-win: Customers found their way to a better support experience (see figure 2.16) and, ultimately, better resolution, and Linksys benefited by removing their most costly service channel from the picture.

CATEGORY #2: *The Customer Found the Information, but It Was Unclear*

The second major category of channel switching occurs when customers find their way to seemingly helpful information, only to realize they don't understand it. It's a hugely troubling but easily corrected problem. The root

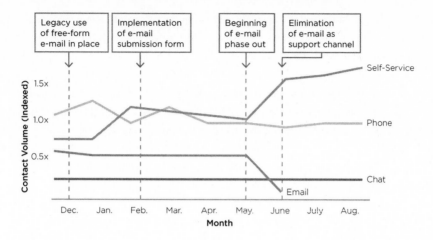

Source: Linksys; CEB, 2013.

Figure 2.16 Linksys's Email Phase-Out Process

cause in most cases is *company-speak*, jargon that is specific to certain industries or companies but that customers rarely understand. And when customers who are trying to solve a problem don't understand what they're reading on a web site, they click the "contact us" button and end up calling.

Here's a question to ask yourself: How well does your service web site reflect the things your team members talk about in meetings, the departments within your company, and the nuanced language that's associated with all those things? Now consider how well it represents your average customer—not a longtime loyalist, but a fairly new customer, someone who has only a marginal knowledge of your company and its products and services. How meaningful is the language, particularly the web pages that are several clicks within your service site, to that person? Chances are your web content makes a lot more sense to people on the *inside* than the *outside* of your company.

Here's a fun exercise that helps illustrate what we mean. In the 1950s, a language simplicity calculator called the Gunning Fog Index was introduced. More than sixty years after it was invented, it still proves a useful benchmark for language simplicity. The scoring represents the years of education a person would need to comprehend a piece of text. Greater use of multisyllabic words and longer sentences ultimately raises the score. To illustrate, here is a statement from the former secretary of the treasury of the United States, Timothy Geithner, delivered to the U.S. Congress as he detailed planned regulatory changes:

> "... create one agency with responsibility for systemic stability over the major institutions and critical payment and settlement systems and activities."

That quote scored a 24 on the Gunning Fog Index. In other words, you need roughly twenty-four years of education to understand what he's talking about. Instead, what Geithner *could* have said was this:

> "Set up an agency that makes sure banks remain stable and follow the law."

The revised quote scores an 8.5 on the Gunning Fog Index.

One of the companies working aggressively toward more customer-friendly language on their self-service site is Travelocity, the U.S.-based Internet travel and leisure services company. Their FAQs and many other sections of their service site had become a compilation of support artifacts that had been written over many years by a wide variety of departments and individuals throughout the company. When Travelocity started to develop a plan to decrease call volume and improve their online experience, what they quickly realized was that a lot of customers were calling to ask about information that was *already* on their web site or in their FAQs. But in many cases, the information was written in a way that made little sense to customers. Sure, frequent travelers might know what a "forced connection" or an "oversold situation" is, but many travelers don't. So Travelocity went on a quest to improve their web site, developing a set of ten rules for web stickiness in the process. Here are a handful of these rules:

Rule #1: Simplify language. Travelocity aims for all customer service support (FAQs) pages to score an 8 or 9 on the Gunning Fog Index. This is an acceptable level for near-universal comprehension among customers. This isn't about dumbing down language, but rather making the information more readable and easier for scanning, which is how most customers read online. This includes removing complex multisyllabic words and shortening lengthy sentences.

Rule #2: Eliminate null search results. This is one of the quickest wins for a company. Travelocity first reviewed lists of null searches (common customer searches that yielded zero responses) as well as low-relevance searches. They quickly discovered that customers often used different words than what the company typically used. For example, if a customer searched for the word "suitcase" (wondering how many suitcases they could bring on a cruise), they received a null result. These customers concluded that Travelocity's self-service was poor and typically felt as if they had no other choice but to call a live rep. However, if that customer had searched for "baggage" (the more commonly used term in the travel industry), they would have been directed to the correct response. Simply rewording and recoding the search strings to accommodate customer-friendly search terms vastly reduced the frequency of these null searches.

Rule #3: Chunk related information. Chunking refers to condensing related information and spacing it apart from other text, allowing readers to scan content more easily. Previously, Travelocity had quite dense service pages and FAQs, which confused customers and led to channel switching. Judicious use of white space between issues better accommodates how most customers scan information online and helps draw readers to the correct section to resolve their issue.

Rule #4: Avoid jargon. Travelocity scanned their most-visited web site pages and FAQs carefully for internal jargon, airline and hotel lingo, and terms that would generally confuse the average customer. Customers researching how to book a multileg trip did not necessarily know what an "open-jaw itinerary" is, and so they would call a live agent to clarify the terminology. (Hint: Searching for jargon is a great activity for new hires within your service organization, as they are probably not yet speaking entirely in your company's lingo).

Rule #5: Use active voice. Travelocity discovered that active voice was much better for reading online. Try this quick experiment— which phrase do you think is easier to quickly read?

- "Airlines may vary on their policies regarding advanced seating."
- "Advanced seating policies vary by airline."

Both say the same thing, but the latter is written in active voice, where the subject takes action (passive voice occurs when the subject is acted upon). In the example above, "advanced seating policies" is the subject. When scanning text, active voice is a lot easier to grasp.

The culmination of these rules has led to a far more simple and intuitive online experience for customers. None of Travelocity's rules in isolation represent a mind-blowing new approach to managing web content. But few service organizations apply such discipline to their service site. And while their service site isn't necessarily dazzling in appearance, it is simple, clean, and clear. Their team's efforts have led to a 5 percent reduction in call volume related to the improved web content. Audit your company's web site against these five rules and see how you fare. A simple Internet search will reveal a variety of free, easy-to-use Gunning Fog calculators that can be used to conduct such an audit. Start with your most-visited web pages, including your home page. We're betting you'll identify plenty of low-hanging fruit.

CATEGORY #3: *The Customer Was Simply Looking for a Phone Number*

What do you do with that 32 percent of your web visitors who are simply looking for your phone number—effectively using your web site like a phone book? This final category of channel switching is clearly the most difficult to mitigate. But for customers who visit the web site just to obtain the phone number, there are some subtle things that can be done to *productively* engage these customers in a way that doesn't create undue customer effort.

Perhaps the most common question we are asked is whether or not phone numbers should be suppressed, even hidden, on service web sites. It is true that moving the phone number just a single click beyond the home screen can create enough of a deterrent to encourage customers to engage in a self-service interaction. However, our advice is that it's far better to incentivize self-service usage than to overtly discourage live service usage. The reason is simple: Most companies have not committed to the principles discussed throughout this chapter such as guiding customers, clarifying language, or even understanding precisely what is causing channel switching in the first place. Moving the phone number without undertaking these actions is a surefire recipe for driving up customer effort. What's more, those companies who have done this work will often tell you that suppressing the phone number isn't necessary. If you provide a low-effort self-service experience, the right issues end up in the phone channel without causing customers grief.

For the majority of customers who *are* hell-bent on calling, our data (and common sense) tells us that they'll probably end up calling. But the fact remains that many of these customers *are* on your service site. It stands to reason that you should be able to engage *a few* of them, despite their original intention. Think back again to the goal we set out for this chapter: Prevent two in ten customers from switching.

One simple idea is to simply feature prominent links to the most common questions customers ask. Add these right on the main service site page or right next to your phone number. You'll be surprised how many of these would-be callers will actually end up resolving their issues in self-service. As an aside, another idea in this vein is to simply move the "contact us" link from the top right of the screen to the bottom right-hand side (below the divider line). In our focus group, we heard that customers tend to view this real estate as "ad space," so they don't look there unless they are actively searching for the phone number.

Another great story of an organization doing some clever things to help lure customers into self-service comes from a company we've discussed once already in this chapter, Linksys. They use carefully constructed language to passively draw likely callers to their different self-service options. This isn't actively guiding customers, like Master-Card or Amazon, but rather attracting them away from the phone number and encouraging them to try self-service.

For years, Linksys invested in new self-service technologies ranging from knowledge bases to online forums to interactive guides. Ironically, none of those were able to affect their call volume because of channel switching. The old adage, "if you build it, they will come," didn't seem to apply. Linksys wisely realized that certain segments of their customer base, namely new customers whom they affectionately called "Newbies," were among the most likely to abandon self-service and call the support center.

Linksys determined that customers who fit the Newbie profile typically have little product knowledge and therefore tend to need significant direction. So, not surprisingly, their first choice was to pick up the phone. But Linksys knew what Newbies need is to learn about their products, and the knowledge base provided clear guidance to these customers. By describing the knowledge base with the words "simple" and "step-by-step" and "tips," Linksys drew Newbies into this self-help channel. This practice spanned other user segments, such as "Gurus," who are highly sophisticated users who tend to want to engage with other Gurus. Linksys used purposeful language to draw these customers into their forums using words like "connect" and "learn" and "other experiences." Again, simple tweaks to help prevent channel switching.

So did the simple changes they made work? In Linksys's case, it certainly helped. In three years, Linksys was able to improve from roughly 20 percent of support incidents solved via self-service to an astounding 85 percent. Additionally, during this period the average time a user spent on their support site went up dramatically from thirty seconds to roughly six minutes, further indicating far greater channel stickiness. These results cannot be solely attributed to this initiative; however, they are indicative of the time and energy that Linksys spent to improve channel stickiness.

We often find that organizations looking to hide or suppress the phone number are typically asking the wrong question. Only after making the changes discussed in this chapter should companies truly consider more extreme actions.

To recap the key lesson from this chapter: The majority of your customers are *starting* on the web and most callers have likely switched to phone as a choice of last resort. Without significant capital investment or massive process reengineering efforts, most companies can mitigate two in ten instances of channel switching, reducing both customer effort and operating costs at the same time. Those are cost *savings that customers actually want.*

But what happens when customers *do* call? How are leading companies reducing effort in the live channel? Without losing sight of our theme of offering simple, near-term things companies can do to reduce effort, that's where we'll go next.

• • •

KEY TAKEAWAYS

♦ *Most customers are perfectly happy to self-serve.* While most service leaders think that customers prefer live service much more than self-service, customers actually prefer to self-serve—a finding that holds across issue types and most customer demographics.

♦ *It's not about getting customers to try self-service, it's about getting them to stay in self-service.* Nearly 58 percent of all inbound calls are from customers who were just on the company's web site, in many cases trying unsuccessfully to solve their issue.

♦ *The key to mitigating channel switching is simplifying the self-service experience.* Most service sites fail not because they lack functionality and content, but because they have too much of it. The best companies aggressively simplify their web site and actively guide customers to the channels and content that best address the issues they have (as opposed to encouraging customer choice).

3

THE WORST QUESTION
A SERVICE REP CAN ASK

"Have I fully resolved your issue today?" It is the most commonly asked question at the end of customer service phone calls. Reps are trained to ask it, quality assurance managers listen for it, and signs hanging in the contact center remind reps that they are there to fully resolve the customer's issues. It's also perhaps the *worst* question in customer service. What's concerning isn't so much the question itself, but the instinctive response it prompts—"Yeah, I *think* so . . ."—which leads the rep to wrap up the call as quickly as possible and move on to the next customer in the queue. But fast-forward several days from this original phone call and it turns out that the vast majority of these customers end up calling back because their issue wasn't, in fact, fully resolved at all.

We've all had experiences like these:

> "So I tried to make that error message go away based on what the rep told me yesterday, and that seemed to work . . . but now I've got this other error message."

> "I just opened my invoice, and I think the credit that I called about last week was applied, but I can't really tell . . ."

> "You told me I would get the refund check shortly, but it's been three days and I still haven't seen it, so I thought I'd better check again."

At the risk of being cliché, customers don't know what they don't know. And companies, well, they know a lot more about the issues they resolve than the customers they serve. It's simply unfair to ask customers if their issue is fully resolved. After all, *how would they even know?* Sure, the *explicit* reason they called may seem like it was resolved, but related issues, secondary issues, or other implications often remain. Customers have no idea these other *implicit* issues exist, and this forces them to call back all the time—certainly a lot more often than companies tend to think.

As we discussed in chapter 1, repeat contacts are, by an order of magnitude, the single biggest driver of customer effort. Having to call a company back because an issue wasn't fully resolved is a customer experience killer. It's also hugely costly—just ask any service leader. So it's no surprise that most executives are squarely focused on the idea of "one and done" service, fretting over the question, "Why aren't we doing a better job resolving issues the first time customers contact us?" Most service organizations obsess over a specific metric—first contact resolution (FCR)—to help assess performance in this area. FCR is a fairly straightforward concept: Did the rep solve the customer's problem? If so, the call is considered a job well done and we put a check in the FCR box.

Companies regularly boast first contact resolution rates of 70–80 percent or even higher. All things considered, that doesn't sound so bad. If only 20 or 30 percent of issues require more than one contact to resolve, it stands to reason that companies must be doing a pretty good job. But when you ask *customers* how well companies are doing, you get a completely different answer. Customers report, on average, that only 40 percent of their issues are resolved in the first contact (see figure 3.1). In other words, there are typically an *additional 30–40 percent* of issues in which customers would disagree with the companies' assessment that the problem was in fact solved. And what happens in those situations? You guessed it: Customers call back—and they're typically frustrated when they do so. As you now know, the result is *at least* a high-effort interaction and an unnecessary cost for the company, but it can also result in disloyalty, perhaps even of the vocal variety as customers take to Facebook, Twitter, and LinkedIn to share their negative experiences and opinions of the company.

The disparity between what companies *track* and what customers

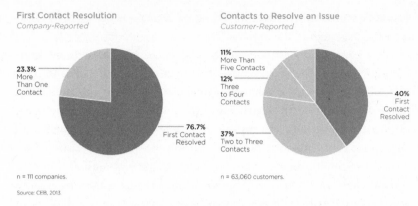

First Contact Resolution
Company-Reported

23.3%
More
Than One
Contact

76.7%
First Contact
Resolved

n = 111 companies.

Contacts to Resolve an Issue
Customer-Reported

11%
More Than
Five Contacts

12%
Three
to Four
Contacts

40%
First
Contact
Resolved

37%
Two to Three
Contacts

n = 63,060 customers.

Source: CEB, 2013.

Figure 3.1 Issue Resolution Rate, Company-Reported versus Customer-Reported

experience is pretty shocking when service leaders hear it for the first time: "That's not what our dashboard says! How did you measure this? Clearly, this must be some sort of mistake." But here's something we've come to appreciate based on all our research: Even if a service organization had 100 percent first contact resolution, they'd still be missing half of the battle to eliminate repeat contacts. The problem here isn't a discrepancy in the data, but a discrepancy in how most companies think about issue resolution.

The concern keeping most service executives up at night is, "Why aren't we resolving issues the first time customers contact us?" But the question that *should be* keeping them up at night is, "What causes our customers to have to call us back?" The differences are nuanced, but hugely important. The former question focuses on reasons why companies fail to resolve the customer's *explicitly* stated issue. The latter question focuses on that as well, but also on the critical issue of why *else* might a customer have to call back.

It turns out that the concept of FCR fails to account for the host of other *related* issues that cause customers to call back. Sure, the customer applied the right software patch, and the issue seemingly went away in that moment. Most companies would consider that issue resolved. But what about when the customer logs on a day later and a related error message awaits them? Sure, the credit was applied to the customer's account, so the issue was considered resolved. But a week later the customer calls back to clarify what "prorated credit" means on their statement. In any one of these instances, both the company and the customer would've ended the interaction feeling the issue was resolved. Yet days later the customer still had to call back.

Most companies only consider the explicit side of resolution—quite literally whether they resolved the customer's *stated* issue. The implicit side of issues gets little acknowledgment at all. These are the related, tangential, or spin-off issues that are often more of an implication of the original issue. Almost always they're unknown to the customer until later. As it turns out, a customer who hears the question, "Have I fully resolved your issue today?" would be better off by responding, "I dunno, is there anything else I should be asking you? Is there anything you can anticipate or clarify right now before I hang up the phone so that I don't have to call back in three days?"

The Other Half of the Equation

We conducted an analysis to better understand why customers have to call back so frequently. By examining call data from a sample of fifty different contact centers, we were better able to understand just how these implicit *and* explicit issues impact repeat customer contacts (see figure 3.2).

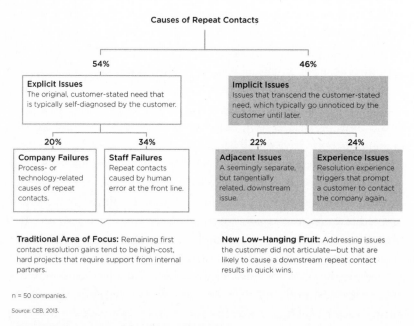

Causes of Repeat Contacts

54%

Explicit Issues
The original, customer-stated need that is typically self-diagnosed by the customer.

46%

Implicit Issues
Issues that transcend the customer-stated need, which typically go unnoticed by the customer until later.

20%

Company Failures
Process- or technology-related causes of repeat contacts.

34%

Staff Failures
Repeat contacts caused by human error at the front line.

22%

Adjacent Issues
A seemingly separate, but tangentially related, downstream issue.

24%

Experience Issues
Resolution experience triggers that prompt a customer to contact the company again.

Traditional Area of Focus: Remaining first contact resolution gains tend to be high-cost, hard projects that require support from internal partners.

New Low-Hanging Fruit: Addressing issues the customer did not articulate—but that are likely to cause a downstream repeat contact results in quick wins.

n = 50 companies.

Source: CEB, 2013.

Figure 3.2 Drivers of Repeat Customer Contacts

Again, explicit issues are the customer's originally stated issue. Think of these as simply "how the issue presents itself to the customer." This could be a billing discrepancy or a question on how to use a device. Repeats contacts for these explicit issues happen when companies simply fail to resolve the issue correctly—and, according to our analysis, these explicit issue resolution failures drive about 54 percent of all callbacks. There are really two main reasons this happens. About 20 percent of the time, a systems error occurs that prevents the customer's stated issue from being resolved. For instance, the billing system fails to apply a credit to the customer's account. Or maybe the systems were down when the customer called (oh—and the sticky note on which the rep jotted the reminder to issue the credit went missing). In these cases, the explicit issue wasn't solved, so the customer calls back. The other major cause of explicit resolution failure is staff failures, which constitute about 34 percent of all callbacks. This is simply human error. For example, an agent keys in the wrong information or perhaps just gives the customer the wrong answer. So again, just over half of all repeat contacts are because a company didn't solve the customer's original stated issue.

On the surface, that may sound like a huge opportunity to improve the customer experience. But most companies have been chasing explicit resolution failure for *decades*. They've invested in better systems, implemented new technologies to support their reps, trained their reps to make fewer mistakes, quality-controlled more interactions to ensure mistakes aren't made, and so on. To say that these explicit repeat contacts can't be further reduced would be foolish, but most in the customer service world would agree that the low-hanging fruit is gone. Process reengineering, Six Sigma initiatives, consultants, system upgrades, training—this is what is required for most companies to substantially decrease these types of repeat contacts.

Implicit issues, on the other hand, *transcend* the original customer-stated need. These repeat contacts happen for two main reasons. The first we refer to as *adjacent issues*, which account for 22 percent of all callbacks. These are downstream issues that might at first glance seem unrelated, but are ultimately connected to the first thing the customer called about. Adjacent issues are best illustrated by way of example. Consider the following from a company we work with in the insurance industry: Their customers often call in trying to lower the insurance premiums on their cars. One way to do that is to raise the deductible from, say, $500 to $1,000. So the premium is lowered, and the issue is marked as "resolved" by the agent handling it. But a couple of weeks later the customer calls back. It turns out the bank holding their car loan only allows a maximum deductible of $500. So the insurance company has to change everything back. Now, you could debate whether anyone was at fault here, but the point is that the customer now feels like dealing with their insurance company is a hassle: "Why didn't the insurance company forewarn me that changing my deductible amount might affect my loan agreement? Surely I'm not the first customer who's had this issue." Not an ideal outcome.

Here's another one: A customer places an order for a high-definition TV and the TV arrives without issue at the customer's house, right on schedule. First contact resolution, right? Not so fast. It turns out the customer didn't know she needed to contact her cable provider to order a special HD converter box. So that's another contact, albeit to a different company. When the cable installer arrives, he tells her that she needs special cables in order for the TV to receive the signal from the box. One more contact, this time with the company she originally ordered the TV from. If you think about it from the companies' perspectives, it's three discrete instances of first contact resolution. But from the customer's point of view it's totally different. She's had to endure three contacts to resolve her *real* issue: being able to watch television in high definition. That's a very high-effort experience, and her loyalty from that point would likely be in serious jeopardy. Now, is it unfair to hold companies accountable for such "customer events"? Maybe so. But try explaining that to a fickle customer who only cares about what *they* experience and how it felt to them. Most all service leaders can think of loyalty-threatening examples like this that happen regularly in their own companies.

The second major source of implicit repeat contacts is experience issues, which constitute 24 percent of all repeat contacts. These are primarily *emotional* triggers that cause a customer to second-guess the answer they were given, or double-check to see if another answer exists. This includes customers feeling like they didn't get all the information they wanted. "Why did the issue happen in the first place? What's the company going to do to prevent that issue from happening again? Are other customers going to be impacted?" And so the customer calls back to get those answers. It also includes instances in which customers just didn't like the answer they were given. This emotional side of the customer experience is hugely important and grossly misunderstood, well beyond driving repeat contact volume. In fact, it's so prevalent that we've dedicated the entire next chapter to this idea, so we'll only briefly discuss the implications here.

Going Beyond First Contact Resolution

The idea of resolving implicit issues as well as the customer's explicit issue is something we call *next issue avoidance*. It's a concept that spans beyond traditional first contact resolution in several important ways. The traditional FCR approach is grounded in the idea of "one and done"—the customer calls in, the issue is resolved as quickly as possible, and the rep moves on to the next caller. Reps are commonly trained to ask themselves, "How do I resolve *this* customer issue?" The company's focus when improving issue resolution performance is to remove the process obstacles for reps and arm them with tools that quickly deliver information and resolve the issue. In this system, measurement primarily focuses on whether or not the rep resolved the customer-articulated issue in that interaction. Most service organizations subscribe to this approach in some way, shape, or form.

Next issue avoidance is very different. It starts with a totally different mind-set. Reps are trained and coached to ask themselves, "How can I make sure this customer *doesn't have to call us back*?" (See figure 3.3.) One important thing to note is that next issue avoidance doesn't necessarily replace first contact resolution. Rather, it's in addition to the traditional FCR approach.

In next issue avoidance, reps don't *just* resolve the issue that the customer articulated; they also resolve the issues that the customer *didn't* articulate but might encounter once they get off the phone—both adjacent issues and experience issues. Now, simply asking reps to resolve issues this way isn't a fair expectation. Companies need to arm reps with sharper diagnostic skills and tools that can help them "forward-resolve" the next likely customer issue. This approach is like chess—you have to help reps think a few moves ahead in the game. It would only stand to reason that this different approach requires not only a different mind-set, but also a different measurement approach—and it does. Companies trying to improve next issue avoidance (not just FCR) should track callbacks—any repeat contact by the customer, for any

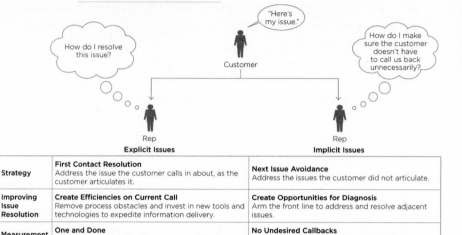

	Explicit Issues	Implicit Issues
Strategy	**First Contact Resolution** Address the issue the customer calls in about, as the customer articulates it.	**Next Issue Avoidance** Address the issues the customer did not articulate.
Improving Issue Resolution	**Create Efficiencies on Current Call** Remove process obstacles and invest in new tools and technologies to expedite information delivery.	**Create Opportunities for Diagnosis** Arm the front line to address and resolve adjacent issues.
Measurement Approach	**One and Done** Success is measured by the company's ability to resolve only the customer-stated issue.	**No Undesired Callbacks** Success is measured by no resulting callbacks from the customer, for any undesired reason.
Wrap-up Statement	"Have I fully resolved your issue today?"	"While I have you on the line, there are a couple other things we should address..."

Source: CEB, 2013.

Figure 3.3 First Contact Resolution versus Next Issue Avoidance

reason, within a specified time period. We'll touch more on that later in this chapter.

But let's first look at how some real companies have made a next issue avoidance strategy work for them and their customers.

Think of Customer Issues as Events

A Canadian telecom company taught us a considerable amount about how to make next issue avoidance part of the operating fabric of the service organization. In one of the conversations we had with their team, they corrected us when we asked them how their best reps tend to handle issues. The word "issue" was something they were trying to eliminate from their vocabulary. "We think in terms of customer 'events,' not issues," one of their managers explained.

Take an everyday type of call that this company's reps deal with—a customer ordering a new mobile phone and service plan. The rep fields the call, completes the order, and the request is considered resolved. But five days later, the customer tries to use their new voicemail for the first time and realizes they can't remember how to access it and can't remember the password they set when first subscribing to the service. So they call, and another rep fields the request and gives the customer the information they need. And this *new* issue is also considered resolved on the first contact. Another week passes and the customer realizes they need more features than the basic plan they signed up for, so they call to upgrade their service. Finally, a few weeks later, the customer gets their billing statement and has questions on how the prorated charge for the new service was calculated since it seems more expensive than the offer they saw in the newspaper ad. So they call again to get an explanation of the bill. Suddenly the total for this customer event—getting a mobile phone service that meets the customer's needs—is four total calls. From the company's perspective, that was four instances of first contact resolution. But from the customer's perspective, it's all connected. In fact, the company shared that the average customer event required 2.5 calls to fully resolve.

Thinking about customer issues in terms of "events" helps, but clearly the company wanted to arm their reps to forward-resolve these likely issues. Imagine the aforementioned scenario in which the rep is fielding a new phone order and service plan setup. What would happen if the rep tried to forward-resolve *all* the potential follow-ups? The customer calls, and the rep places the order. The rep starts to tell the customer how they'll access their voice mail. At this point, the customer is trying to find a notepad to write down what's being said. As the conversation continues, the rep realizes that this customer might be much better off with an upgraded plan instead of what they ordered, so the rep starts to upsell the customer. By this point, the customer is completely overwhelmed as she listens to the rep drone on about the first billing statement and what that will look like. The whole interaction starts to enter a death spiral. The handle time goes through the roof. The customer is completely confused and decides to hold off on the order, questioning if they even want to give their business to the company at all. It's all very high-effort.

The company knew these were real risks, so they worked hard to create a simple approach to forward resolution that wouldn't harm rep productivity or the customer experience, and would be fairly easy to implement. They analyzed their most common issue types to help determine the opportunities they had to forward-resolve any related issues. The first part of this analysis was to assess which issues most commonly had associated adjacent issues. For this, the company created an "issue taxonomy." Three analysts working for eight months compiled information from call logs, quality assurance recordings, and phone trunk and IVR data and pieced it together to build out these issue maps.

While the time and effort required to conduct an investigation like this would give most companies pause, the returns this company has seen have more than justified the level of resourcing. Still, if you don't have a few analysts at your immediate disposal, we think there's an easier, "good enough" way to get the issue-mapping exercise started. We affectionately call this the "pizza and beer" approach, since that's all it requires to get started. Ask a small group of tenured frontline service reps and managers to stick around after their shifts end to help create your own issue taxonomy.

Start with the ten most common call types and answer this question: In your experience, why would a customer who calls us about this issue have to call us back? Urge the team to think through adjacent reasons only—in other words, not "because the last rep screwed up" or "because they didn't like the answer and wanted to shop around." Ask the group to agree on the ten most common types of repeat contacts—instances where customers start the call by saying, "I just spoke with another rep the other day about this issue . . ." Once you've settled on the list, answer this question: What could the *last* rep this person spoke to have done to prevent this call that *you* had to handle? The results of this exercise certainly won't be comprehensive, but they will serve as a solid starting point for awakening your team to the power—and necessity—of next issue avoidance.

As this telecom company built out their issue taxonomies, they simultaneously assessed how often these adjacent issues were happening. The adjacent issues that only happened, say, 5 percent of the time, were poor candidates for forward resolution, whereas issues that created callbacks 20 percent of the time or more were prime candidates. Put differently, they opted not to waste their time forward-resolving issues that rarely come up. They opted to just stick with the low-hanging fruit.

This analysis allowed the company to create triage maps for forward resolution that they could provide to their frontline reps. Let's revisit the new service order example to help shed light on how this company compiled their analysis and put this concept of forward resolution into practice (see figure 3.4).

In this illustrative example, the company's analysis indicates that customers placing a new service order had a *75 percent likelihood* of calling

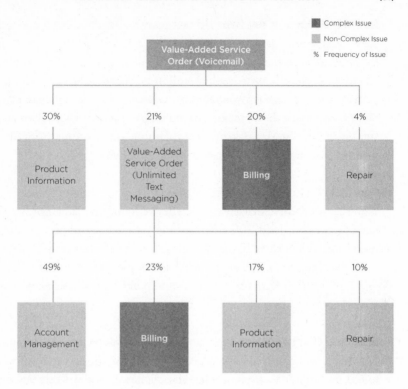

Figure 3.4 Canadian Telecom Company's Repeat Contact Triage Map (Illustrative)

back as part of that one event. This 75 percent likelihood consists of four frequently cited adjacent issues. The first is a follow-up request for product information (e.g., "Can you remind me how many MB of data I get per month with my plan?" or "What is the rate I'm charged for international calls on this plan?"), which occurs 30 percent of the time. The second, upgrading to an enhanced service package, occurs 21 percent of the time. The third, billing-related follow-up calls, occur 20 percent of the time. And finally, they have service repair calls, which happen only 4 percent of the time. These triage maps inform the company's systems, which push forward-resolution tips to reps as they input case information.

You could imagine that this would be an effective practice simply knowing how often these adjacent issues occur, but this company has added in some really smart rules to make sure that they're balancing simplicity of forward resolution with effectiveness and thereby avoiding the confusion that forward resolution of adjacent issues might create:

Rule #1: Down one, not two. The company realized that even though they could confidently predict two or three calls into the future—such as the likelihood that a new service setup would eventually turn into an enhanced service order such as unlimited text messaging, and ultimately the customer would have related account management questions—it just didn't make sense to forward-resolve more than one step at a time at the risk of overwhelming the customer. So they forward-resolve only the *immediate* adjacent issues.

Rule #2: Pick winners. The company only forward-resolves the highest-probability adjacent issues. They've found that adjacent issues have to occur at least 20 percent of the time to qualify for forward resolution. If less than 20 percent of the time, it's better (for the company and for the customer) to just roll the dice and see if the issue *might* arise rather than use call time (and potentially confuse the customer) trying to forward-resolve it.

Rule #3: Don't forward-resolve complex issues on the phone. For their more complex issues, such as billing questions, the company found it difficult to explain what the customer would likely see on their upcoming statement. So instead of confusing customers during a phone call, the rep explains how they'll follow up with a simple e-mail that details what to expect on the billing statement.

So how does this work in practice? Let's use two hypothetical interactions to explain. In the first example, a customer calls in with a straightforward request to correct their address. The rep handles the issue, and there aren't any high-probability adjacent issues for correcting an address, so the call simply ends. In other words, some issues are just "one and done" calls.

But what happens when a customer calls to initiate new service? The first thing that happens is the rep handles the explicit customer issue, which in this case is setting up new service. As the rep completes this request, her system recognizes that there are a few adjacent issues she should also resolve while on the phone with the customer. First, the rep asks the customer to go to the company site so she can show the customer where to find basic plan information and FAQs. Second, the rep attempts to upsell the customer an enhanced plan since that's something new basic plan customers often call back about. And finally, the system prompts the rep to get the customer's e-mail address so the company can send a follow-up e-mail about the bill. This call doesn't end with, "Have I fully resolved your issue today?" Instead the rep proactively says, "If you have a minute, I'd like to go over a couple of things with you now that you might not be thinking about, but will help save you time and effort later." It's *such* a different way to interact with customers.

As an aside, it's worth mentioning that these follow-up e-mails that the company sends customers on complex issues (such as billing) are extremely clever (see figure 3.5). The company has three simple criteria that all forward-resolution e-mails follow. First, keep these e-mails short. Only critical information should be included. These e-mails can be kept short because of the second criteria—push customers to self-service. If customers need more information, they can read a knowledge article or FAQ that has that detail. Finally, the company times the e-mail delivery for maximum impact. Often this is immediately after a call has completed, but for other issues the company will delay sending the e-mail until later (e.g., for billing; the company also sends e-mails that arrive just a few days before a bill arrives).

Dear [Field: First Name] [Field: Last Name]

We hope you're enjoying your Call Answer service. Find out more about using all the features this service has to offer.

As with your other telephone services, this feature is billed one month in advance. On your next bill, you'll see a charge for the time between when your service was activated and your bill date, plus a charge for the full month ahead. Learn more.

Did you know that **voicemail manager** can enhance the capabilities of your service? Find out how!

**If you're not happy with your purchase, visit our Web site anytime within the next 30 days to cancel the service hassle-free.

Thank you for choosing us!

Newsletter Subscription | Legal Notice | Security and Privacy | Contact Us

---

Source: Canadian telecom company; CEB, 2013.

Figure 3.5 Canadian Telecom Company's Proactive Billing E-mail (Illustrative)

This practice on the whole has led to some huge successes for this company. Running a controlled pilot group allowed them to isolate the impact of this forward-resolution approach and the impact it has on both their customers' expenses and their own operating costs. The pilot showed a net reduction of 16 percent in phone calls per customer event—a call reduction that allowed them to recover their initial investment within six months. Anecdotal rep feedback has also been positive, since reps feel they are better able to help customers but also are dealing with fewer frustrated customers who are calling back for entirely controllable reasons.

As you can see in this company's example, the concept of next issue avoidance also has significant potential in a service-to-sales or inbound sales setting. In this case, one of the forward-resolution opportunities is to recommend an enhanced service upgrade. Upselling and cross-selling so often take the form of the "offer of the week" that gets pushed to every caller. But understanding precisely what additional products or services will help customers make the most of your services and avoid a need for them to call back can result in far more meaningful upsell conversations. Which approach do you think would result in more converted sales? Consider the following example, where an extended product warranty is being offered to a customer buying a new mobile phone:

Example #1: "Would you like to extend the phone original warranty, covering any manufacturing defects for two years?"

Example #2: "I know that replacing a phone is a huge pain. One thing I'd suggest that'll help save you time and effort is to add our extended protection to this phone. If there are any defects—like the speaker issue you had with your old phone—in the next two years, we'll replace it with the most current version that exists, or let you pick another phone of equal value."

Positioning next issue avoidance, even in a sales setting, as a way to save the customer time and energy will not only help reduce customer effort, it may even lead to a sale. In the next chapter we'll explore this emotional side of customer effort further. Simply letting a customer know that you are trying to save them from having to call back later and deal with another related issue goes a remarkably long way. So there's clearly a human element to next issue avoidance.

But think back for a moment to all the analysis that the telecom company conducted. Clear patterns emerged in their data that helped them arm reps for forward-resolving customer issues. It would only stand to reason that next issue avoidance could also be automated to a certain degree, particularly in self-service channels.

Fidelity Investments is another company that has done just that—applied next issue avoidance principles in their online service channel. Similar to the "pizza and beer" exercise mentioned earlier, Fidelity has their service team brainstorm recommended next steps for their most popular online issues. For example, one of the most common issues resolved in self-service is updating an address. Most organizations' web sites simply confirm the interaction and thank the customer. But Fidelity realized that an address change likely means there are other implications for this customer. So after updating an address, a customer is prompted to take up to three additional actions—two service-related and one sales-related. On the service side, the customer is prompted to order new checks and update their electronic fund transfers, since Fidelity knows these are common adjacent issues. On the sales side, the customer can learn about homeowner's or renter's insurance with a partnering organization. It is a very targeted cross-sell offer.

Another example occurs when a customer opens a new retirement account. Once that's completed, they are prompted to transfer money, roll over other accounts, or learn about mutual fund pricing. Since these prompts are so targeted, *an entire quarter* of all Fidelity's self-service interactions started with another self-service interaction. Because Fidelity is making it easier for customers to further engage in self-service, this practice helped them recognize a 5 percent decrease in calls per household.

Measuring Next Issue Avoidance

As the old saying goes, *what gets measured gets done*. In the operationally focused world of contact centers, seemingly *everything* gets measured. The idea of measuring issue resolution success is no different—but as we've established, the traditional first contact resolution metric has some serious flaws. In most cases, FCR is measured based either upon the customer indicating the issue is solved while on the call, or through a post-call survey. The customer is always right, right? So it's little surprise that 60 percent of companies measure FCR based on one of these customer-indicated approaches. But we also established that customers often don't know if they'll need to call back for an implicit issue. So what's a company to measure?

Before revealing what we believe is one of the better approaches to measuring next issue avoidance, let's take a moment to lay out our general philosophy on measuring issue resolution rates. The reality is that there is no silver bullet. An absolutely perfect metric for measuring first contact resolution, or next issue avoidance for that matter, doesn't really exist. Any conceivable way to measure resolution success has at least some flaws. That leads to the second principle: You should measure *something* consistently. Don't become paralyzed searching for the perfect metric, or debating the flaws of your current metric. Here's the dirty little secret of measuring issue resolution: Companies that actually reinforce their metric through their service ethic, their culture, and their performance management have 4.9 percent better resolution performance *regardless of their metric* than organizations that simply pay lip service to issue resolution.

So what is the best metric for tracking next issue avoidance? We worked with a lot of companies to understand the pros and cons of different measurement approaches. In fact, we created an entire issue resolution toolkit (see appendix B) that captures all that we've learned, accounting for different technology limitations, process limitations, and other environmental factors for different service and support organizations. Out of all the companies we've observed, one U.S.-based home mortgage company is among the most progressive. This company tracks a remarkably simple metric: repeat calls from any customer within a seven-day period. This metric is tracked not just on a companywide basis, but right at the individual rep level.

This company chose a seven-day window for a couple of reasons. First, in their analysis, they realized the vast majority of repeat calls occur within five days of the initial call. A small but significant number of repeat calls occur up to seven days out. Second, in order to effectively coach, reps need to be able to recall the service incident. Beyond seven days, this company found that reps had a difficult time remembering the situation. In fact, they formerly used a thirty-day window, but found that coaching wasn't terribly effective when reps couldn't remember the customer situation. Interestingly, the company still tracks repeat contacts on a thirty-day basis at the company level, but not the rep level. This allows them to create standardized reports by teams and to benchmark team performance and relative improvement over time.

The company also found that most callbacks seldom occur beyond seven days. Other companies in other industries have reported very similar findings, so our general guidance is to consider a seven-to-fourteen-day window for tracking callbacks. (A word of forewarning: The longer the measurement window, the lower your issue resolution rate is going to appear.) Keep in mind that, as this company taught us, the longer the window, the less powerful the coaching interactions will be, since reps forget the specifics of given customer interactions.

A natural objection that often arises when we teach this company's approach is that *it seems unfair to track this at an individual rep level.* Obviously there are a lot of things completely out of any one rep's control that might make some customers call back. The customer might not have written down the information they needed. Perhaps the customer did something wrong. The customer might have been confused and didn't ask the rep to clarify. And so they call back. Surely that isn't fair to the rep who tried to help. But here's the thing—every other rep is up against the same uncontrollable issues, and over the course of the many calls that each rep handles week to week, it becomes very clear which reps are creating repeat calls, and which reps are indeed forward-resolving issues. Over time, this company is able to set an average performance threshold for repeat calls. In this way, they're able to see which reps are the better performers, learn the approaches these reps take, and see who needs coaching (see figure 3.6).

Other companies that have tried this approach do something very simple to make it feel even fairer to reps—*they don't show them their raw performance data.* The reps don't need to know the precise number or average number of repeat calls they're driving. Instead, they need to understand their general tendencies—whether they are failing, meeting, or exceeding the overall performance threshold. This way, reps will be less inclined to debate whether or not specific callbacks were within their control.

What's most remarkable about this metric is that it focuses attention on the issue in a way that no other method could. Granted, whenever new metrics like this are introduced, reps will try to game the system, so

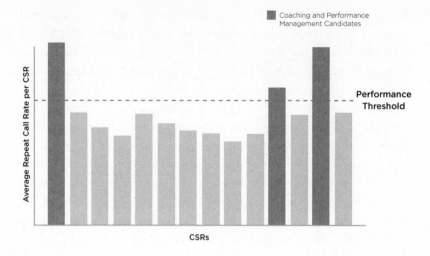

Source: US-based mortgage company; CEB, 2013.

Figure 3.6 Repeat Call Rates by Representative at US-Based Mortgage Company (Illustrative)

quality assurance teams should be on high alert to ensure that bad habits aren't developing (e.g., reps transferring any remotely complex issue to another rep). But among the organizations that do measure callbacks, we've heard great stories about how their best performers start to suggest improvements to company policies and processes to avoid repeat calls. "Hey, I'm not taking the heat for that bad policy—I better tell my team lead that this is a problem and is forcing customers to call back." The other significant improvement this drives is on the emotional side of the customer experience. Reps take on the mind-set of truly being on the customer's side and ensuring they don't need to unnecessarily call back. Customers sense that reps are doing all they can to make sure the customer is all set and ready to move on with their lives.

Remember the emotionally driven repeat contacts we discussed earlier in this chapter, those instances when customers call back just to be sure the issue was solved, or perhaps because they didn't like the answer they received? The best reps quickly figure out that the emotional side of the customer experience matters a lot too, particularly in driving up repeat contacts and customer effort. They adjust their behavior almost immediately. You might be thinking, *Of course, they're the best reps. But I need the majority of my reps to serve customers that way.* As it turns out, it is very possible to teach reps new ways to connect with customers in a way that makes them feel more confident about the resolution and lowers their perception of the amount of effort required to resolve their issue. This is such a powerful idea, we've dedicated the entire next chapter to some specific practices that every company can and should be employing.

KEY TAKEAWAYS

♦ *Nearly half of all repeat contacts go unseen by the typical company.* Customers who had their issue resolved often call back for reasons indirectly related to the original issue. The most common sources of repeat contacts are adjacent issues (i.e., downstream implications linked to the original issue), and experience issues (i.e., "emotional" disconnects between the rep and the customer—for instance, when the customer doesn't like the answer they've received).

♦ *Don't just solve the current issue, head off the next issue.* The best companies think of issues as events, not one-offs, and teach their reps to forward-resolve issues that are related to the original issue but typically go unnoticed by the customer until later.

♦ *Measure callbacks, not just first contact resolution (FCR).* FCR is a flawed metric because it expressly focuses on resolution of the customer's stated issue, rather than related, downstream issues. The best companies instead measure callbacks within a limited time frame—assessing whether the rep solved the stated customer issue, as well as forward-resolved adjacent and experience-related follow-up issues.

4

JUST BECAUSE
THERE'S NOTHING YOU CAN DO
DOESN'T MEAN THERE'S
NOTHING YOU CAN DO

t's 7:30 a.m. and you've just arrived at the airport for your 9 a.m. flight. But as the departures board clearly indicates, your flight's been canceled. So you take a deep breath, compose yourself, and call the airline to see about rebooking on a later flight.

When you reach the reservation agent you're told the following: "We regret the inconvenience of this flight cancellation. We can rebook you on the 9 p.m. flight tonight." How would that make you feel—especially if you could see on the departures board that the airline has multiple earlier departures you could catch? You probably wouldn't be very happy.

Now, imagine instead that the agent says, "We regret the inconvenience of this flight cancellation. I know I can get you on the 9 a.m. flight *tomorrow,* but let me see if I can get you a seat on a flight out today." A brief hold ensues and then the agent comes back on the line: "Great news—I managed to get you a seat on the 9 p.m. flight. I know you'll have to kill some time, but at least you'll get to your destination today."

While the outcome in both examples is exactly the same (getting rebooked on the 9 p.m. flight), we're betting the second response felt a lot better than the first. Why is that?

It has to do with a concept we call "experience engineering"— managing a conversation with carefully selected language designed to improve how the customer interprets what they're being told. In this chapter, we'll help you understand how and why experience engineering works, and also provide several practices from real companies that will help you learn how to use these techniques in your own organization.

As you'll recall from chapter 1, we found that the customer's own *perception* of how effortful the experience was stacked right up against more tangible effort sources like repeat contacts, channel switching, transfers, and repeating information.

How much does perception matter? Quite a bit, it turns out. Our original study gave us an inkling that this "soft side" of effort matters to some degree, but when we went back and studied it in depth, we were shocked to learn that the customer's perception of the experience actually counts for fully *two-thirds* of the overall "effort equation." Put differently, how the customer *feels* about the interaction matters about twice as much as what they actually have to *do* during the interaction—a hugely important finding we'll discuss in more depth later in this chapter.

Ironically, while the "feel" side of effort—the emotional, perceptual side—matters a huge amount in the overall effort equation, it's something that most companies pay very little (if any) attention to. Instead, most companies immediately focus on the "physical exertion" side of effort. When we asked customer service executives around the world, "What specifically are you doing to reduce effort?" we discovered that all the top responses fell into the category of "general process improvements"—for instance, streamlining processes, simplifying interactions, and generally making things easier for customers (see figure 4.1).

If you think about it, it seems to make a lot of sense. The logical approach to reducing effort is to minimize the number of steps a customer has to take. In fact, almost three-quarters of companies we surveyed reported that their effort reduction approaches were squarely targeting these hard, tangible effort drivers. Of course, if effort was mostly about what customers have to *do* to get their issues resolved, you'd see a near-perfect correlation between exertion and the level of effort customers reported having gone through in a service interaction. But that's not what we found at all.

We analyzed the service interactions of more than 4,500 customers and looked at their exertion levels—in other words, what customers had to *do* to resolve their issues. This included things like the total number of interactions required for them to resolve their issues, the number of

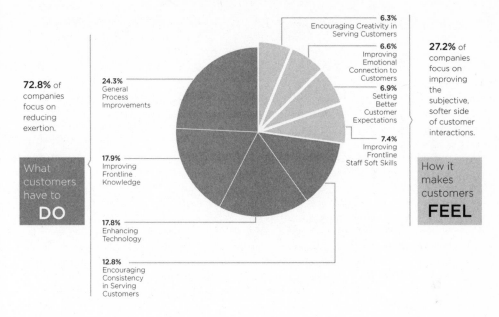

72.8% of companies focus on reducing exertion.

What customers have to **DO**

24.3% General Process Improvements

17.9% Improving Frontline Knowledge

17.8% Enhancing Technology

12.8% Encouraging Consistency in Serving Customers

6.3% Encouraging Creativity in Serving Customers

6.6% Improving Emotional Connection to Customers

6.9% Setting Better Customer Expectations

7.4% Improving Frontline Staff Soft Skills

27.2% of companies focus on improving the subjective, softer side of customer interactions.

How it makes customers **FEEL**

n = 26 companies.

Source: CEB, 2013.

Figure 4.1 Company-Reported Effort Reduction Focus Areas

transfers from one agent to another, whether they had to switch channels, and the frequency with which they had to repeat information.

When we plot the exertion levels reported by these 4,500 customers, we get a normal distribution curve, which is what you'd expect. In other words, some customers put forth little exertion (e.g., no callbacks, no channel switching, no repeat contacts), and some put forth a lot, but most folks put forth a moderate level of effort (see figure 4.2). But when you plot this curve against reported effort (we used our Customer Effort Score metric, which we'll discuss in more detail in chapter 6), there's very little overlap.

The exertion curve actually peaks nearest to the lower end of the scale. This indicates that the majority of service interactions do not require that customers *do* a lot of seemingly effortful things to resolve their issues. However, when we map out the effort curve—the amount of effort customers *perceived* during those exact same transactions, we find that it peaks much farther toward the higher end of the scale.

Like most companies, we assumed that *exertion* and *effort* were synonymous, so this data was quite an eye-opener. If customers primarily

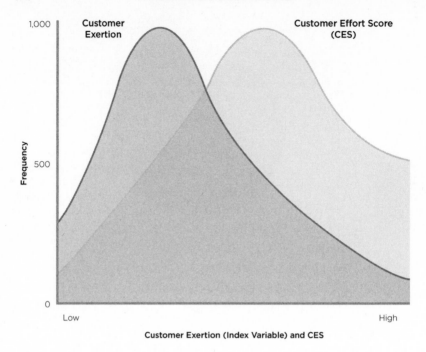

Customer Exertion (Index Variable) and CES

n = 4,589 customers.

Source: CEB, 2013.

Figure 4.2 Customer Exertion vs. Reported Customer Effort

experienced effort based on their degree of exertion—the number of things they had to do to resolve their issue, and the difficulty of those things—these two curves (the customer exertion curve and the Customer Effort Score Curve) would have overlapped almost entirely. But they don't. There are two things we can conclude from this.

First, it is clear that a lot of interactions that don't require a lot of *exertion* still feel like a lot of *effort* to customers. Lots of interactions that were low exertion were still scored as high on the effort scale. That is not a positive sign for customer service leaders. This is bad news for companies that are losing the loyalty battle with a lot of customers who don't have to exert much effort to get to a resolution but still come away thinking to themselves, "That was a lot of effort." It's as if service organizations are handling "easy" situations in the wrong way far too often.

Second, the way most companies have been strategizing about how

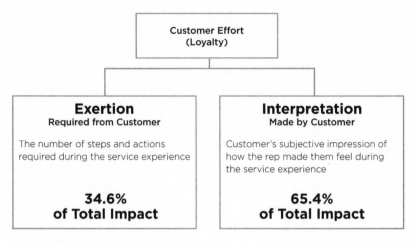

n = 4,589 customers.

Source: CEB, 2013.

Figure 4.3 Regression Drivers of Customer Effort

to reduce customer effort isn't quite complete. In fact, companies on an effort reduction journey run the very real risk of being blindsided by a huge driver of effort that they're not at all focusing on: the customer's perception of the experience (see figure 4.3).

Effort, it turns out, isn't mostly about what customers have to do. While that's certainly a critical part of the effort story, customer effort is actually mostly about how customers *feel*. The exertion required from the customer makes up only 34.6 percent of how they evaluate customer effort. But the interpretation side—the softer, more subjective elements based entirely on human emotions and reactions—make up a shocking 65.4 percent of the total impact. Put simply, what matters most to customers when it comes to evaluating effort isn't what they have to do to get their issue resolved, but rather how they feel during and after the interaction. *It turns out that effort is one-third "do" and two-thirds "feel."*

To create the biggest, fastest impact in improving the customer experience at your company, your goal should be to do exactly the opposite of what most companies instinctively think of when it comes to reducing effort. While it is important, don't overinvest in streamlining the physical side of the service experience. Instead, focus on the interpretation or "feel" side of effort.

Of course, the knee-jerk reaction for most companies would be to double down on "soft skills," but we have come to learn that leading companies are in fact focused on something very different.

Overreliance on "Soft Skills"

Classic customer service soft skills training is fundamentally about teaching agents to be polite, warm, and empathetic to customers, in a way that reflects well on the company. But there is compelling evidence that if the goal is effort reduction, just getting reps to be nicer to people doesn't have much of an impact at all. In fact, when we dig into the data, we find that six of the variables most closely associated with classic soft skills have either marginal impact or no impact at all:

Variables with Marginal Impact on Customer Effort (Less Than 5 Percent):
- Rep communicated clearly
- Rep demonstrated confidence

Variables with No Statistical Impact on Customer Effort:
- Rep showed concern
- Rep was non-scripted
- Rep understood customer
- Rep listened well

Now of course, these four areas that registered as having no impact on reducing effort are still obviously essential for any live interaction. Being rude and obstinate can make a call go in a bad direction quickly. But what the data tells us, in no uncertain terms, is that these skills alone aren't enough to move the needle at all on effort reduction. Even doing all six of these things at a world-class level won't make your company a category leader in effort reduction. If you're betting on soft skills training, you're very likely to lose the battle for customer loyalty.

So if the "feel" side of effort isn't simply about reps being nice or being good listeners, then what *is* it about? To get some leads, we spoke to a small minority of companies that reported investing heavily in the emotional side of the service experience. Here are two verbatim quotes from customer service leaders who are part of that minority:

"We see our best reps really taking control of the conversation—they anticipate moments when the customer is likely to have a negative reaction, and do their best to get ahead of it."

"There are lots of times when we can't give the customer exactly what they want. But our best reps guide customers to a point where they feel pretty good about an outcome that most likely wasn't their first choice."

That sense of anticipation—of somehow being a step ahead of the potential negative moments of a service interaction—is a trait we believe the best reps are born with at some level. And we know that this kind of anticipation can make a huge difference in reducing a customer's interpretation of effort. But is it *learnable*? Could a company get the average rep to do this seamlessly and with regularity? The scenarios where a customer has no choice but to accept an outcome they were not hoping for are typically *very* high-effort situations. These are the calls that end in escalations, arguments, and multiple callbacks. Learning to operate a step or two ahead of the customer and take control of how they interpret a bad news scenario could never be acquired through soft skills training. What we're talking about here is far more than just being friendly and nice or using a customer's name or empathizing with their personal situation.

But if not that, then what? Where does it come from? How do you teach it? What do you even call it? What we discovered is that this thing has many names. It's rooted in psychology, sociology, and behavioral economics. We call it *experience engineering*, since that is precisely what is being done—managing or engineering a conversation using carefully selected language to improve how the customer interprets what they're being told.

While experience engineering is still a nascent idea in customer service, there are a host of strategies employed by sales and marketing organizations, labor unions, and political parties that have been used for years and even decades to influence the thoughts, feelings, and reactions of customers, employees, and voters.

We tested some of the specific techniques that we believed could be used in everyday customer situations, ideas that would be simple enough to teach and flexible enough to employ in a wide variety of situations. Among those we explored:

- Advocacy—demonstrating clear alignment with the customer and supporting them in an active way.

- Positive language—resisting the use of words or phrases (like "no" or "can't") that convey an inability to reach a productive outcome with the customer.
- Anchoring—positioning a given outcome as more positive and desirable by comparing it to another less desirable one.

For each of these techniques, we conducted experiments to test customer reactions and then compared their reactions to those of a control group which did not experience any form of experience engineering. In three experiments, we showed a test group of several hundred customers the same exact service scenario, but in each case, half the subjects were shown "Rep Response A" and the other half were shown "Rep Response B." We then asked all the subjects to rate that transaction for overall quality of experience and for customer effort, using a scale based on the Customer Effort Score (CES) which we'll discuss in chapter 6. What the customers in each group were required to *do* was exactly the same, and the steps the customer endured in each situation represented a relatively high degree of effort. Rep A and Rep B offered the same solutions in each scenario, but the language they used to take control of the experience, as you will see, was very different.

Advocacy

Customer Scenario: You have a new bicycle that you've only been using for a short time, but there is some issue with the brake cable that is making the bike unsafe to ride.

Rep Response A: "It's really difficult to tell what's happening over the phone. You should just bring it into one of our certified repair shops to have it looked at."

Rep Response B: "I know that can be frustrating, so I'll definitely pass your feedback on to our engineering team. Okay, let me check to see if other customers have had a similar issue with that bike model—that should tell us if it's a repair issue or if it just requires a break-in period. Okay, I'm not seeing many instances of customers having the same issue, so I'd recommend bringing it back to the shop and having them take a look at it, especially since it's still under warranty."

So, the same answer from both reps—you're going to have to bring the bike in to the shop, there's no getting around it. The difference, though, is the degree of advocacy shown by the two reps. The impact on the customer's interpretation was dramatic.

The customers who heard Rep B's response said the quality of that experience was 67 percent higher than what was reported by the control group who received the Rep A response. When we asked them to rate the interaction for customer effort, the B group reported 77 percent lower effort.

Positive Language

Customer Scenario: You're having trouble transferring funds from one online bank account to another account.

Rep Response A: "Well, you can't transfer funds from this online account to a non-authorized account. There isn't much I can do until you authorize the other account. You'll need to go back to the Account Management tab, and under that you'll see the Authorization menu. First, click on . . ."

Rep Response B: "I see the issue—it looks like we need to get that other account authorized for you. That should only take a few seconds and I'll walk you through the process. Can you go back to the Account Management web page? First, let's click on . . ."

The B group judged the quality of their experience 82 percent higher, and the degree of customer effort was judged to be 73 percent lower—a huge difference considering that the two responses differed only slightly.

Anchoring Expectations

Customer Scenario: You've having connectivity issues with a new cable TV box and the issue can only be resolved by a technician who will need to make a home service call.

Rep Response A: "We can send a technician out tomorrow, but it's an all-day window and someone will have to be home from 8 a.m. to 8 p.m. would that work?

Rep Response B: "Well, it looks like our next guaranteed two-hour window is next week. Or it looks like I *could* have the technician there tomorrow. Now, it would be an all-day time slot, so you'd need to make sure that somebody would be available to let our technician in from 8 a.m.

to 8 p.m., but at least it's tomorrow instead of next week. I know it's short notice, but would that work?"

In this example, the B group rated the overall quality of the experience as 76 percent higher and the degree of customer effort as 55 percent lower. And again, the outcome was exactly the same.

In all three of these scenarios, the rep could not do anything to reduce the actual amount of physical exertion required to resolve the issue, but Rep B was able to create a very different result—not by being nicer, but by actually *engineering* the customer experience through the purposeful use of language.

In customer service circles, soft skills are typically defined as "A code of behavior created to consistently handle customer issues in a friendly, personable, and professional manner that reflects positively on the representative and the company."

Let's break this definition down. First, soft skills are about *consistently handling* customer issues, practicing the same approach with all customers across the board with a fairly standard protocol. Soft skills are not considered an option or choice, but are designed to be applied with every caller, every time. Next, soft skills are based on the rep being *friendly, personable, and professional* by focusing on the interpersonal elements of the exchange. Lastly, they are about engaging the customer in a way that *reflects positively* on the rep and the company they are representing. When companies invest in soft skills training, they are betting that if their reps are professional and nice to customers, they'll be more tolerant of the experience and ultimately more likely to remain loyal to the company.

The concept of experience engineering is very different. We define experience engineering as "An approach to actively guide a customer through an interaction that is designed to anticipate the emotional response and preemptively offer solutions that create a mutually beneficial resolution."

Again, let's break it down. First, experience engineering is purposeful. It's about *actively guiding* the customer. It involves taking control over the interaction through a series of deliberate actions, like the ones demonstrated in our experiments. Second, experience engineering is designed to *anticipate the emotional response* of the customer. It's like peering into the future—recognizing the moment when a negative situation is just about to develop, typically when the customer is about to be told they cannot have exactly what they're asking for, and easing them into that answer. Next, reps who engage in experience engineering are trying to *preemptively offer* solutions that the customer will find agreeable. In other words, it's not about explaining why the customer *can't have* what they want (which is a recipe for increased escalations and sometimes four-letter words from customers), but rather focusing exclusively on what solutions *are* possible. And finally, an experience engineering approach is focused on finding a *mutually beneficial* resolution to customer issues. This means matching the customer's actual (often unstated) needs with what the company can offer. It's not about giving away the store or paying customers with lavish givebacks to ensure their loyalty, but rather arriving at a true win-win outcome that is both acceptable to the customer and the company.

Experience Engineering: Opportunity and Payoff

In the midst of any service experience, customers are constantly assessing (in their own way) how much effort went into the experience. Customers at the highest end of the effort scale are likely experiencing a severe, complex, multifaceted issue that's influenced by a lot more than just the attitude of the rep or the words they use in the interaction. More often than not, there's something seriously wrong that the company has to fix. And of course, that something is probably obvious. So the concept of experience engineering is not a tactic for avoiding the *worst* kinds of customer disasters. Rather, it is a purposeful approach designed specifically to impact the customers who've experienced *above-average* levels of effort.

That's why experience engineering is so valuable, because the difference between a moderately high-effort experience and a moderately low-effort one is not very obvious. Most companies' initial forays into effort reduction are aimed at reducing customer exertion. Once most high-exertion situations are discovered and fixed, it can feel like there's nothing else left to do. But just because there's nothing you can do, doesn't mean there's *nothing* you can do.

One thing we're very certain of is that there are plenty of lower-exertion interactions that were judged as higher-effort strictly on the basis of customer interpretation—which could have been influenced in a more positive way. That's where experience engineering can significantly change outcomes, by preempting a high-effort interpretation and instead getting the customer to feel like it was really very little effort at all.

Now, to be clear, this isn't simply about improving survey scores. Remember, lower effort translates to less disloyalty, which translates to strategic and financial success. Reducing the interpretation of effort, particularly in situations where there's nothing else that can be done to reduce exertion, is the ultimate win-win-win—best for the customer, best for the company, and best for the individual reps who are in the hot seat delivering bad news on a daily basis.

Nature or Nurture?

Can experience engineering be taught? Is it something that only the highest-performing service reps can do or could it be practiced by everybody on the front line? It's a perfectly fair question. The good news is that we've uncovered a number of companies that are teaching their reps how to do this in ways that are simple to understand and relatively easy for even inexperienced staff to use. For the remainder of this chapter, we'll take you behind the scenes with three such companies:

- Osram Sylvania, the global lighting manufacturer, which has created the simplest imaginable framework for teaching its frontline reps how to harness the power of positive language.
- LoyaltyOne, a loyalty rewards program vendor, which has developed a repeatable framework to help its reps to position "alternative offerings," in ways that allow even a second-best choice to be just as acceptable—or even more so—than what the customer originally called to request.
- UK-based mortgage lender, Bradford & Bingley, which provides reps with a simple model for diagnosing each customer's dominant personality characteristics, so that the service experience can instantly be customized to that person's preferred interaction style.

Reframing "No"

You can't always say yes to every customer request. It would be great if you could, but there are many situations in which the thing a customer wants and the thing you have to give are not the same. Then what?

Well, of course, the opposite of yes is . . . *no*. So let's consider the word "no" for a moment. How do you react when you hear that word? For most of us, "no" is a trigger that sets in motion an entire chain of negative emotions. Anger, outrage, argumentation. These are all baked into our DNA. Somewhere between your sixth and twelfth month of life, you first made a realization that has stuck with you until this day:

If Mommy says no, you have three options:

- Accept it and move on (unlikely).
- Go ask Daddy (since you've still got a 50/50 shot of getting a yes from him).
- Or kick and scream to show your displeasure, hoping your outburst will change the no into a yes.

In a service interaction, when most customers hear "no," they do one of a number of things—all of which are pretty bad outcomes for the company (and not all that different from how we responded when we were children):

- Engage in some emotional response: Argue with the rep, get angry, use foul language, create some kind of outburst.
- Hang up, call back, and try again with another rep, often called "rep shopping." This, of course, is the customer version of the "go ask Daddy" reaction.
- Escalate the call: By asking the rep to transfer you to their supervisor, you're playing a more savvy version of the rep-shopping game, since most customers have learned that the supervisor has more authority to waive annoying fees, substitute higher-priced products without an additional charge, and generally bend the rules.
- Threaten to never do business with the company again: Sometimes this is just a veiled threat, and sometimes it's sincere. Regardless, as we saw in chapter 1, even if it's just bluster, it's bluster that a customer can easily share with anyone and *everyone* who will listen, thanks to the digital soapbox that social media gives us.

That's a lot of bad outcomes just because of one word. So, of course, it only makes sense that you'd want your people to avoid using it as much as possible. Reps need to find a way to both be truthful (because the answer in many cases *is*, unfortunately, still no), but in a way that doesn't trigger the negative emotional reaction and all the bad outcomes that come along with it. This is where the use of positive language can make such a big difference.

For example, some hospitality companies teach their representatives how to reengineer their thought processes when dealing with guests, and to think entirely in positive terms. According to legend (at least customer service legend), at Walt Disney World all "cast members" learn the art form of positive language (no one is *just* an employee, no matter their job; *everyone* is part of the cast of a big show—not just the guy in the Goofy costume, but every bus driver, ride operator, and funnel-cake maker). This skill is exemplified through a game called "What Time Does the Park Close?" Cast members are challenged to answer even the simplest questions in the most positive way possible. In their first attempt at positive language, many people struggle:

> "Uhhhhh, the park closes whenever the magic stops." (No, the park actually closes at 8 p.m.)

> "The park closes whenever you leave." (No, if you're still here at 8:01, you'll probably get some Disney version of the bum's rush.)

Ultimately, the most correct answer is some version of, "The park *remains open* right up until 8 p.m. Then we reopen for even more fun tomorrow morning at 9 a.m. Hope you can join us then!" How could a customer possibly have a negative reaction to *that*?

What's the big deal here? It's not just a matter of trying to make the answer *sound* better—but if we know that the thing we're just about to tell a customer has the potential of creating a negative reaction, wouldn't we want to instead use words that mitigate that possibility?

That strategy is exactly what Osram Sylvania has developed with their frontline contact center reps. But rather than try to get all their reps to master the art of positive language and completely rewire their brains about how to react when talking to customers about every imaginable scenario, the company has created a simple tool that helps reps avoid negative emotional reactions in only the situations that occur most frequently.

They started by analyzing their highest-volume incoming customer requests—the issues that come up most often—and then they listened to how frontline reps responded when it became apparent that the customer was not going to get what they wanted. What they discovered—and we think this is very likely similar for most companies—was that the top ten most frequently occurring negative scenarios represented approximately 80 percent of their total volume of "no" situations.

So if they could just teach their reps how to use a simple response substitution when these situations came up—try saying this instead of saying that—not for every customer issue, but for these ten specifically, it would have a significant impact on a customer's interpretation of effort and a positive impact on future loyalty. This is all presented in the form of a simple chart that every rep has pinned up in front of them at their workstation (see figure 4.4).

All this is nothing more than another manifestation of the classic lesson of service: "Don't tell customers what you *can't* do, tell them what you *can* do."

CUSTOMER: Can I have a Coke, please?

SERVER: I'm happy to get you a Pepsi, will that work for you?

Top 10 "Negative Language" Scenarios	From Negative Language	To Positive Language
1. Backordered product	"We **don't** have the item in stock."	"We **will** have stock availability on..."
2. Order placement	"We **can't** ship the order until..."	"We **can** ship the order on..."
3. Pricing dispute	"You **have to** talk with sales for pricing issues."	"Our sales department may be able to **help you** with this issue."
4. Shipment error or damage	"We'll **need to** order you a replacement."	"The **best way** for me to handle this is..."
5. Check stock	"We **don't** carry that item."	"We **do** carry..."
6. Provide order status	"Your order **won't** be ready until..."	"Your order **will** be ready on..."
7. Pricing incorrect	"You'll **need to** have your sales rep check pricing."	"Your sales rep **can** verify..."
8. Explaining a late shipment	"You **didn't** get your order in on time."	"To allow timely delivery, **please submit** your order by..."
9. Product return process	"You **need to** write your return number on your package."	"**Please be sure to** include your return number on your package."
10. Where to buy	"We **don't** sell to end users."	"You **can** buy from..."

Source: Osram Sylvania; CEB, 2013.

Figure 4.4 Osram Sylvania's Positive Language Guidance

No lie. No deception. No Jedi mind tricks. Just move the conversation forward toward resolution. It's incredibly simple. One hundred percent of what will come out of my mouth is what you *can* have.

In Osram's case, instead of saying, "We don't have that item in stock right now," their cheat sheet instructs them to say "We *will* have availability on [date] and I can get that out to you immediately once it comes in."

The rep acts as the customer's advocate—she's the person who's on *your* side and is doing everything she can to make this an easy, low-effort experience. Sure, she can't *create* stock that doesn't exist and hand it to you over the phone, but here's what she *can* do—create a positive conversation that moves forward rather than backward. It's a seemingly tiny little thing, but think about how these situations become amplified over thousands and thousands of customer interactions every day, mitigating the corrosive effect of negativity and its impact on customer loyalty. It all adds up and has a meaningful impact on customers.

Osram Sylvania discovered that while there might have been a case for teaching their reps how to use positive language on every single imaginable interaction, even just providing a simple tool that covers only the ten situations that come up most frequently still had a markedly positive result. Once the tool was in place, escalation rates (the percentage of calls that required the intervention of a supervisor) decreased by about half, and the overall Customer Effort Score reported by its customers improved by 18.5 percent, putting them well above average for similar B2B organizations.

Again, this isn't just about being nice to customers. Nor is it just about using positive words. It works because Osram Sylvania teaches its reps the best way to react in the most common situations where we are very likely to be entering into the high-effort zone, since saying no (as well as words like "can't," "won't," "don't," etc.) is such a huge effort trigger.

The management team at Osram Sylvania claimed that one side benefit is that the reps themselves love this idea. Rather than feeling like they're being scripted or told exactly what to say (the company never forces their reps to use verbatim scripting), this tool is seen as another way the company is supporting them and positioning them for success. To help get you started, we've provided a Negative Language Toolkit for Trainers in the back of this book (see appendix C).

The worst kinds of calls most reps have to deal with every day are the "argument calls"—the ones in which customers get angry, hostile, or confrontational. As customers, these calls make our blood boil, because we've all been in a situation where we're so frustrated with the company we're calling, we could scream. But the rep on the other end of the line doesn't like that kind of call any more than we do. Think about it from the rep's perspective: As customers, we might have one of these kinds of interactions every once in a while; for a service rep, this sort of thing can happen many times in a single day. But since the use of positive language mitigates a significant percentage of these hostile interactions, the job of talking to customers all day long becomes easier and more manageable—particularly in the cases where a customer can't get what they want.

Just because there's nothing you can do, doesn't mean there's nothing *you can do.*

Positioning Alternatives with Customer Benefits

How could a rep possibly get a customer to agree to some alternative option that is clearly their second choice, and not just to grudgingly accept it, but to come away feeling just as good—or even *better*—than if they were able to get what they wanted in the first place?

That's what the concept of *alternative positioning* is all about. Beyond using positive language, this is a strategy designed to explore additional options with a customer—in many cases before the customer even knows they are not going to be able to get their first choice. The best example we've seen comes from the Canadian company LoyaltyOne. The framework they've developed is relevant to every company in every industry, because it is all based on simple human psychology.

You probably haven't heard of LoyaltyOne, but they are a unique B2B/B2C hybrid that provides analytics, customer loyalty services, and loyalty solutions to Fortune 1000 organizations around the world. They own and operate the Air Miles Rewards Program, Canada's premier coalition loyalty program spanning numerous high-profile consumer brands, with more than two-thirds of Canadian households engaged in it. Its coalition partners issue reward miles to build long-term relationships between partners and their end consumers. These consumers can select from over 1,200 reward options. So, for example, a retail store's customer who is calling a toll-free number to redeem the reward miles they've earned from their purchases will actually be speaking to a Loy-altyOne customer care rep. That makes these redemption calls tricky for a number of reasons:

- Consumers want to use their reward miles in exchange for free goods and services, such as airline travel or other leisure and entertainment.
- Inventory for these services is limited. For example, with airline travel not all open seats on all flights are available for re-demption.
- LoyaltyOne wants to create a successful redemption for end consumers, ensuring value for their partners.

So in the case of a customer who wants to use reward miles to book a specific flight with no available seats, if the LoyaltyOne rep can't help get the customer to some version of "yes" by the end of the phone call—by creating some other acceptable alternative—the result is a customer who goes away disappointed, with potentially a longer-lasting impact on program engagement. This is why alternative positioning is so critical for them. But what they learned from these all-or-nothing mo-ments turns out to be very applicable to any company when facing the kind of high-effort situations where a customer can't get exactly what they want. Indeed, we often find best practices from companies that have been forced to think creatively due to their unique circum-stances.

LoyaltyOne has developed a call handling model dubbed the "Expe-rience Blueprint," designed to explore and uncover a customer's primary motivation for their request—to learn what's *really* going on in their mind—and then suggest available alternatives that are likely to be just as satisfactory as the initial request. And the whole process starts with the way their reps interact with consumers trying to redeem miles.

Unlike most companies, whose reps place customers on hold while they look for the answers to their questions, LoyaltyOne reps strategi-cally use those moments when a rep is looking at their screen for infor-mation as an opportunity to learn something about that customer and their needs that could become useful later in the call.

Now, just based on that description, this might seem to be a hard thing to teach the average rep, but much like the positive language framework taught by Osram Sylvania, LoyaltyOne has created a repeatable methodology that can be used effectively by any rep.

As you would imagine, almost all redemption calls start with a customer stating their request. They want something, and very likely it's a specific flight to a specific destination on a specific day and time. And from the first second the request is uttered, the rep already knows two things:

- It will take a few moments to determine whether the exact flight the customer wants to book will be available or not.
- And if not, the rep is going to have to make some other suggestion to see if they can get the customer to be willing to accept some other flight—possibly on another day or time, or even to another destination.

Here's where the alarm bell goes off (inside the rep's head), and here's where the process of alternative positioning begins. As the rep is checking for availability—keystroking in the destination and date requested—they attempt to engage the customer in (what feels like) some innocuous small talk. This most often takes the form of a very gentle question: "So, what's taking you to Vancouver?"

Instead of putting the customer on hold (which, by the way, a vast majority of customers dislike, because they're uncertain if the rep is still there on the call with them or if they are going to be abandoned or disconnected), the rep is trying to *use* that moment in a way that could be helpful later.

Is this customer planning to travel for business? Do they plan to combine a business appointment with some personal time at the destination? Is this a vacation trip? Are they traveling solo, or with a spouse or family members? Are they truly excited about this specific destination, or could they be open to other suggestions? The rep doesn't know exactly what they might learn during these moments, but they are already starting to formulate a backup plan. In the event that the system tells the rep they can't offer this exact flight to this destination, what *could* they offer that might work just as well for this customer?

Of course, if the customer's exact request *can* be fulfilled, then they get the flight they wanted—that's easy. But if they cannot, before the customer even knows there's a "no" coming, the rep is already working several moves ahead to envision some suggested alternative that *could* work. And all those inside-the-rep's-brain machinations start with just some friendly chitchat. In the moment this all seems so subtle, it's just two people talking. But what's actually happening is the difference between failure and success.

Here is an example interaction that typifies how this process can work:

CUSTOMER: I'd like to book a flight to Vancouver on Monday morning.

REP: Sure thing, I can check on that for you. (Keys clicking in the background) So, what's taking you to Vancouver?

CUSTOMER: I've got an important business meeting on Monday afternoon.

REP: Okay, got it—can you bear with me just a sec while I check availability for you?

(The rep then realizes there are no Monday morning flights available to Vancouver. However, there are a number of good options on Sunday morning and afternoon, so she continues the discussion rather than placing the customer on hold, which is the knee-jerk reaction of most frontline reps.)

REP: So, do you go to Vancouver often? Have you had a chance to explore the city?

CUSTOMER: Actually, this is my first trip, but I've heard good things.

REP: Absolutely, it's beautiful there. Are you going to have much free time while you're there?

CUSTOMER: I'd like to, but unfortunately I'll be too busy on Monday with my meeting.

REP: Well, as I'm checking here, what I'm seeing is that we do have good availability early Sunday afternoon—turns out the Monday flights are sold out—but this way you could get into town early enough to do some exploring, and also you won't have to worry about any flight delays during the Monday rush that might cause you to miss your meeting. How's that sound?

There are a number of key lessons inherent in this process that we believe have broader applications. Let's explore these below:

Don't be so fast with the "no." The key to making an alternative suggestion work for a customer is to avoid immediately sharing what is *not* available. Take a little extra time. The customer has no idea how long it takes for your system to process their request. Use those precious moments to focus on the customer's *actual interests*, not just their stated request. Try to figure out what's going on inside this person's head, and begin to determine just how flexible they might be.

Don't encourage reps to try to explain their way out of a high-effort situation. The average rep at the average company wastes way too much of a customer's time and mental energy by explaining *why* the customer can't have the thing they want. While that usually seems like the fair thing to do, it typically comes across to the customer as defensive or even combative. "All you're doing is justifying why your company can't give me what I want. How's that helping me?" And of course, in customer service, when you're defending, you're losing.

Don't take the customer's request quite so literally. In a great number of cases, the service the customer is requesting and their actual issue may be very different. Often, by understanding the full context, a very different need emerges. For example, when a cable TV customer is demanding that their service be restored in the midst of an outage, their underlying issue may be that they have friends coming over to watch a big game tomorrow. If the rep was aware of that, the customer could be reassured that their service will very likely be back up and running by game time if not sooner, and perhaps the customer's anger about the immediate outage will quickly pass.

The airline customer who is upset about their canceled flight to Chicago may actually be reacting to the fact that their daughter is performing in a dance recital the next day. So the issue isn't rescheduling the flight or even getting to Chicago per se, it's fulfilling a promise to a child to be present for her big event. There may be a host of alternatives that could be acceptable to a customer in that kind of desperate situation (e.g., flying to a different city and driving the rest of the way, or taking ground transportation to another city and flying to Chicago from there). Again, the rep would never know to suggest any of these other alternatives if they didn't understand the context of the customer's request.

Now, of course, this approach does not work with every customer and every issue. Not everyone is willing to engage in small talk with a service rep. And not every issue can be satisfied by some alternative service offering. But the percentage of situations in which alternative positioning *could* work is more than high enough to make it worth at least attempting.

LoyaltyOne says that in its own experience, a good percentage of customer requests can be satisfied exactly as requested—and obviously, for those people, no further alternatives would even need to be suggested. (However, because the rep doesn't immediately know whether the customer's request can be met, they are still asking conversational questions about the context of the request, just in case).

Of those customers whose first request cannot be fulfilled, approximately 10 percent simply refuse to engage with the rep in any discussion of the reasons why they need to travel. In these cases, the frontline rep still does their best to suggest potential alternatives—using positive language skills—and working for the best outcome. The ability to match some other different choice to that customer's needs is compromised, of course, by their unwillingness to share more information. But that's the customer's loss, and the rep still knows they're doing everything possible to try to reach a successful resolution.

But among the remaining requests, a very high percentage of customers are willing to at least consider—and in many cases accept—a different flight, either on a different day or time, or to another destination. And all of this is achieved simply by a rep who is willing to keep the positive momentum going—buying himself enough time to learn a little bit more about the customer, not going straight to the "no." This is simply understanding the context of the customer's request, then waiting until some alternative solution can be presented that might appeal directly to the very motivations the customer shared.

The reason for doing this is to benefit the customer—to help them get something *they* want. This is not manipulation or mental trickery. Yes, the company wins by completing a redemption, but the driving motivation is to create a superior low-effort experience for the customer.

In order to measure the success of this alternative positioning approach, LoyaltyOne taught the idea only to a pilot group, then compared their results with those of a test group of reps who continued to serve customers in the more traditional way. When customers were asked about their overall satisfaction with the call, the pilot group was rated 8 percent higher. Their rating for "caring about me as a customer" was 11 percent higher. Additionally, they saw a 7 percent rise in first contact resolution, which is impressive in and of itself, but also creates the indirect benefit of fewer callbacks and escalations. This has a significant economic impact on the overall cost of the service operation.

But one additional benefit that came as a very fortuitous surprise was a small reduction in their average handle time. At first glance this seems completely counterintuitive. Wouldn't the process of attempting to engage in small talk with customers—probing a little deeper about the underlying reasons for their request—take *more* time per call?

Well, in some cases, yes. Asking a few more questions definitely does add time to some calls. But it greatly *reduces* the time they used to spend on the worst kinds of calls. The argument calls. The escalated calls. The ones where the customer was so annoyed when they didn't get the exact thing they wanted that their reaction was to argue with the rep and demand to speak to a supervisor.

So while alternative positioning is not a silver bullet, it is effective in taking much of the negativity and pain out of calls, not just because it allows more customers to have a lower-effort resolution experience, but because it also mitigates at least some of the worst, most emotionally draining calls frontline reps have to deal with every day.

Personality-Based Issue Resolution

What if, instead of constantly striving for absolute consistency in the way live customer interactions are handled, a rep could create a more customized approach to service? What if there was a way to identify the basic personality characteristics of each customer live and in the moment, and tailor the interaction to that one customer? That skill would undoubtedly create a superior service experience and lower the effort required to resolve issues. But is it possible?

Surely, within every major service organization, there are some individuals who seem to have a more finely tuned mechanism for being able to get on the same wavelength with the customers they deal with. Some people just "click" better with people who are having a problem or issue. They seem to be able to understand the other person—what they need, where they're coming from—and provide the kind of interaction that feels right at a visceral level.

Sometimes that ability is chalked up as superior empathy skills, and sometimes it appears as an almost maternal interest in helping others, but whatever it is, it works for those select few who seem to possess it. Being on the same page as the customer goes a long way toward reducing customer effort and mitigating disloyalty.

But here's the frustrating thing—if you ask these very special service reps how they do what they do, their most likely response is, "Do *what*?" That's because, for these top performers, this behavior is just intuitive. If organizations could find more people with this skill, they would probably want to hire them. But these skills are very hard to see on a résumé, or test for in an interview. That's why the idea of a teachable, scalable approach to personality-based issue resolution is so necessary. It is, in essence, a way to enable even the least attuned service reps to emulate the kinds of behaviors—and results—that otherwise would be restricted to the few who have these special people skills.

While there have been a number of methodologies and systems for identifying personality types, the best we've ever seen was originally developed by the UK financial services company Bradford & Bingley. The concept they used is rooted in the Myers-Briggs Type Indicator assessment. Many of us are familiar with this basic construct, which analyzes a person's dominant preferences in perception and thinking style. The Myers-Briggs test assesses each person based on four "dichotomies" and then creates a four-letter code to distinguish that individual's personality. With four different dimensions in play, the Myers-Briggs framework is expressed as a four-by-four grid with sixteen unique characterizations.

Compared to the myriad personality styles we have all encountered in the course of our lives, condensing down to just sixteen seems like a very small number to identify and understand. But in the span of a two- or three-minute customer conversation, having to juggle sixteen different profiles would be overwhelming for most frontline reps. So working with PowerTrain (a UK-based behavioral change consultancy), Bradford &

Source: Bradford & Bingley, plc.; PowerTrain (UK) Ltd.; CEB, 2013.

Figure 4.5 Bradford & Bingley's Personality Framework

Bingley used their framework, which tightens this up to just four—a far more manageable number for the average rep to navigate (see figure 4.5).

Building a Profile

Imagine the whole world of customers, divided into four basic categories:

- The Feeler, who leads with their emotional needs.
- The Entertainer, who loves to talk and show off their personality.
- The Thinker, who needs to analyze and understand.
- The Controller, who just wants what they want, when they want it.

At first glance this appears simple enough, but it would not be very useful to a customer service rep. Without some kind of tool or guidance to understand which personality profile an individual customer is expressing, and how to treat that individual, this framework would be nothing but a slightly more accessible version of intuition.

The real magic of the process Bradford & Bingley used is that it is a *process*. It's a methodology that allows even an average rep to make an educated guess about the personality profile of any customer, typically within no more than thirty to sixty seconds. And the best part is that getting it right doesn't require reps to ask a whole multitude of questions of the customer. Instead, the reps put all of this into action based exclusively on the words that a customer uses to describe their issue or problem—not their tone of voice per se, or any other more subtle characteristics, but simply how they choose to articulate their reason for calling the company in the first place.

To help reps do this, Bradford & Bingley arms them with a simple decision tree (see figure 4.6).

The process requires a rep to be able to answer no more than three questions in the course of their diagnosis, starting with:

1. Is the customer's issue complex? If the answer is no—that is, if it's a simple issue—the rep doesn't need to go any further down the diagnosis path. If a customer's issue can be resolved quickly and easily

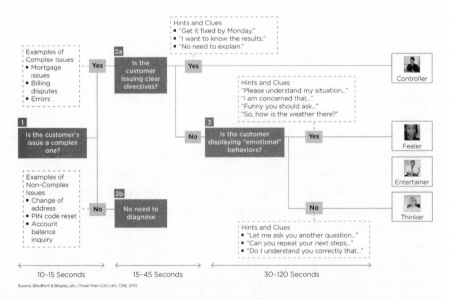

Figure 4.6 Bradford & Bingley's Customer Profile Identification Tool

with little additional interaction (e.g., a change of address or balance inquiry), then there's no real point in customizing the resolution process in any distinct way beyond just being courteous and professional. In fact, in these simple-issue situations, reps are asked to treat all customers as Controllers—just get them what they need, and get them off the phone as expeditiously and politely as possible. But if the customer's issue *is* a complex one (e.g., a billing dispute), then the rep listens carefully to the words the customer uses to describe their issue.

2. Is the customer issuing clear directives? If the answer is yes, then the customer is likely a Controller. No need to further assess the profile—instead, the rep begins to promptly and succinctly answer the customer.

3. But if the answer is no, then comes the third and final question: Is the customer displaying "emotional" behaviors? If not, they are probably a Thinker. If the answer is yes, then they are likely either an Entertainer or a Feeler—distinguished by the source of their emotional need. (Entertainers, not surprisingly, like to socialize, joke, and have a chat. Feelers want for their personal point of view, even their feelings, to be taken into consideration.)

Of course, identifying a customer's personality characteristics is one thing, but tailoring the delivery of service to that individual customer is the real key. Bradford & Bingley has simplified that element as well with a series of cheat sheets that become tools of the everyday experience for their frontline staff, a series of simple reminders that guide reps toward the specific service approach that is most appealing for each personality profile, and that ultimately create the lowest-effort interaction for that individual customer (see figure 4.7).

One somewhat surprising element of the process is that frontline reps are strictly prohibited from leaving notations in their CRM system about their personality diagnosis of a customer. Now, it would seem to be a good idea to pre-alert the rest of the team to that customer's personality profile, as a benefit for the next rep who will interact with that person. However, Bradford & Bingley chooses not to do this, because they've learned that a customer's profile can vary based on a number of factors (e.g., how urgent the issue is or how busy the customer is at the moment), and the company wants therefore to avoid having their reps prejudging customers who may act very differently the next time they call.

Source: Bradford & Bingley, plc., PowerTrain (UK) Ltd., CEB, 2013.

Figure 4.7 Bradford & Bingley's Customer Issue Resolution Tailoring Guide (Abridged)

Is it really worth the time and effort to teach an entire frontline customer service team how to recognize different personality characteristics, and expect hourly or part-time employees to develop some degree of proficiency in this skill? Our analysis, based on observations with the Bradford & Bingley team, as well as the dozens of other companies that have begun to adopt this smart process over the past few years, points to a resounding yes.

Consider the potential impact on customer loyalty. When a customer feels that the rep they're interacting with "gets" them, a lower-effort experience is much more likely. This is the essence of experience engineering. Remember, a customer's general perception of effort is a major driver of disloyalty, as is the perception of generic service delivery. Bradford & Bingley's strategy enables reps to deliver service in a way that really *feels* customized and tailored to the customer.

The results attest to the power of the approach. The company reported a 20 percent increase in "willingness to recommend." What's more, a number of additional benefits accrued over time, several of which were ancillary ones that no one ever expected. Within the first year of practicing personality-based issue resolution, repeat customer calls were down *40 percent*. If you recall from our earlier discussion of next issue avoidance in chapter 3, a huge chunk of callbacks stem from implicit experience issues—for instance, when a customer doesn't trust the information provided to them or simply doesn't like the answer they received. Handling customers in a way that is tailored to their personality helps Bradford & Bingley put a big dent in these emotional drivers of unnecessary callbacks, and has resulted in a massive positive impact on the economics of the service operation.

In addition, the company reported dramatically higher engagement scores from frontline employees. When we asked them about this, they explained that personality-based issue resolution not only makes the job a lot more fun for reps, but frontline staff also feel liberated to handle calls in the way they think best fits the customer they're dealing with, thereby creating an environment that's very different from the scripted, checklist–driven, "command and control" culture of most service organizations.

Again, the win-win-win. Best for the customer, best for the company, and best for the reps.

In conclusion, the move from "consistent service," in which the customer service management team defines what "good" is and then expects all frontline reps to conform to this standard, to "consistently tailored service," where each individual customer is treated individually, is a cultural change. It cannot be accomplished simply by telling employees what to do in every situation. It is readily apparent that this notion of consistently excellent service will require a serious rethink about how to *manage* customer service employees.

So with that in mind, we did what we always do—launched yet another research project, this time specifically around management of the customer service function. Our goal was to understand how low-effort companies manage their frontline reps. What do they do differently? How exactly do they gain control in a world where absolute control and dictating employee behavior couldn't possibly be the right answer to creating a customized, personalized service experience?

Ultimately, we were very surprised by what we discovered. And that surprise created yet another breakthrough for us, and for the hundreds of companies that have embarked on the journey of delivering a low-effort experience to their customers.

• • •

KEY TAKEAWAYS

♦ *Effort is one-third "do," two-thirds "feel."* Much of customer effort is driven by a customer's perception of whether the service interaction was effortful, not whether they actually had to exert undue effort during the interaction.

♦ *Managing the customer's perception isn't about just being nice.* "Experience engineering" is a way to manage the customer response. It significantly differs in both form and purpose from traditional soft skills. It's rooted in behavioral economics (using techniques such as advocacy, alternative positioning, and anchoring), relying on purposeful language to generate a positive response to an outcome that may not be good news.

5

TO GET CONTROL, YOU HAVE TO GIVE CONTROL

For those who have spent a lifetime in customer service management, we've had to recognize one harsh fact: For all the science and strategy that is put into creating an optimal customer experience, the everyday *delivery* of that experience is typically in the hands of hundreds, if not thousands, of reps. It's well beyond the control of the leadership team.

Achieving goals like mitigating disloyalty by creating a low-effort customer experience are entirely dependent on the execution of frontline customer service representatives, most of whom are hourly-wage, often part-time employees. Put another way, the brilliant battle plan created by the generals at company headquarters will either succeed or fail based on the actions of hundreds or even thousands of foot soldiers whose investment in the success of the operation may be limited to simply needing a steady income. It's a reality check that many companies choose to avoid thinking about in such stark terms.

As far as the company and its strategic and financial interests are concerned, there is clearly a lot riding on the skills and abilities of any one rep. There is no supervisor listening in (unless the call is escalated by the rep), and so there is no safety net. And so, in the majority of customer service operations the prevailing people-management strategy is to do everything possible to limit the company's risk exposure by keeping an extra-tight rein on *everything*. It's not uncommon to see companies still mandate the exact words customer service reps must use in all their interactions. Most still focus on antiquated productivity measures like driving down average handle time (AHT) and employing checklists masquerading as quality assurance (QA) assessments that dictate every move every rep must include in every interaction. It's clearly an environment designed to *control* employees. Some companies (particularly those in regulated industries) feel this particularly acutely.

What we've discovered, however—the fourth pillar in creating a world-class customer experience—is that low-effort service organizations run their operations very differently and manage their people very differently. If you walk around the offices and work areas of a low-effort customer company, it doesn't feel like a typical call center operation. There's no AHT clock signaling reps to get off the phone as fast as possible. There's no QA person checking boxes to measure service consistency. There's nobody telling reps to make sure they say the customer's name three times, thank the caller for being a loyal customer, or otherwise "smile through the phone."

In a low-effort service organization, reps determine for themselves how best to handle the unique issue being experienced by *this* unique person. In other words, the best customer service organizations recognize something most companies don't:

In order to get *control, you've actually got to* give *control.*

This isn't some sort of idealized aspiration achievable only on paper or under laboratory conditions. What we're describing is real and is already happening at progressive service organizations around the world. What the leaders of those companies are realizing, faster than average companies, is that the world of customer expectations and demands is changing much more rapidly than it ever has in the past. The service strategies of yesterday's successful companies are fast becoming antiquated and are either no longer sufficient or, in the worst cases, actively harmful. For longtime customer service leaders, it's easy to understand why many are in a state of denial, wishing things were *the way they used to be.*

But for those who are willing to see things *as they are,* the differences are shockingly apparent. Over the past two decades there have been significant shifts in both customer expectations and the frontline customer service skills required to meet those expectations. The world has evolved from one in which most customer issues were routine (and customer service could therefore be managed much like a factory) to one in which

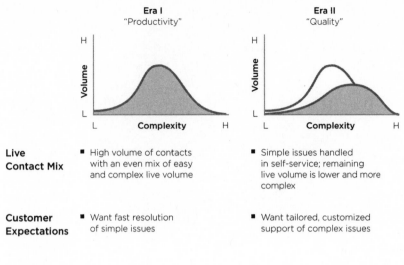

	Era I "Productivity"	**Era II** "Quality"
Live Contact Mix	■ High volume of contacts with an even mix of easy and complex live volume	■ Simple issues handled in self-service; remaining live volume is lower and more complex
Customer Expectations	■ Want fast resolution of simple issues	■ Want tailored, customized support of complex issues

Source: CEB, 2013.

Figure 5.1 The Three Eras of Customer Service

the easy issues have gone the way of self-service and what's left is more complex. Add to this the rapid rise in customer expectations and their ability to quickly punish companies via social media for failing to meet their expectations, and it's clear that the stakes and challenges for service reps are much higher than they used to be (see figure 5.1).

So amid this backdrop it may come as no surprise that in a recent survey we conducted, 80.5 percent of service organizations say their rep performance has not improved noticeably over the past couple of years (see figure 5.2).

It's depressing news at some level. For all the management that goes into creating an excellent customer experience—for all the care and energy that (most) service reps put into achieving the best possible outcomes for customers—the result is often no real progress at all. It's like trying to go up the down escalator. No matter how hard you try, you never seem to get anywhere. This inability to increase frontline rep performance—or worse, face the very real potential of declines in performance—has left service leaders with many big questions and few answers. One director of customer service for a large bank told us, "Reps can't seem to keep up with customer expectations. When you couple this with our 30 percent annual employee turnover, it means that I'm always onboarding new people, only to see them leave—often due to burnout from demanding customers and an inflexible system."

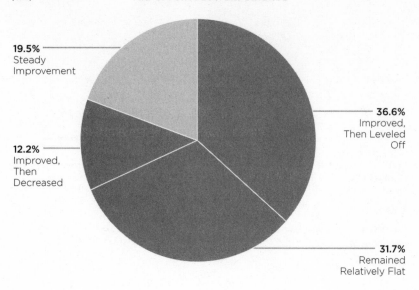

19.5%
Steady
Improvement

36.6%
Improved,
Then Leveled
Off

12.2%
Improved,
Then
Decreased

31.7%
Remained
Relatively Flat

n = 41 companies.

Source: CEB, 2013.

Figure 5.2 Rep Performance Improvement Trend (Company-Reported)

How do we prepare staff for this very different world of customer expectations and demands? Exactly what kinds of frontline employees are best suited for today's customer environment? Who should companies be hiring into their frontline positions? What kinds of skills and behaviors have the biggest impact on performance—particularly when it comes to reducing customer effort? What kinds of training, coaching, and incentives reap the biggest payback? To boil it down to two questions: How can companies position their reps for success in today's world? If we want to deliver a low-effort experience, what skills matter most?

These are the questions we endeavored to answer as we launched one of the most comprehensive and wide-ranging studies ever conducted in the area of frontline service rep performance. Our goal was to learn exactly what skills and behaviors have the biggest impact on improving customer loyalty and creating a superior customer experience. And while the scope of this task was enormous and the logistics very complex, the central proposition was quite simple: What if we could learn about the skill set and dominant behavior characteristics of a number of individual frontline reps, and then match those skills and behaviors to their individual performance levels? If we could know what any one person is good at, and then learn how well that person performs compared to their peers—and if we could then repeat that process hundreds of times with hundreds of different frontline reps—we could begin to develop a much clearer conclusion about what matters most for driving superior performance.

In order to learn more about individual frontline reps, we put out a global call for help to the people who know reps best—their immediate supervisors. When all was said and done, we were able to enlist the assistance of 440 customer service supervisors from a wide variety of companies, comprising a representative sampling of various industries, business models, company sizes, geographies, and cultures.

Each of these supervisors was asked to provide detailed information about three randomly chosen frontline reps with whom they worked directly and knew well. This gave us a total pool of 1,320 reps to analyze. The supervisors were asked to assess each one of their three reps based on their expertise in more than seventy-five different skill areas—an exhaustive laundry list of behaviors that we hypothesized might contribute in some way to strong execution in today's customer service environment.

After the skill analysis, the reps were then assessed for their individual performance—where does this person rank among all other reps against the success metrics employed by that company (customer satisfaction, Net Promoter Score, first contact resolution, Customer Effort Score, etc.)? Are they a top performer? An average performer? A low performer?

Finally, by comparing the individual skills of 1,320 reps to their performance stack rankings, some very clear conclusions emerged—some of which confirmed suspicions and hypotheses we'd predicted, and others that came as dramatic surprises.

Our findings came as the result of two analytic processes. By performing factor analysis, we were able to see that this long list of skills clustered very neatly into four statistically defined categories, each of which had common characteristics and natural relationships.

Then, by conducting regression analysis, we were able to answer the key study question by clearly seeing which one of the four factors has the biggest impact on increasing rep performance in today's customer environment.

We'll reveal them in inverse order of impact. The first clustered factor consisted of four skills:

- Curious
- Creative
- Capable of critical thinking
- Experimental

These four, grouped together, fell neatly into the area most of us think of as *advanced problem solving,* or IQ for short. And our analysis shows that being better than average in this area increases rep performance by 3.6 percent. (All the increases in rep performance we'll be showing you are comparisons from reps at the 25th percentile of a given skill or behavior to those at the 75th percentile—so, not absolute worst to absolute best, but rather a more meaningful comparison of "not very good" to "pretty good.")

Think of this as a 3.6 percent improvement in CSAT or in Net Promoter Score, or a 3.6 percent reduction in customer effort. And virtually every company we've ever worked with has told us that a 3.6 percent improvement in rep performance would be a significant lift in their overall customer experience metrics. And remember, IQ ranked the *lowest* of the four groupings—so the news only gets better from here.

The next grouping consists of six skills:

- Demonstrates product knowledge
- Demonstrates technological expertise
- Communicates confidently
- Communicates clearly
- Asks good questions
- Capable of multitasking

We describe this cluster as *basic skills and behaviors*—these are the foundational skills most leaders would expect service reps to have. Reps who are superior in this area perform 5.1 percent better. And that only makes sense. If you're better than average at the basic skills of customer service, you'd perform somewhat better than reps who are not as good.

But as important as the basics are, the third factor represents a slightly bigger lift. This one is also comprised of six skills:

- Empathetic
- Able to flex to different personality types

- Has customer service ethic
- Extroverted (i.e., comfortable interacting with strangers)
- Advocates for the customer
- Persuasive

This factor is best characterized as *emotional intelligence,* or EQ for short. The impact of this factor represents a performance boost of 5.4 percent.

EQ has a slightly bigger impact than IQ or basic skills and behaviors, but the difference is marginal. And if there were only these three focus areas to consider, it would be hard to make a strong recommendation that *any one of these* would be the obvious logical choice for companies to emphasize in their hiring and training. If a company were to invest all its resources into any one of these directions—or to hedge their bets by splitting their energies into thirds—the result would likely be somewhat positive, but hardly earth-shattering.

But we've discovered there aren't just three choices. There is a fourth. And this fourth factor—a previously unidentified "missing link"—has a significantly larger impact than any of the other three. In fact, its impact is bigger than any two of the others combined. It is made up of five skills and behaviors:

- Resilient
- Able to handle high-pressure situations without becoming burned out
- Takes responsibility for own actions
- Responds well to constructive criticism by managers
- Able to concentrate on tasks over extended periods of time

Again, these five skills clustered statistically with each other, and broke apart from all the other factors. This was a finding we certainly did not expect, so we spent considerable time looking at this cluster of skills and coming to some hypothesis about why it is so important. We call this fourth factor the *control quotient,* or CQ for short. Let's talk about why we call it this, and why we believe it is so impactful in today's customer service interactions (see figure 5.3).

It has become increasingly obvious that one of the key elements for success in today's complex customer environment is a frontline rep's ability to take control over their interactions with customers. They *must*

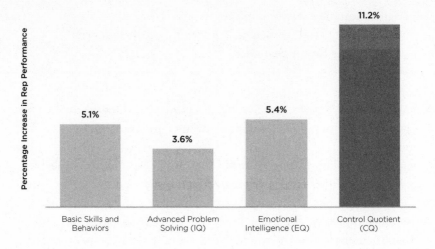

n = 440 supervisors, 1,320 reps.

Figure 5.3 Performance Impact of Rep Skill Categories

be able to engage—fully—in often challenging personal situations with people who may be having an emotional reaction to a problem or issue. Often the emotions of the moment are exacerbated by the inability of the company to fully resolve that issue.

Envision a situation where a customer is told that their broken product is no longer under warranty, and the company cannot help them beyond selling them a replacement. Or where a hotel guest is told that the extra rooms they need for a big family event are not available, and the best solution is to send the additional family members to a different hotel across town.

The ability to keep one's cool in situations like those—to use positive language skills and alternative positioning in order to create an emotional connection with customers in complex, challenging situations—requires a great degree of personal control. More importantly, frontline reps quickly realize that it is impossible to fully satisfy *every* customer request. Sometimes the company simply cannot offer a customer the solution they need, and the best that can be done is to empathize and wish them well. The backlash and emotional outbursts from customers in situations like this can groove a deep scar in the psyche of some reps, particularly those who are not resilient and are unable to control their own emotional reactions.

What's most important in today's customer environment, however, is not just how well a frontline rep can handle one particularly challenging interaction with a tough customer, but how they handle the next call. And the one after that. And so on.

Some frontline reps experience a kind of emotional deflation following a tough interaction. They glaze over or retreat into a self-protective bubble. We've probably all experienced customer service people like this. They're the ones who speak in a flat monotone and assume the robotic persona of someone who is acting professionally, but without any human qualities. Interacting with reps like that just requires more energy from the customer, and is almost always a substandard experience. That kind of rep behavior leads directly to poor-quality customer service and degrades a company's ability to achieve its loyalty goals. That's why these five qualities that comprise CQ are so important to success in today's customer environment.

The more we explored this idea of CQ, the more we realized that these qualities are similar to the qualities present in the best performers in other professions where high-pressure and emotionally charged situations are normal in the everyday course of business.

Consider nursing. Nurses must often engage with patients who are experiencing life's biggest challenges. Some patients are victims of horrible accidents. Two hours ago they were healthy and carefree. Now they're in a hospital bed suffering. Some patients are suddenly aware of their mortality in a way they weren't yesterday. But the best nurses are able to engage fully and completely with a patient in one room, and then—regardless of the outcome of that interaction—move on to the patient in the next room and engage just as completely with that person, as if the bad thing next door never happened. That's the essence of personal control.

In fact, nurses have a catchphrase for this—a four-word mnemonic they offer each other in moments of support, or just silently repeat to themselves—when they experience a particularly bad or emotional interaction with a patient. It's called QTIP. Not the cotton swab, but rather an acronym: *Quit Takin' It Personally.*

One longtime nurse who has spent a career working in emergency rooms and psych wards for more than two decades told us, "When you have a negative emotional experience, you can't allow that to affect your performance with the next patient. That next person deserves everything I have to offer, and it's not fair to give them any less than my best just because I happened to have a bad experience with someone else a few moments ago. So I *don't* take it personally. I do my best in each situation, and when I'm done with that patient, I start fresh all over again with the next person."

As we considered what it takes not just to engage with one patient (or customer), but to be able to *disengage* immediately afterward in order to be fully effective with the next person, it became more apparent to us that this previously undefined cluster of five skills and behaviors is really a missing link that needs to be separately explored and defined.

The impact of CQ is abundantly clear from the regression analysis—it can propel companies from mediocre rep performance to the eventual delivery of a world-class low-effort customer experience with all the loyalty benefits and economic advantages that come along with it.

Boosting CQ in the Contact Center

Obviously, once customer service leaders become aware of this very powerful driver, their natural reaction is simultaneously both *in*quisitive and *ac*quisitive: "How can I get some more of this CQ on my team?"

The natural assumption is that the way to acquire more CQ is to hire differently—to somehow screen for it, to find reps who naturally have "high CQ". The vast majority of companies we spoke to want to know how to spot high CQ in a person's employment application, and what screening questions or tests could be applied in an interview situation to find the highest-CQ candidates. That would make complete sense, were it not for an important wrinkle in the story.

In our analysis of these 1,320 reps, we made a rather startling discovery. Only about 6 percent of reps have little to no CQ.

Of the remaining 94 percent, we found that 30 percent already have high CQ. These people are naturally better at "control." They have an innate sense for being able to bounce back following a negative experience. In sports this psychological quality is called "a short memory," typified by the golfer who misses a two-foot putt to win a tournament, only to come back the next time without dragging along the negative baggage of that bad experience in a way that impacts their future performance. *As if the bad thing never happened.*

But fully 94 percent of all reps—typical, average core employees—have at least moderate CQ, or at least a latent CQ "gene" that can blossom under the right conditions. It's easy to understand why this is the case: There's a natural selection of sorts in the contact center—those who don't have any CQ potential quickly leave.

However, while CQ doesn't vary all that much by *individual*—from one person to another—it varies significantly from one *company* to the next. In other words, while most reps possess some baseline level of CQ, the story from a corporate perspective is much more stark: There are definitely high-CQ and low-CQ companies (see figure 5.4).

At first glance you might think this would be easily explainable by segmenting the types of companies that fall into the high-CQ category. Maybe they are all web start-ups that let employees do whatever they please. But what we found is that the highest-CQ companies don't look very similar at all on the surface. They don't hire people who are very different, or screen them in different ways than the average company. They don't pay their people any more. They don't have crazily relaxed work rules, like "bring your dog who wears a bandana to the office and let him sleep under your cubicle" day. In fact, if you walked into a high-CQ service company, you wouldn't see anything different. But there is a *huge* difference.

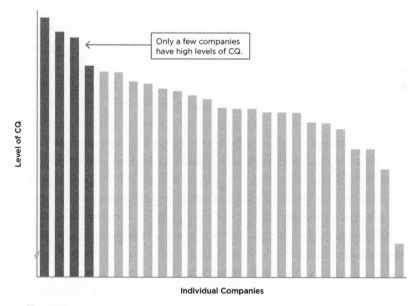

Only a few companies have high levels of CQ.

Level of CQ

Individual Companies

n = 33 companies.

Source: CEB, 2013.

Figure 5.4 Average Level of CQ Attributes Across Companies

We conducted a series of in-depth interviews with frontline employees at both high-CQ and low-CQ companies. One of the key questions we asked was, "What is it that you like *best* about your job?" As you can imagine, that question is specifically engineered to elicit a positive response. We didn't want to ask *whether* people like their jobs. We weren't looking to open up some Pandora's box of complaints and pent-up negativity.

But in today's more complex, more demanding customer environment, we wanted to learn what keeps people coming back to work every day. What motivates them to *want* to do this very tough job of handling challenging issues and emotionally charged customers?

See if you can detect the difference in the responses. Here are typical quotes from frontline employees at *low-CQ* companies:

"I like the hours I work and not having to work on weekends."

"I like helping customers—whenever I can."

"I like the benefits and the incentives the company provides."

"Two words: job security."

"I am paid well for a customer service rep."

The important thing to observe here is that these employees do not hate their jobs. They work hard, they get a decent wage for their time on the job—and of course, there is nothing wrong with enjoying that your job is secure and pays well.

But contrast that reaction with the general sentiment of frontline employees at *high-CQ* companies, responding to what they enjoy most about their job:

"I appreciate that my supervisor trusts that I can handle my job on my own."

"It is a very good work environment."

"I have the freedom to reach goals in the way I feel is most helpful to customers."

"I like that our management team trusts my judgment when it comes to handling customer issues."

"This is the first place I've ever worked where I don't feel like I'm being micromanaged."

Again, remember, these employees are no different than those who work at other, lower-CQ companies. They don't have demonstrably higher IQ or EQ. They are not paid that differently or trained that differently. They aren't all graduates from top universities. So, what *is* so different?

In addition to the initial research that surfaced the control quotient, our search for answers also included an extensive survey of an additional 5,667 frontline service reps created to allow us to see and explore the similarities and differences in their overall work experiences. We tested things like how people are managed, relationships with supervisors and executives, the nature of interactions with peers, and the nature of "rules" and policies in their organization.

Out of all of this, we discovered one fundamental difference—that makes *all the difference*. It is the key that unlocks CQ potential: *The environment*.

It's not the training, it's not the people. It's the work environment those people are subjected to on a daily basis that enables higher rep performance, a lower-effort customer experience, and ultimately loyalty benefits for the company. In fact, it wouldn't be a stretch to say that if you were to transplant the entire frontline workforce of a low-CQ company into the environment of a high-CQ company, their performance would *immediately increase*. By the same token, shortly after transplanting the entire workforce of a high-CQ company into a lower-CQ work environment, you would likely start to see signs of lower performance—regressing back toward the mean.

So what is it exactly that is so different from one environment to another? The difference is not physical or obvious. It's not about brightly colored call centers, ergonomic chairs, or free soda machines. It's about something else entirely.

Creating a High-CQ Environment

When we dig into the data, we find that there are three distinct keys to unlocking CQ—three environmental factors that are completely within the control of customer service leadership to enable:

- Trust in rep judgment
- Rep understanding and alignment with company goals
- A strong rep peer support network

These three factors—with all other things being equal—are the difference makers that transform average organizations into world-class low-effort service providers (see figure 5.5).

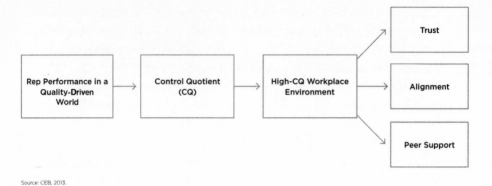

Source: CEB, 2013.

Figure 5.5 Environmental Drivers of CQ

Let's examine each of these three factors in further detail and then share some practical examples of each of these concepts featuring real companies.

CQ KEY #1: *Trust in Rep Judgment*

At high-CQ companies, frontline reps are made to feel that they are free to do whatever is right to serve that one customer they are interacting with right now. Now, there's no question that for many management teams this is a scary proposition. Permitting reps to do *anything* they think is best for that customer would seem to open the company up to a wide range of potential abuses by both reps and customers. Which is why "trust" needs to be defined more clearly.

Yes, total freedom to do anything with any customer at any time— open-ended, unchecked, and without any guardrails—would seem to be the exact opposite of the concept of management. But there is a middle ground between tightly restricting every action of every rep, and permitting total anarchy in the contact center.

Consider the notion of delivering "consistently excellent service." To customers, this term is used on a nearly universal basis by service organizations in every industry—and why not? What management team *doesn't* want to be working toward a goal of consistently providing the highest-quality service to the highest percentage of customers?

But the big difference from one company to another is how the concept of *consistency* is applied. At low-CQ companies, there is an inherent understanding (whether stated or unstated) that consistency is achieved by "treating all customers the same." Managers preach the value of greeting each customer with consistent language, using the same techniques to diagnose all customer issues, and resolving all similar problems with the same predetermined solution set. Individual reps who stray from the preferred, prescribed resolution path are reminded that they're acting in a way that is inconsistent with the company's service standards. Repeated incidents of inconsistency are dealt with through performance management.

The understanding at low-CQ companies is that management has already determined how a frontline rep should solve customer problems, which means the job is to stick to the game plan. *Consistently.* To be fair, this certainly seems like the safest approach. For companies that have hundreds or thousands of reps dealing with millions of customer contacts every year, it seems like the best way to de-risk service delivery. And risk management is clearly one of the chief responsibilities of any service management team.

Except for one thing. A heavy-handed approach—which may have worked perfectly well five or ten years ago when customers' issues and their service expectations were straightforward and fairly uniform—is doomed to create subpar results in today's customer environment. This is why at high-CQ companies, the achievement of consistently excellent service could never—by definition—be accomplished by *treating all customers the same.* Because all customers are *not* the same. Customers have different personalities, different needs, different expectations. Their ability to understand and verbalize their problems and issues is very different. Their level of experience with your company and your products is widely variable. If there's anything that's consistent from one customer to the next, it's that they each want to interact with a rep who understands them uniquely.

Trust in rep judgment has a 14 percent impact on CQ. In other words, greater trust equates to more CQ. It is a major factor with a significant impact on overall performance. So it would only seem natural in a discussion of trust in the workplace environment to ask the obvious question: "Do you trust your employees?" And—not surprisingly—when we've conducted surveys of customer service executives, the percentage who say they *never* trust their employees or even only *rarely* trust them is exactly zero.

But we've learned that this is the wrong question to ask.

The more important (and troubling) issue is, "Do your employees *feel* trusted?" And the answer we continue to hear from frontline customer service reps is a resounding "not so much." This too is hardly a surprise. Many work environments (especially those with a large number of front-line customer-facing staff) have a general overtone of mistrust. Just ask anybody who has ever worked in a retail environment about the random "bag checks" they've experienced where personal handbags and back-packs are subject to searches in order to reduce "shrinkage." Some com-panies subject employees to random polygraph testing to probe for misdeeds of one sort or another. You don't think those surveillance cam-eras in banks are just there to catch bank robbers, do you? If you've ever been to a casino, you've seen all those hundreds of smoked-glass bubbles that line the ceilings. While those serve as a none-too-subtle reminder that cheating the house will be dealt with "the old-fashioned way," the true purpose of the extensive surveillance camera network is to protect the casino from its own employees. As casino boss Ace Rothstein (played by Robert De Niro) says in the Martin Scorsese film *Casino:*

"In Vegas, everybody's gotta watch everybody else. The boxmen are watching the dealers. The floormen are watching the boxmen. The pit bosses are watching the floormen. The shift bosses are watching the pit bosses. The casino manager is watching the shift bosses. I'm watching the casino manager. And the eye-in-the-sky . . . is watching us all."

In the typical customer service environment, Big Brother is more like the *ear*-in-the-sky. Calls are recorded and many are listened to af-terwards by the clandestine quality assurance team, which grades each rep according to a checklist system of regimented performance ele-ments that must be included in every call:

- Did the agent use the proper standard greeting?
- Did they verify all customer information to ensure security?
- Did they diagnose the customer's problem according to the standard issue resolution map?
- Did they close the call the right way (for instance, by assuming we'd fully resolved their issue and then thanking the customer for their loyalty)?

Many quality assurance checklists include dozens of mandatory ele-ments that must be demonstrated in every phone interaction, some of which may even be scripted and spoken verbatim with no variation whatsoever from one customer to the next.

This is the exact opposite of trust.

One example that we personally witnessed took place a at a contact center of a major consumer electronics manufacturer. At that location, there had been a recent management emphasis to remind frontline reps to always obtain the postal code of customers during each call. Apparently there had been a number of quality issues in one assembly plant, so the company was trying to isolate the geographic patterns of product failures to determine if they were occurring with more regularity in some regions.

Here is a sampling of one customer call we listened to as it was being graded by the quality assurance team:

> CUSTOMER: Wow, I'm so glad I got you on the line. I really need your help. I'm at my daughter's dance recital, and my video camera isn't working. Here's the thing: My wife is away on a business trip and she's so sad to be missing this event, so if I don't record this recital on video, I'm telling you, I'm a dead man. The show starts in less than five minutes and I have no idea what to do. Can you possibly help me?
>
> REP: Certainly, sir . . . what's your zip code?
>
> CUSTOMER: Zip code? Who the hell cares about my zip code—I need you to help me now!

This is a classic example of what happens when companies don't trust their frontline employees. When a company mandates that every customer call include all the standard, company-imposed criteria, and takes away the rep's ability to deal with the customer at a more natural, spontaneous, human level, the interaction is reduced to a mechanical, rote exchange.

And what's so unfortunate is that based on the rules and scoring criteria of the average company, this type of interaction is often graded as "excellent." The rep did exactly what they were told to do. They followed the rules. They ticked off the boxes of the checklist one by one. They performed their job as management dictated they should.

But to the customer, this kind of depersonalized, robotic service is the exact *opposite* of excellent service. (Note: The quality assurance team at this company later confessed to us that this is the kind of call they personally *hate* the most. They were painfully aware of how bad this interaction must have felt to the customer, but because the system forces them to score the call based only on the criteria specified by the checklist, they had no choice but to score the call as excellent.)

ELIMINATE THE CHECKLIST MENTALITY

In our survey of service organizations around the world, we found that 64 percent of all companies have performance criteria that are regimented and unwavering. Just over two-thirds of companies monitor their agents to ensure consistency. We've shown how this approach stands in direct conflict with what customers really want from us. But clearly, total anarchy and unbridled rep judgment isn't the likely answer either. So where does that leave us?

We are seeing an increasing number of companies doing away with the standard checklist approach to quality assurance and substituting broader frameworks that allow reps far more flexibility in their interactions with each customer. One very smart example of this kind of approach was originally developed by a UK-based bank. Their reps are assessed based on a broad array of competencies tied to specific outcomes (which vary by service department or function).

This "adaptable quality framework" identifies five different "mastery levels," with clear definitions for each. During coaching sessions with each rep, supervisors listen to previously recorded calls and agree on which level the rep is achieving with that customer. As an example, an agent in their collections department is evaluated on six competencies:

- Interaction with the customer
- Identification of opportunities to create a mutual solution
- Call control
- Negotiation skills
- Urgency to resolve the issue as soon as possible
- The communication of consequences if the issue is not resolved

There are specific criteria to define the mastery levels for each competency. For example, there are five levels based on the competency "interaction with the customer" (see figure 5.6).

The message here to the front line is very clear: *You know what we need to achieve as a company, and your goal should be to become increasingly excellent at the skills required for you—and all of us—to succeed. Because*

Sample Competency Guidance: Interaction	
Mastery Level	**Description of Competency**
Novice	• We are distracted, interrupt, or ask the customer to repeat information provided earlier. • We talk over customers and dismiss their feelings.
Emerging	• We partially practice active listening skills but race the call too quickly. • We fail to probe warning signs that we may be on the wrong path, strategy, or education.
Effective	• We use a collaborative and assertive tone during negotiation. • We ask questions to clarify.
Advanced	• We use empathy to gain trust and motivate a payment or desired outcome from the customer.
Expert	• We make a real connection through developing exceptional rapport. • We show real insight into customers and their individual priorities.

Source: UK-based bank; CEB, 2013.

Figure 5.6 UK-Based Bank's Rep Competency Guidelines (Abbreviated)

every call and every customer is different, there's no one set of rules or directions that apply to every situation, but the basic competencies required to have a successful interaction will always be the same. The company trusts you to do what is best with each customer, and to work to improve your skills over time. If you're doing these two things, you will always be on the right path. No one is going to tell you what to do, but you need to drive yourself toward continual improvement based on the competencies and outcomes that everyone else here is also working toward. And your manager and coaches and peers are all here to help you in whatever way is best for your personal development.

There is no checklist. Instead, there is commonsense guidance. Nothing more.

This switch to a much more flexible competency-based approach has paid significant dividends for the team at this bank. Within just a year, the company's collections team saw an 8 percent increase in customers paying their overdue balances on the spot. They also reported a 50 percent increase in customers who were willing to commit to a specific payment plan. These are very impressive results that fly in the face of the conventional wisdom that the only way to manage customer service reps is to orchestrate their interactions and critique them based on a long list of objective criteria.

REMOVE THE PRESSURE OF TIME

Historically, call centers have operated under an unchallenged assumption—the faster the call, the more efficient the operation. Shorter calls mean more calls per hour, which can be handled by fewer reps. Efficiency is tracked through a metric known as AHT—average handle time. It's the average length of all calls from all customers, and it's measured in a wide variety of ways:

- Overall AHT for the entire operation
- Handle time of various customer segments or among users of various company products
- AHT by shift, or by individual supervisors, and down to the level of each individual rep

Regardless of how it's measured, every person in the service department knows that every call is being timed. It's like the clock is always ticking, and no one can escape its scrutiny. This measurement system is omnipresent, and creates both a subconscious pressure as well as a contradictory set of goals for every rep. It doesn't take long for people who are new to the service operation to realize that if they're doing a good job of serving customers, but they're taking longer than the average rep to do so, then what they're doing isn't considered a good job.

But as the simple issues have been siphoned off by self-service and customer expectations for personalized service have begun to rise, service executives have recognized that the *quality* of the interaction is in fact much more important than just squeezing every drop of productivity out of every rep. How could a rep possibly be concentrating on providing unique, customized service to each individual customer when that clock is ticking louder and louder in their brain every second they're still on the line with the customer?

In fact, longtime QA managers tell us that they can always tell what is going to happen with a rep who has just completed a more complex call with a customer who required significantly more time to resolve their issue. The very *next* call is going to be a *really* short one. Even if that next customer also has a complex issue, the rep will purposely do everything they can to make that call as short as possible, since they don't want to blow their personal AHT.

If a rep has too many longer calls, they assume it will be just a matter of time before their supervisor comes a-calling with a "friendly reminder" to keep their AHT in check. What's worse is that even if the supervisor never brings it to their attention, the rep typically experiences their own sense of time pressure—sometimes without even knowing they're doing it. That's why high-CQ companies are abandoning the measurement of AHT—either removing it from the dashboard of each individual rep, or in the most extreme cases, just abandoning it entirely.

This may seem unimaginable to service leaders who've been working in contact center environments their entire careers. ("How could we ever give up that degree of control? Wouldn't our call length—and therefore our costs—skyrocket?") But we're seeing increasing evidence that throwing AHT measurements out the window is, in fact, no less efficient.

A perfect example comes from a major pharmaceutical company that recently took drastic steps to improve the quality of its service by counseling its reps to simply "do whatever you have to do to take care of the one customer you're talking to right now." The implicit understanding was that if *this* customer has a complex issue, and needs more time, then we'd want to give it to them. And if you happen to get seven calls in a row from customers who need more time, that's fine. What matters most isn't your average handle time; what matters is the customer outcome.

However, they were also very careful not to totally abandon efficiency. Instead of reporting AHT at the rep level, they simply introduced a new dashboard metric called Available Talk Percentage:

ATP = (talk time + idle time) / (shift length - (lunch break + other breaks))

ATP measures the sum of all talk time *and* idle time (the times when a rep is ready to take a call but there isn't one in the queue waiting to be answered) and divides that by the length of the rep's scheduled shift (minus lunch time and other permitted breaks). ATP is essentially, then, a measure of how efficient a rep is with all the other work they do that *isn't* talking to customers—things like after-call work, follow-up, and other administrative duties.

Instead of the message, "Work quickly, because time is money," the message at high-CQ companies is, "Do your non-customer-facing work as efficiently as possible so you can have more time to talk to customers who need your help." The results of the AHT-to-ATP conversion have greatly exceeded the expectations of the customer service management team. In a period of just one year, overall customer satisfaction (this company's primary customer metric) went up 15 percentage points. As reps became increasingly more efficient with their after-call work, they were able to buy themselves additional time to spend on customers—without the pressure of the clock ticking in their heads. It's a great example of *gaining* control by *giving* control.

Other companies that have tried similar approaches to suppress AHT also report an interesting knock-on benefit. They get fewer repeat calls. Spending an extra sixty seconds with a customer in that first interaction avoids a subsequent four-minute call days later. Suppressing handle time allows for the next issue avoidance we discussed back in chapter 3. The deep irony is that the cost driver most service leaders prioritize above all else—talk time—is actually costing many of them more by tightly managing it.

It may seem counterintuitive to the standard operating procedure in many company cultures, but that's the nature of trust. And that's where trust needs to be both balanced by and supplemented with alignment. Reps who are aligned by having a firm grasp on the company's goals and its mission are much less likely to simply give away the store to appease one dissatisfied customer.

CQ KEY #2: *Rep Understanding and Alignment with Company Goals*

This concept is about helping individuals see the clear connection between their own daily work and the achievement of the organization's bigger goals and objectives. Reps who understand exactly how customer service ties directly to customer loyalty, which ties directly to strategic and financial outcomes, are much more likely to take control over their own individual interactions. And again, this sense of control is the essence of CQ and the key to greater performance.

Anyone who has ever explored the topic of employee engagement is generally familiar with the concepts of alignment and connection. The value of engagement is that employees are more likely to try harder to perform at a higher level—to exhibit what's called *discretionary effort*—if they understand and appreciate the direct connection between their everyday work and the overall big-picture mission of the organization.

When a person can see how what *they* do impacts *everyone* in some positive way, this serves as a powerful positive motivation. The power of this connection is often taught via a parable known as "The Two Brick-layers:"

> **A young boy is passing a construction site where two men are working side by side laying bricks.**
>
> **The boy asks the first worker,** *"Excuse me sir, what are you doing?"*
>
> **The man replies gruffly,** *"I'm laying brick. What does it look like?"*
>
> **The boy then asks the second worker,** *"And what are you doing, mister?"*
>
> **The other worker says,** *"I'm helping to build a beautiful new cathedral."*

This sense of connectedness to the bigger mission is critical to awakening an employee's sense of control—to maximize their CQ—and it is critical that companies take active steps to ensure that each frontline staff member has every opportunity to feel so connected. Frontline employees need to know that in every interaction with customers they are literally representing the fate of every other employee of the company, and that the collective success or failure at that moment is entirely in their hands.

Now, because of the human element of customer service, that connection might seem easier to achieve than in other professions—back-office functions like accounting, for instance, where the work is typically done silently and alone. How could you not feel more connected when you're dealing one-on-one with another person?

But our research shows that because of the often mind-numbing repetitiveness of dealing with customer after customer, hour after hour, it is all too common for employees to quickly lose all sense of the human qualities of the job and regress into a robotic trance, unmotivated by any mission higher than "somehow getting to the end of my shift."

In order to break employees of this tendency, it only makes sense to enable them to see that connection in ways that are more obvious, more visible, and more personal. Of course, to make this work on a personal level would seem to be completely nonscalable. Any practice that brings the higher goals and purpose of the organization all the way down to an individual level would have to be very time-consuming and require hundreds or even thousands of one-on-one meetings and discussions across an entire service organization.

It's for this reason that we were so excited to learn about the methodology pioneered by one Canadian financial services company. They created a process by which each individual customer service rep is able to internalize the service mission of the company in their own unique way, and is then offered an opportunity to commit to a number of specific focus areas to which they can personally contribute.

The process starts not at the individual level but at the team level. A number of frontline reps are enlisted—on a voluntary basis—to form a Rep Committee charged with setting service goals for the entire frontline workforce. The committee participates in a series of workshops during which they examine the individual elements of the company's corporate values and overall strategic mission, then break those down into component parts to determine the exact contribution customer service can offer in achieving them. (We will explore how all this translates down to the level of each individual rep shortly.)

The lesson here is that the typical corporate mission, vision, and values seems so high-level and "oh-so-corporate" to the average employee. *What exactly does any of that ivory-tower stuff mean to me?* That's the Rep Committee's charge—"You guys go off into a private room and figure out what it should mean to us." A facilitator is assigned to lead these committee sessions, introducing the group to each corporate value and strategic goal one by one, and then guiding them through a four-step process for each:

Step 1: Norming.

The committee starts by examining each value and coming to some common agreement about what it means in real terms—level setting, synchronizing definitions, and ensuring there is no misconception or misalignment within the group. Depending on how corporate values are written, this step can be harder or easier. We often see corporate goals that are written in a way that is so lofty or so generic, they really do require some degree of interpretation.

Step 2: Brainstorming.

The committee members then create a comprehensive list of the specific things a customer service rep could do that would have some impact on the achievement of a single corporate goal. Here is where the connection begins. The discussion now shifts from the mission of the company to the everyday actions of the customer service division. But as in any brainstorming exercise, during this phase "there are no wrong answers." The only objective at this point is to create the longest possible list of actions a frontline rep could take that could contribute to success in each specific area. Sample outcomes from the brainstorming phase might include things like active listening, using clear language, aligning to the customer's communication style, or demonstrating empathy.

Step 3: Refining.

Here is where the temperature in the committee room really starts to heat up. From the entire brainstormed list of things a rep could do, the group tries to narrow down to those ideas that drive the highest value, are the most practical, and are achievable under normal—not exceptional—circumstances. This step requires the facilitator to exercise their own sense of control, because this stage of the discussion can easily degrade into arguments, tangential sidetracks, eruptions of negativity, or other emotional forces that are counterproductive to the process. With the help of the facilitator, the group arrives at a much smaller list of no more than three or four ideas per corporate value.

Step 4: Polishing.

The final step is to turn each of the refined ideas into specific actions or behaviors that a frontline customer service rep could commit to in their daily work, that are clearly tied to the achievement of a much bigger corporate objective. The final output from the committee's work is a document that is distributed, with some degree of fanfare, to the entire frontline rep population. "Here are the conclusions of a group of your peers about how we in customer service can directly contribute to the success of the company. This does not come from management. This comes directly from people exactly like you, who do exactly the same job you do." For example, when relating strong communication skills to the service team, the final stated goal from the committee might be: "Identifying customer traits, and communicating with each individual in a way that appeals most directly to them."

As the committee's document is shared with each individual frontline employee, it is presented with a direct "ask." Not, "Take a look and see what you think," but rather, "Which of these behaviors are you personally willing to commit to? You don't have to choose all of them—in fact, you shouldn't choose more than a few. Select the specific ones you like best, that you can achieve in your own personal interactions with customers on a daily basis."

This personal discussion about goal setting and commitment is then taken to the level of individual one-on-one sessions between each employee and their supervisor—not in some unique one-time-only meeting where contracts are agreed to and signed in blood, but in the normal course of the typical coaching sessions that frontline reps have with their supervisors.

This idea, in many ways, is nothing more than the classic three-step technique of employee management:

1. Ask each employee how they plan to personally improve.
2. Ensure that their improvement ideas make sense and are aligned to the mission of the organization.
3. Hold that employee responsible for their self-selected goals— push them a little harder when they're not living up to their own commitment, praise them when they are.

The company has learned that the output of the committee process is a list of behaviors that are almost identical to what would have been created if the exercise had been performed by customer service management. But the fact that these goals are "of the people, by the people, and for the people" makes a huge difference. And while it might be somewhat easier and more scalable for management to simply proclaim, "Now that a committee of your peers has decided how you will be held accountable, these are the new standards for everyone," it is the personalized element of this process that makes it so powerful.

Consider the following quotes from people throughout the company service organization about the impact this is having on their culture.

From their director of customer service operations:

"We have witnessed tremendous results. Engagement has increased, absenteeism has decreased, and client compliments have increased more than 20 percent."

From a customer service supervisor:

"Our reps now have greater clarity into what their daily work means to the organization and how they play a significant role in driving the business forward."

And from a frontline rep:

"I now feel like management actually values me as an employee. I get to have significant input and control into my own goals, that I can tie directly to my own job."

That strikes us as "the voice of CQ." And again, executives and leaders did not *make* any of this happen. In fact, if they had tried too hard to make it happen, the whole effort likely would have backfired. But they did *enable it to happen* in a natural, organic way that has paid great dividends in improved frontline rep performance and its downstream impact on customer loyalty.

Reps who support each other at a peer level are much more likely to conform their behavior to what they see others around them doing—not at the level of cookie-cutter, robotic consistency, but with a reasonable set of self-imposed guardrails that still allow for a resolution that is best for both the customer and the company.

CQ KEY #3: *A Strong Rep Peer Support Network*

One important lesson we've learned about creating an environment where trust, alignment, and peer support are critical to success: You can't *make* any of these things happen. You cannot make people trust you, or force them to be better aligned to the bigger mission of your company, or insist that your employees support each other better. If you *could* make these things happen, you would. But you can't.

However, you *can* definitely enable them. You—as a manager and a leader—can make changes in the work environment that make these three conditions much more likely to happen on their own. Which is the only way they will ever happen.

Having a strong rep peer support network has a 17 percent impact on CQ, meaning it has even more impact than the other two drivers (trust and alignment). But according to our firsthand observations of hundreds of companies, it is also the hardest to get right. Based on what we see the best companies doing, we believe there are three conditions that must be met—simultaneously—for the maximum benefits of peer support to be realized:

Condition 1: Adequate time.

If supporting one's peers is considered an extra burden or a hassle at any level, it is very unlikely to occur with any regularity. Companies need to concentrate on methods that make it easy for reps to participate in supporting one another and ensuring that this support is considered part of the job and not something a rep should only do in their spare time.

Condition 2: True best-practice sharing.

There's no question that frontline staffers share ideas with each other all the time—typically in unstructured settings like the break room, the outdoor smoking area, and the bar across the street from the office. The real question is whether those ideas being shared are positive and beneficial, or just suboptimal shortcuts, workarounds, and ways to "cheat the system." It is critical that what the support reps are offering each other is based on how best to serve customers, particularly in more complex situations where there may be no one right answer, or where a customer's issue may be unique and has never been addressed before.

Condition 3: Receptive reps.

There's nothing more painful than trying to help someone who doesn't want to be helped, or to share information with someone who has zero interest in listening. That's why some companies have created systems and structures that enable reps to help each other, in forums and settings that are not controlled by management. Receptivity of assistance is directly related to the source of the help, and if reps feel that any form of peer support is nothing more than an alternative form of micromanagement, it will be doomed.

Two ideas we've seen in practice strike us as meeting all three of these conditions. The first of these occurs in the "live" world—peer coaching. And the other exists in the "virtual" world—team discussion forums. We believe every customer service organization should seriously consider implementing both of them.

REP DISCUSSION FORUMS

This is a solution that didn't exist five or ten years ago, but is now very possible at most larger companies—and we believe it makes great sense. Providing reps with an online outlet that enables them to ask each other questions, compare notes on common problem resolution situations, and simply vent about customer issues creates at least three significant benefits:

- Peer support of this kind takes the pressure off time-oppressed supervisors, as frontline reps can seek answers and suggestions from a wider variety of sources than simply having to ask their boss every time they have an issue they're unsure about.
- A discussion forum allows frontline reps to identify problems and issues that might not be obvious to management, but could easily be corrected.
- It becomes a platform for better-performing reps to take a greater leadership role within the customer service team, positioning them for additional responsibility over time.

We have seen a variety of solutions that fit this general category, and of those, the one developed by Fidelity Investments strikes us as the best model for other companies to follow. Fidelity has created a fully rep-owned forum called "Spaces" that has produced some excellent results—largely because of three elements that make it unique:

- *Although it was created by company management, it is operated exclusively by frontline reps.* This is not a "company" site per se, but a free exchange of ideas and suggestions that only frontline staff participate in.
- *It is moderated by a single frontline rep.* One team member is designated as the Spaces moderator, spending approximately 90 percent of their work time in this role, in a rotation that typically lasts for about six months. The moderator is charged with creating discussion topics and then generating reports about key rep issues and suggestions that are presented to management, as well as reporting back to the front line about decisions and improvements being made by management.

- *Each workplace location or shift designates a "team champion" to maintain the buzz.* That person encourages their coworkers to participate more actively, and shares information with the team about issues that are most directly applicable to that worksite. During the first year of its operation, Spaces generated over 3,000 comments from frontline reps throughout the global Fidelity service organization. The moderators advanced a total of more than 350 ideas and suggestions to management, of which 100 became action items in which some specific improvement or modification was made.

Fidelity says the suggestions covered a wide variety of issues, including suggestions for how to reduce unnecessary customer call volume, and how to increase operational efficiency. The total savings realized as a result of these successful implementations represented a significant cost reduction for the company, while increasing the degree of peer support and CQ for its frontline staff.

These discoveries about driving increased frontline rep performance and "setting our people up for success" in today's more demanding and challenging customer environment lead to a clear conclusion:

We need to manage differently, and set different expectations for what "success" looks like.

This cannot be accomplished through a "program" or a "campaign." You can't just hang new posters in the break room and expect to achieve any significant results (e.g., "March Is CQ Month!"). In fact, just the opposite—if your movement toward creating a world-class low-effort service operation is perceived as the flavor of the month, you'll find yourself constantly pushing the rock uphill. What you need to undertake is a thorough reexamination of what you and your people are there to accomplish—what you do, how it impacts customers, and how it's measured. One service leader we work with said that shifting the organization toward a strategy of effort reduction "isn't a sprint; it's a marathon. In fact, it's probably a series of marathons."

But again, like tracking your pace in a marathon, another great benefit of creating a low-effort experience for your customers is that effort can be directly measured. Rethinking the culture of your contact center environment might sound like a daunting, overwhelming process—at first. But it begins with a relatively simple step: Ask customers about the effort required for their issue to be resolved, and when they experience high effort, try to understand how and why. In this next chapter, we'll show you why "effort" is more than just a concept. It can—and should—be an important component of the measurement system you use on a daily basis to determine your own success in serving customers.

KEY TAKEAWAYS

♦ *Judgment and control differentiate today's best reps.* In this era of increasingly complex live service and heightened customer expectations (due to simple issues being resolved in self-service), the most important competency for reps to possess is "control quotient" (CQ). CQ is the ability to exercise judgment and maintain control in a high-pressure, complex service environment.

♦ *CQ isn't learned, it's enabled.* While CQ is the greatest differentiator of rep performance, the reality is that most reps have moderate to high CQ potential. The problem is that most companies inhibit reps from exercising CQ due to the environment of strict adherence they've created and reinforced for years. Judgment and control are not welcomed in these environments.

♦ *Give control to get control of the front line.* To allow reps to activate their latent CQ potential, companies need to demonstrate trust in rep judgment. Approaches include deemphasizing or eliminating handle time and the QA checklist, clarifying reps' alignment between what they do and what the company is trying to achieve, and allowing reps to tap into the collective experience and knowledge of their peers to make smart decisions.

6

THE DISLOYALTY DETECTOR—
CUSTOMER EFFORT SCORE V2.0

I f ever there was a function prone to hand-wringing over how to measure things, it's the customer service department. There is endless contention about how best to measure the customer experience. Take first contact resolution. Does the customer who called back to "shop" for a different answer count as a resolved issue or not? How should you record the time it takes to resolve an issue? Do we measure individual call length or aggregate resolution time across multiple calls, web site visits, e-mails, and other forms of contact? How should we assess the quality of the service we deliver? Should we have an internal team listen to recorded calls and score them, or should we actually ask customers to score us? Which metric is best for that? Customer satisfaction? Net Promoter Score? Something else?

While debate will likely continue to rage around service experience metrics, one thing we can say with absolute certainty is that measuring customer effort can help any organization improve the customer experience and better support loyalty initiatives across the company. At a more systemic level, measuring customer effort shines a spotlight on the service experience and can bring new levels of clarity to what we can do to improve it. In our research, we found that measuring effort can be quite powerful indeed (see figure 6.1). For instance, 94 percent of customers who had low-effort experiences reported that they would repurchase from the company, while only 4 percent of customers experiencing high-effort interactions reported an intent to repurchase. And 88 percent of

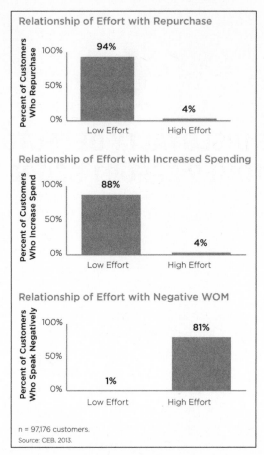

Figure 6.1 Impact of Effort on Repurchase, Share of Wallet, and Customer Word of Mouth

customers with low-effort experiences reported an intent to increase spend with the company, compared to just 4 percent of those customers with high-effort experiences. Only 1 percent of all customers with low-effort experiences said they'd spread negative word of mouth about the company, compared with a staggering 81 percent of customers with high-effort experiences who said they'd do the same. Understanding how we're doing on the effort front, in other words, is powerful stuff. Not only can it help us to ascertain how we're doing when it comes to service, but when employed as a post-interaction survey question, it can serve as a "divining rod" to identify customers at risk of defection and who represent a potential source of negative word of mouth to others.

As with anything we want to improve, the real first step in the journey of reducing customer effort is measuring it. In this chapter, we'll show you two techniques we recommend. First is a survey-based metric we call the Customer Effort Score (CES). Second, we'll show you how to systematically track the most common indicators of customer effort. For this, we'll share the principles of an audit we've helped companies put in place called the Customer Effort Assessment (CEA). Measuring effort using the CES survey metric, when coupled with a more in-depth audit like the CEA, creates a clear picture not just of how you're doing when it comes to effort reduction but, more important, specific actions you can take to improve it. Along the way, we'll share some of the data and benchmarks we've surfaced since we started to track CES and monitor customer effort for companies around the world, and we'll share some views on "dos" and "don'ts" when it comes to measuring effort in your own organization.

The Customer Effort Score

In customer experience circles, there's a lot of attention paid to single, incisive survey questions that are designed to predict future customer loyalty—most notably, customer satisfaction (CSAT) and Net Promoter Score (NPS). Customer effort also has a question, one we call the Customer Effort Score (CES), a survey question that's received a lot of press in the customer service world since we first publicly unveiled it a few years ago.

When we pored over our data and looked at the predictive power of different metrics for understanding customer loyalty, we found some pretty surprising things. First, as we discussed in the earliest pages of this book, we found (just like Fred Reichheld before us)[1] that CSAT is a poor predictor of a customer's intent to repurchase and to increase spend. Conversely, we found that NPS was a much better predictor of loyalty.* Like the many companies that employ NPS in their customer

---

* NPS is a metric pioneered by Reichheld and described in his book *The Ultimate Question: Driving Good Profits and True Growth* (Harvard Business School Press, 2006). It is based on a single question: "How likely is it that you would recommend [your company] to a friend or colleague?"

experience measurement programs, we too found it to be a powerful leading indicator of future customer behavior.

Let's examine NPS for a moment as it relates to customer effort. NPS is a "big question" that captures a customer's holistic impressions of their relationship with a company—and it does a great job doing so. The problem is that it isn't the best metric for understanding customer service performance at a transactional level. NPS, particularly when used correctly,* is a fine measure of relationship-level loyalty—the net sum of a customer's interactions with a company, its brand, its products, its channels, and all other touchpoints—but it can mask effort in service transactions since it is such a *big* question.

You can imagine, for instance, customers enduring high-effort service interactions nevertheless reporting that they would be likely to recommend the company to a friend. The customer service might be awful, but the product's still great, so the customer gives the company a decent NPS score and effectively masks the improvement opportunity in the service channel. Or, conversely, we deliver a terrific, low-effort service experience to a customer who hates our product, so we get a bad NPS score that makes us scratch our heads, wondering what went wrong in what seemed like a great service experience. Our data suggests that these reactions occur often enough that it's worth exploring other ways to measure the specific impact of the service experience.

We found that we could actually sharpen the ability to predict loyalty—at least in customer service interactions—by measuring effort at the transactional level. This raises an important distinction in the quest to measure loyalty. Loyalty is influenced by many touchpoints a customer has with a company and its brands. Service happens to be one of those touchpoints—and one we know is far more likely to drive *disloyalty*. While companies need to know the health of broader *relationship loyalty*, service executives need to apply a laserlike focus to the *transactional loyalty* impact of their service interactions. The challenge for service leaders relying primarily on NPS or other relationship metrics is that they often lack visibility into which specific service levers they can pull to positively impact the service experience, and therefore

---

* Fred Reichheld and other NPS practitioners are clear in their guidance that the NPS question itself is a directional indicator, not a be-all, end-all metric. Used properly, it's part of an overall customer loyalty "operating system"—as we'll discuss later in this chapter, this is the same guidance we've given service leaders when it comes to using CES.

loyalty. And that's really where the Customer Effort Score shines—it helps us understand the actual impact of the service experience (and only the service experience) on customer loyalty. CES is a simple question that tries to gauge how hard a customer feels like she had to work to get her issue resolved by the company—was it an easy experience or did the customer feel like she had to run through a gauntlet to get her problem solved? Typically, it is asked in a post-transaction survey (for instance, in an IVR survey, a pop-up web survey, or an e-mail survey).

By this point in the book, you should know that delivering a low-effort experience is the Holy Grail of customer service. CES gives managers a simple way to understand whether they've accomplished this from one interaction to the next, across different channels and divisions in their organizations, and over time. And, importantly, it offers a way to immediately spot customers at risk of defection.

The exact wording of CES has evolved since we first released it in a 2010 *Harvard Business Review* article entitled, "Stop Trying to Delight Your Customers."[2] In its first iteration—"CES v1.0," if you will—we phrased the survey question in the following way: "How much effort did you personally have to put forth to get your issue resolved?" We measured it on a five-point scale ranging from "very low effort" (1) to "very high effort" (5). In our cross-industry studies, we found that the answer to this question provided a strong measure of the impact of an individual customer service interaction on loyalty.

While this was certainly encouraging, implementing CES wasn't as straightforward for all companies as implementing a CSAT or NPS metric. First, we found that CES could be prone to false negatives and positives simply because of the inverted scale it uses. In a post-interaction survey, most customers are conditioned to associate low scores with "bad" and high scores with "good." So when you ask the CES question at the end of the survey, you sometimes see customers offering a knee-jerk response ("I gave them a four on the last question asking how satisfied I was, so I'll just give them a four on this one too").

While this could be rectified by reversing the scale (as many companies have done in their own deployments of CES), there were other, harder-to-fix problems with the original wording. For instance, some customers misinterpreted the CES question as asking not how difficult their resolution experience was, but how hard they personally *tried* to resolve the issue on their own. Some customers felt the question had an accusatory tone, not unlike the parent chiding his child by asking, "Did you *really* look for the milk in the refrigerator before asking me where it was?"

The word "effort" can also prove hard to translate for companies that serve non-English-speaking customers. While there are acceptable alternative terms, there is some debate as to the right ones in some languages—a factor that makes benchmarking difficult across companies that have used different translations, and within companies with global operations.

Finally, there was the challenge presented by a lack of "priming" before the CES question. In other words, after enduring a battery of questions that all ask, in some way, shape, or form, how much the customer liked or disliked certain elements of the service experience (e.g., how knowledgeable, courteous, or polite was the representative), it can throw some customers off to suddenly ask them about effort when everything they'd been asked up to that point pertained more to satisfaction.

This isn't to suggest that companies haven't had success using CES as an experience metric in the service organization. Quite the contrary. Most of the companies we work with who've implemented CES report that it works very well in their service environment, especially as a way to pre-empt customer defection. But a number of companies struggled with one of the aforementioned problems, and that was enough to send us back to the drawing board to see if we couldn't do better.

As we've collected more data on customer service interactions and customer effort, we started piloting different versions of the CES question. This book represents our first public unveiling of our new effort metric, which we're calling CES v2.0.

The new CES metric is based on a statement, "The company made it easy for me to handle my issue," after which the customer is asked to answer (on a common 1–7 scale used in most customer service surveys) whether they agree or disagree with statement.

This new question, CES v2.0, is a variant of the original question, but one we found produces much more reliable results, is less prone to misinterpretation, is less arduous to translate into multiple languages, and requires less priming to get the customer to accurately respond. The notion of effort is still front and center, but is phrased in terms of "ease," which is simpler for most customers to understand. And because it's on an agree/disagree scale, it fits with other questions the survey is already asking (e.g., "Do you agree or disagree that the rep was knowledgeable, courteous, or polite?").

Running this question with a panel of thousands of customers produced some fascinating and powerful results. First, we found that the new question wording was very strongly correlated to customer loyalty, explaining approximately one-third of customers' repurchase intent, word of mouth, and willingness to consider new offerings (i.e., increase spend). While this may not sound like much, consider that we are only measuring the experience of resolving just a single service issue (statistically speaking this is extremely powerful). If one-third of a customer's loyalty intentions are driven by merely one service interaction, that is a pretty intimidating fact for most service organizations.

When comparing this CES v2.0 to CSAT, we found the effort measure to be 12 percent more predictive of customer loyalty.[*] So there is a strong case for—at the very least—adding CES to the dashboard to help provide a more detailed perspective on the customer interaction.

Something else we discovered is that customers' time sensitivity matters quite a bit when selecting the right outcome metric for customer service. We found that the accuracy of CSAT in predicting customer loyalty drops precipitously for customers who are more time-pressed, whereas customer effort, on the other hand, remains a strong predictor.[†] In fact, for those customers who feel significant time pressure in their daily lives, customer effort was more than twice as accurate a predictor of their level of company loyalty than CSAT. This finding is particularly relevant for B2B companies, whose customers often face tremendous time pressures at work every day, and B2C companies serving segments like multichild households, busy professionals, or working parents.

One more bit of discovery: It turns out that the impact of the service experience on loyalty is greater when either of the following two conditions are true:

---

[*] We defined accuracy here by comparing the R-squared measure from two bivariate OLS regression models with customer loyalty as the dependent variable.

[†] We measured time sensitivity through one to seven agree/disagree questions such as, "I feel like there aren't enough hours in the day," and "I feel rushed to complete the things I need to get done (e.g., at work, at home, etc.)."

1. The customer does not have an extremely strong attachment to the products or services the company provides, and/or
2. There are lower perceived switching costs in your category.

From the product standpoint, this explains why some companies with huge product followings have been able to nevertheless thrive with inferior customer support. If customers perceive a product to be that much better than the alternatives, it may outweigh one's poor service experience. The impact of perceived switching costs also makes intuitive sense—if the customer can easily switch providers, one high-effort service experience could be all it takes for them to defect. In fact, customer effort has about twice as much impact on customer loyalty for customers who perceived low switching barriers from that company.

While companies are often very interested in how they compare to peers and competitors on CES, take caution in knowing that the average score is far less important than the distribution. Averages hide important discrepancies in data—and CES scores aren't unlike other data in that regard. But since it is a newer metric in the customer service space, organizations often focus *only* on the average score. The better way to examine CES is against a normal distribution—in other words, some (10–20 percent) interactions score as very high- or very low-effort, but most should be somewhere around the mean. Looking at the distribution to understand areas of opportunity can be far more instructive than just considering how your average CES compares to others in your space.

Here's a brief example to illustrate: One company was surprised that their CES indicated lower effort compared to their industry benchmark. This didn't align with what the head of the service organization sensed when thinking about the overall state of things. He believed that his group needed to make some serious improvements based on a high number of complaints, but his team kept highlighting their stellar average CES. When he examined the data distribution, he learned some surprising things: First, an extremely high number of low-effort experiences relative to the industry benchmark indicated that something was off the mark. Further, there were very few moderate-effort contacts and a relatively small number of higher-effort experiences. In turns out this skewed distribution suggested that too many simple issues were making their way to the phone channel and not being solved in self-service. So customers were calling in with very simple issues—classic "one and done" calls—that felt easy to resolve. So, again, making sense of CES often has a lot to do with the distribution.

Regardless of the wording (CES v1.0 or CES v2.0), it is important to be reminded that CES is not the same kind of metric as CSAT or NPS, and as such, comparing them against one another is a bit of a fool's errand. As one industry expert observed, comparing CES with these other metrics is a bit of an apples-to-oranges comparison: "Whereas CES is designed to evaluate the 'micro-experience' of a given customer service event, both NPS and CSAT are measures of the 'macro-experience,' the overall sentiment, and take the entirety of the customer experience into consideration—not just a single interaction or event."[3] We see that not as a criticism, but as a clear indication of the true value of measuring effort. CES is not intended to measure the overall health of the broader customer relationship, but rather the transactional health of the most significant driver of disloyalty—effort in service interactions. As this expert goes on to say, CES is "a useful addition to a "well designed and executed customer experience management program." We agree fully.

That being said, one of the clear benefits of measuring effort at the transactional customer service level is that it helps service leaders to gauge the actual impact they are having on broader loyalty improvement efforts across the company.

But even NPS shops should consider adding CES to their measurement dashboard. Here's why: Many companies we talk to about effort buy into the broader concept but then halt when we introduce CES. "We're an NPS shop," they tell us. Our response? That's great—this isn't a religious debate. If they are measuring NPS in customer service, what are the true service-related drivers of NPS they're tracking? Are they trying to improve NPS by reducing things like callbacks, transfers, channel switching, repeating information, and so on? If so, then they're reducing effort—they're just flying under the NPS banner rather than the CES banner. But measuring CES can help service leaders discuss the impact they are having on broader NPS objectives. In some of our latest research, we found that only 3 percent of customers who had low-effort experiences were "Detractors" (a customer scoring from zero to six on the NPS likelihood-to-recommend survey question), compared to 82 percent of customers who endured a high-effort experience. This is a *huge* difference and really speaks to the power of reducing customer effort in order to mitigate disloyalty. If your company measures NPS, you should strongly consider introducing CES into your customer service survey as a way to understand whether you're helping or hurting the NPS cause.

Many companies who've implemented CES have had success using it as a measure of overall customer service effectiveness and as a way to spot at-risk customers. But here's the thing: It's just a question. Make no mistake, it's a powerful directional indicator, but that's really all it is. CES is not the be-all, end-all, or silver bullet of customer service measurement, but rather part of a larger transactional loyalty measurement system. To really understand what's going on in the service experience, you've got to look at it from multiple angles and through many lenses. You've got to collect a lot of data. In other words, figuring out how to improve the experience you deliver to your customers is less about simply taking your temperature and more like undergoing a complete physical. This is where coupling the CES metric with a more systemic monitoring of the sources of effort in your service experience comes into play.

Systemically Finding and Eliminating Drivers of Effort

A robust customer effort measurement system is composed of three parts (see figure 6.2). First, at the highest level, you want to understand the customer's overall loyalty to you as a company—this is best measured by using high-level metrics such as NPS (in part because it's simply a better approach to measuring loyalty at the highest level, but also because it helps link the service organization's role and impact to broader loyalty outcomes, not to mention providing valuable context that your customer experience and marketing teams can use). One level down from this is to understand the amount of effort in the service transaction. The reason is quite clear: It's about trying to better understand what, specifically, the service organization can do to contribute to company-level loyalty. CES is a good way to measure that, and we recommend that companies cross-check their CES results by looking at some of the operational data that underpin effort—for instance, number of contacts to resolve an issue.

Finally, the next level down is to understand how the customer's service journey unfolds—in other words, the number and type of touchpoints

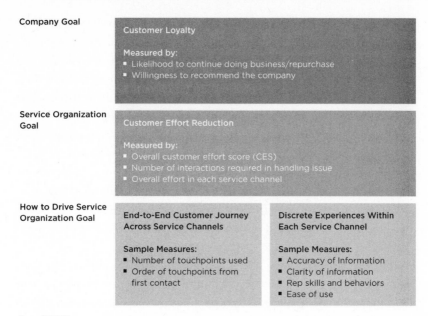

Company Goal

Customer Loyalty

Measured by:
- Likelihood to continue doing business/repurchase
- Willingness to recommend the company

Service Organization Goal

Customer Effort Reduction

Measured by:
- Overall customer effort score (CES)
- Number of interactions required in handling issue
- Overall effort in each service channel

How to Drive Service Organization Goal

End-to-End Customer Journey Across Service Channels

Sample Measures:
- Number of touchpoints used
- Order of touchpoints from first contact

Discrete Experiences Within Each Service Channel

Sample Measures:
- Accuracy of Information
- Clarity of information
- Rep skills and behaviors
- Ease of use

Source: CEB, 2013.

Figure 6.2 Connecting Company Loyalty Goals with Customer Service Strategy and Objectives

they used to resolve their issue, in what sequence those service touchpoints occured (e.g., did the customer just call the contact center or had they first visited the web site?), and the discrete customer experience within each channel (for example, assessing the clarity of information delivered by a service rep or the ease of finding information on the web site).

Collecting data at all three levels will help assess overall loyalty performance, the impact of customer service on loyalty, and the specific action steps a company should take to reduce effort in the service experience.

Acme Company: A Customer Effort Journey

Let's take a look at how we pulled these effort measurements together for one company to really understand their "effort profile". The data is from a real company, but to protect their confidentiality, we'll refer to them as Acme Company.

When we began working with Acme, they told us that they felt they'd done a really good job of developing their phone channel and it had paid off—indeed, they had great effort scores, as expected. They wanted to see what next steps they could take on the phone to really differentiate themselves, but once we conducted a deeper assessment for them, we were able to show them some powerful multichannel data that changed their strategy entirely. The counterintuitive finding for Acme's leadership team was that incremental spending on phone improvement clearly wasn't going to get them the same kind of returns as investment in the web site. Coming out of the diagnostic exercise, they suddenly had a new sense of where the next big thing was for them. They walked away feeling like they'd opened up a whole new field of low-hanging fruit—something they'd never seen before because of the siloed approach they'd always taken to collecting customer experience data.

In the pages that follow, we'll spend some time taking you through this journey and how we arrived at this conclusion, and along the way we'll share a number of the analytic techniques and survey questions we

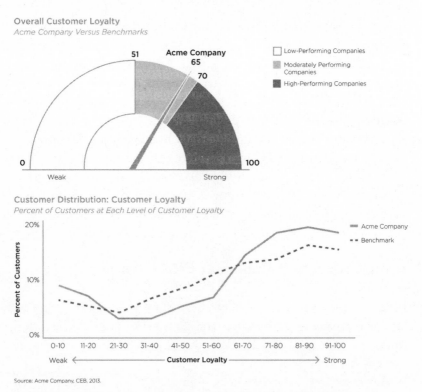

Source: Acme Company, CEB, 2013.

Figure 6.3 Acme Company's Overall Loyalty and Customer Distribution

used to uncover the best improvement opportunities for their company (see appendix E for a sample of survey questions used in our effort diagnostic). We think you can learn something directly from the Acme story, but more importantly, this case will provide great context about searching for the greatest points of customer effort in your customers' experiences.

Per our framework, the first thing we wanted to understand was overall loyalty. Initially it appeared there was little to be concerned about—in fact, Acme boasted a level of overall customer loyalty that was above average and very close to what we were accustomed to seeing from high-performing organizations (see figure 6.3). Similarly, they had a distribution of loyalty scores in line with peer organizations. This side of the story was misleading, however, and this becomes a good object lesson in why relationship-level loyalty metrics often mask underlying operational issues that force customers to endure higher-than-necessary levels of effort.

Beyond the loyalty scores, Acme's overall customer effort profile seemed fairly average too (see figure 6.4). Most Acme customers reported moderate to low levels of effort in their service interactions with the company, and very few of its customers reported that they were forced to endure high-effort experiences.

But while the top-line summary presented a healthy diagnosis, all wasn't well at Acme. When we started to look at channel-specific effort levels and map them against contact volume, two clear findings stood out, one of which was hugely troubling (see figure 6.5):

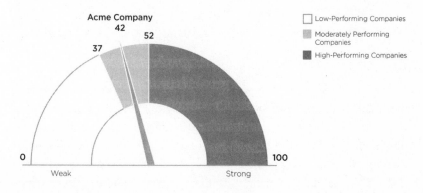

Source: Acme Company, CEB, 2013.

Figure 6.4 Acme Company's Customer Effort to Resolve Latest Service Issue

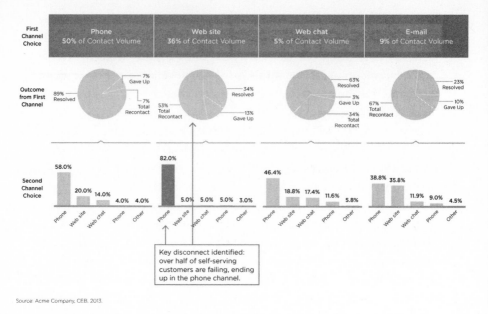

Source: Acme Company, CEB, 2013.

Figure 6.5 Acme Company's Customer Issue Resolution Journey

1. On the plus side, Acme was clearly doing a great job getting its customers to self-serve on their issues, driving 36 percent of first contacts to their web site. But . . .

2. . . . customers weren't staying online once they got there. Indeed, 53 percent of those customers who first went to Acme's web site reported having to recontact the company—and when they recontacted, they didn't stay in self-service. In fact, 82 percent of those customers who failed to resolve their issues on Acme's web site ended up picking up the phone and calling.

The net outcome of this wasn't just disloyalty for Acme customers, but much higher operating costs. It turned out that the failures in the web were driving a huge volume of secondary contacts back into the phone channel. So if Acme had focused on phone channel improvements as they initially planned to, their efforts would have likely yielded little. This was due to their customers entering phone conversations having just endured a high-effort web experience. A bad web experience (especially one the rep doesn't even know took place) isn't something improvements in the phone delivery would have fixed. It was clear that Acme needed to fix the root cause of the problem, which was their web site.

Accordingly, we found that customers reported a much higher level of effort in Acme's web channel—roughly 20 percent higher—than what we see in the benchmark. This was a relatively large disparity compared to where most organizations benchmark against web CES score. So web, not phone, was the sore spot in the customer experience for Acme. This was something Acme's leadership team had never thought about before—largely because their various systems didn't communicate in an integrated fashion, so they had no way to track a customer's entire issue resolution journey. As we discussed much earlier in this book, service leaders tend to think of customers as single-channel users ("phone customers" versus "web customers"), not as channel switchers. So, not surprisingly, this one piece of analysis produces many "a-ha!" moments for companies' leadership teams.

So let's summarize the Acme findings for a moment. If we step back and think about how Acme's customers typically contact them for service, and then compare the different service channels by looking not just at their efficacy (does Acme actually deliver resolution to customer issues in the channel?) but also the kind of experience delivered (does Acme deliver a high- or low-effort experience in the channel?), we get a much clearer picture of where Acme should focus (see figure 6.6).

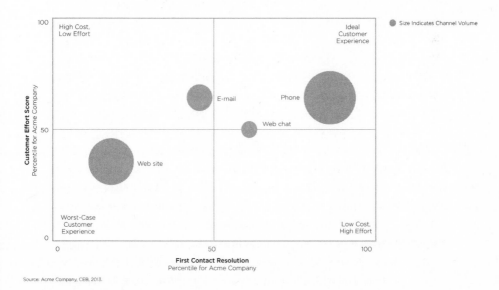

Source: Acme Company, CEB, 2013.

Figure 6.6 Acme Company's Channel Performance and Volume

This exercise highlighted just how detrimental the web interactions were for customers, driving significant repeat contact volume and high levels of customer effort.

Before we launched our diagnostic exercise, Acme told us that they felt they had a significant opportunity to improve the phone channel experience for their customers. By the same token, their team hypothesized that they were doing a relatively good job on the web. They knew from their own research that their percentage of customers self-serving on the web was higher than the norm.

Of course, the customer effort journey didn't stop here. This was really just where it started. While the data presented thus far helped Acme to think more critically about the entirety of the customer experience, it didn't tell them what to do about fixing it. Here's where the value of digging deep really came into play. As part of the diagnostic exercise, we looked into the top drivers of effort within each channel to try to understand what specifically to focus on. Not surprisingly, Acme was performing worse than the benchmark on a few key effort drivers within the web channel.

As it turns out, Acme's customers really did want to self-serve. The issue for Acme is that their customers report some pretty significant problems when it comes to finding what they're looking for on their web site. Sixty-four percent of the customers who went to Acme's site reported that they couldn't find what they were looking for, and even if they could, much of the information was presented in an unclear manner (see figure 6.7).

Our first recommendation to the Acme team was that they immediately invest in a simple customer voice collection mechanism, similar to what Fidelity does (see chapter 2), to determine whether customers who are calling in are actually coming from the web site, and if so, why they left. This would help Acme quickly ascertain the exact nature of the problem. What are customers looking for? Is it content or functionality that's not available on the web, and if so, would it be a good investment to start offering these things in the self-serve channel? If it is something that's available on the site, why can't customers seem to find it now—or, if they can find it, what makes it so hard to understand in the way it's written and presented to the customer?

As starting points, we also suggested thinking about what Master-Card and Fidelity (see chapters 2 and 3 for more detail on their practices)

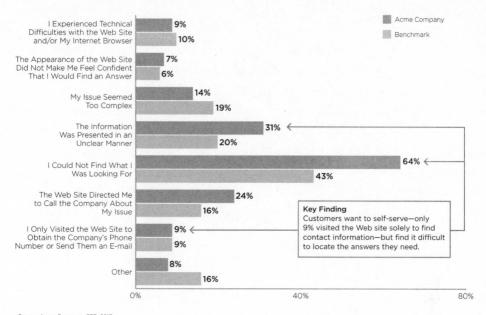

Source: Acme Company, CEB, 2013.

Figure 6.7 Acme Company's Drivers of Issue Reolution Failure in the web

have done in terms of channel patching and next issue avoidance on the web. We also recommended that Acme should perform an issue-to-channel-mapping exercise (see appendix A) to identify where on the customer service home page a customer should go based on their issue type, and then use page placement and task-based guidance to assist the customer in quickly choosing the best path to resolution (i.e., the lowest effort to the customer and lowest cost for the company). Lastly, in terms of making content more consumable and easier for customers to understand, we strongly recommended that they adopt some of the principles of Travelocity's 10 Rules for World-Class FAQs (see chapter 2).

Okay, so what's the potential payoff from these actions for Acme Company?

Fortunately, the years of data we've collected on this topic allow us to do some unique modeling where we can show a company the potential gains to their business from reducing effort in the way we recommend. Knowing the overall loyalty of a company's customers and the level of effort they put forth in the service channel allows us to plot the relationship—in this case for Acme specifically—between the two (see figure 6.8). If there's a business case for actually reducing effort, this is it.

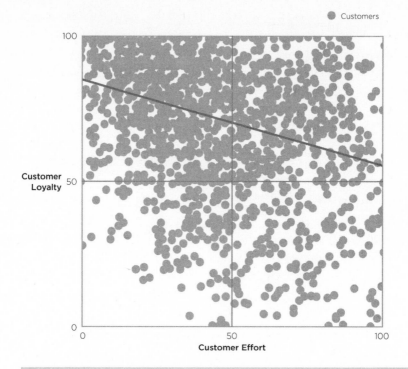

For Acme Company customers, a 10% reduction in the effort required to resolve their service issue corresponds to a 3.5% increase in their loyalty to Acme Company.

Source: Acme Company, CEB, 2013.

Figure 6.8 Acme Company's Impact of Customer Effort on Loyalty

We know that decreasing effort means higher intent to repurchase, to increase spend, and to advocate for a company. In Acme's case, we found that *a 10 percent reduction in effort—an easily attainable goal—would correspond to a significant 3.5 percent increase in customer loyalty*. What would it mean to your company if your customers were 3.5 percent more loyal to you than they are right now? In Acme's case, it means millions. This is a hugely powerful analysis for most companies—a glimpse into the future and the near-term attainable loyalty boost they can get by reducing effort.

In the end, Acme's team completely blew up their strategic plan, redrew it, and committed to making customer effort a regular part of how they measure their performance and how they're doing on their experience improvement initiatives.

At CEB, we've come to appreciate the role of customer effort in the service experience from its infancy in our data and research. Over the past five years, we've applied this idea as more of an "operating system" for service organizations. And now we have amassed an incredible amount of data, modeling, and analysis, and are helping companies take precise actions to reduce effort that will yield the greatest loyalty benefit.

Our team has been focused on continuing to refine the science of effort measurement and learning from companies that have gone down the effort reduction path so that we can better advise those organizations just embarking on the journey. Regardless of whether we do this work for you or you do it on your own using the tools and methods described in this book (we've provided a do-it-yourself effort audit tool in the back of this book; see appendix F), the point remains that effort should be measured consistently across channels and the sources of effort systematically monitored. This will allow your service organization to continually determine ways to positively impact enterprise loyalty objectives.

As we wrap up this measurement chapter, a point made earlier in the chapter bears repeating: There is no silver bullet out there. Reducing effort is hard work and demands that a company collect data—lots of it—often from sources and in ways they hadn't previously considered. In some respects, it means upending the way they currently measure the customer experience and the performance of the service channel, but it doesn't have to be that hard. Most companies we work with will tell you they're "NPS shops" or "CSAT shops." That's okay. This isn't a debate about what the be-all, end-all customer experience metric is. It's about improving the experience you're delivering to your customer, reducing your own operating costs along the way, and ultimately improving the loyalty those customers show to you as a company. Getting that right means asking lots of questions, not just one.

The business cliché of "what gets measured gets done" certainly holds merit, but that's rarely enough. While measuring effort can serve as a powerful guiding force for managing a service operation, only until the people within the operation embody an effort reduction mind-set can real improvement begin. Armed with an understanding of effort, practical advice we've provided throughout this book, and approaches for measuring effort, let's turn our attention to driving the transformation to a low-effort organization.

KEY TAKEAWAYS

♦ *Measure the Customer Effort Score (CES).* Use the Customer Effort Score to assess the ease of resolution in post-service surveys. CES provides a powerful indicator of transactional customer loyalty, clearly highlights friction points in the customer experience, and helps companies to spot customers at risk of defection due to high-effort service interactions.

♦ *Use an effort measurement system.* While CES is a powerful tool, there is no silver bullet when it comes to measuring customer effort. The best companies collect data at multiple levels and from multiple sources to understand not just whether customer effort is happening, but also the root causes of effort.

7

MAKING LOW EFFORT STICK

educing customer effort can't just be the "flavor of the week." In order to really take hold it must become an operating philosophy. It represents a cultural shift in how your team engages with customers and how you'll prioritize the projects you undertake. But while it's easy to say, any shift of this nature is difficult to accomplish, mainly because change in a large organization can be an arduous undertaking. For this reason, we've dedicated this chapter to sharing some lessons learned from our research on driving new frontline behaviors as well as key lessons from American Express and Reliant Energy, both early adopters of customer effort as their operating philosophy.

Taking the First Steps

Let's start the journey by summarizing some key findings on driving change at the frontline level. These basics will prove helpful both in setting up a pilot effort and creating engagement with an effort reduction strategy. Further, these fundamentals will help your organization in driving effort reduction beyond the pilot teams, to senior executives and the remainder of the frontline rep population alike.

First, having a compelling "change story" is critical to communicate why a new approach is needed. In many ways, you must teach frontline staff (both reps and supervisors) a new way of thinking about their roles. Too often organizations attempt to hold tight to past approaches, providing little rationale as to why change is necessary. The message of "reduce customer effort" just becomes more noise—it's simply another thing that has to be done, competing against others that seem equally pressing and critical. A compelling change story breaks the "more of the same" cycle by sending a message that creates urgency and stark contrast with how thing are done now. Done well, it helps to make the business case for change, down to the individual level. A good change story serves as the backbone of all communication, training, coaching, and general reinforcement.

Below is a sample change story that can be tailored to your unique organization and situation. Take note of how the change story establishes the current approach that your organization takes, discusses why this approach is no longer appropriate, presents a compelling (and data-backed) explanation of the new way forward, and expresses how the organization will support this transition. The change story is meant to take your team through both an emotional and a rational journey—it's not a script, but rather key points that should be continually emphasized as your team starts down the effort path.

- **What's happening:** The world of customer service is changing, and customer expectations seem to be increasing on a daily basis. There are many reasons for this, but the most notable is that self-service is changing how customers interact with us. They no longer call us with simple and easy issues; instead we deal with more and more complex issues where customers are more frustrated and the stakes are higher. And while it might feel unfair, the reality is that customers compare us not only to our competitors, but to any company they do business with. The experience we offer is compared to companies like Zappos and Amazon. And when we don't hit that bar, the web has made it incredibly easy for our customers to tell the whole world—a disgruntled customer only needs to go to YouTube or Twitter or Facebook to tell every person they know that we failed to deliver a positive service experience. (Note: This part of your change story should capture the pain that your frontline teams feel. They know this challenge all too well. You're simply bringing clarity to what is happening.)[1]

- **The old approach:** For years, we've managed the customer experience more as a checklist than not. This made a lot of sense when most of the calls we fielded were very similar. It's not that we didn't care about each individual customer, but since we could quickly serve them and move to the next customer, it made a lot of sense to run the service organization in a more disciplined way. When issues are all the same, you can run customer service like a factory and just focus on efficiency and consistency. This approach served us well for many years. (Note: Here you provide a candid account of how things have been managed, and why. There was a lot of good rationale for managing the operation in this way in the "old world.")

- **The old approach no longer works:** Trying to keep pace with the new complexity we're facing is hard—and we've put a lot on your shoulders. We're asking a lot of you to drive customer loyalty in these increasingly difficult interactions. Managing the customer experience as a process doesn't always work, and the data out there suggests that companies are struggling to deliver effective customer service in this new environment. A study by a leading business advisory firm, CEB, recently found that customer service is four times more likely to drive disloyalty instead of creating positive gains in customer loyalty. We need to shift our focus to reducing disloyalty, first and foremost. (Note: Here you are explaining why the old approach no longer works and providing data to help support this claim. You are providing rational justification for why the customer service organization needs to move in a different direction. This is a great place to use data from your own organization to show how tough it's getting to deliver on customers' increasingly high expectations.)

- **A new way to think about service:** CEB's research shows that the biggest reason customer service makes customers disloyal is the amount of effort a customer has to put into the actual service interaction. When we make an interaction harder than it has to be, or make it feel harder than it should, customers leave those interactions more disloyal to us. It makes lots of sense when you think about it. We've all had service interactions where a company made us jump through too many hoops, where we had to call back multiple times, where too many transfers and too much repeating of information made us really frustrated. In many cases, it wasn't the rep's fault, but the rep could have made it seem like less work on our part. (Note: In this part of the change story, you are focusing on effort reduction as the new way forward and using stories and anecdotes from your own organization to drive the point home.)

- **The solution:** Our job as a management team is to help you and support you in making it easier for customers to get resolution and move on with their lives. We're committing to making it easier for customers to interact with us. While reducing effort might feel like it's out of your control, we're going to arm you with approaches to help bring some control back into the customer interaction. As part of this approach, we need to place greater trust in your judgment to serve customers and remove some of the obstacles—such as our checklist approach—to help you do this. In return, we need all of you to learn and master the techniques to better managing the customer experience. It won't be easy, but your supervisors will be supporting you in every way they can. We will teach you techniques for reducing the likelihood that the customer has to call us back for related issues. We'll help you use specific language designed to help customers to feel like it was less effort and less frustrating to get their problems fixed. We'll track different performance metrics so you can focus on doing the right things with customers. And we'll offer you a lot of training and coaching to help make this transition smooth. This is one of our most significant strategy shifts, and we need your support to make it work. It will be difficult and it won't happen overnight, so we all need to commit to making it easier for customers to get issues resolved each and every day from here on out. (Note: You are laying out the vision of what your organization is committing to long-term, and how you will support the reps in this transition. Ground this part of your change story in how this shift empowers reps and allows them to have impact on the customer in ways they traditionally haven't been able to.)

The change story is something your entire management team needs to know extremely well. The talking points should be continually reinforced by them. This is particularly the case as you're undertaking pilot efforts and initial launches are occurring. The simple notion of "the old way doesn't work anymore, we need to instead reduce effort" is the main point of the narrative that needs to stick with all frontline staff. Coaching interactions must center on it. It should be discussed at team meetings. This central thesis needs to serve as a rallying cry for the service organization as you build momentum.

The Most Important Change Agent

Undertaking such a dramatic shift in the service philosophy of your organization requires a diligent focus on changing frontline behavior—where the rubber meets the road in customer service. We've analyzed what the best ways are to change frontline staff behavior and drive performance. Generally speaking, there are two main approaches to developing new skill sets in your frontline talent: training and coaching.

To better understand these two development levers, we conducted an analysis of over 3,600 frontline reps and over 300 frontline supervisors from fifty-five different companies spanning the globe. In this study, we captured detailed information around the types of training and coaching reps received as well as performance data from the full set of individual reps, which helped us to really understand which development levers had the greatest impact on rep performance.

Before we divulge the details of this analysis and explore the implications for an effort reduction strategy, let's quickly baseline how most service organizations focus on developing their frontline staff. The preponderant approach, both in terms of total spend and total time, is *training*. And by training, we mean formally structured one-to-many teaching. This often occurs in classrooms or virtually (sometimes in the form of e-learning modules). Regardless of how training occurs, when most service organizations embark on a new initiative, the natural response is to "train 'em up." New product launch? Training. New QA scorecard? Training. Building soft skills? Training.

This isn't to say that coaching doesn't occur in contact centers—it does, at some level. But frankly, it's often more of an afterthought, a reminder of what was learned in training, if anything. More commonly, coaching is synonymous with "performance management," which is really just code for *getting my behind kicked by my supervisor.*

So what does this focus on training get organizations? Well, not much. As it turns out, organizations that disproportionately focus on training generally have lower-performing rep populations (see figure 7.1). Conversely, organizations that place greater emphasis on coaching tend to drive higher performance levels from their teams. Given the importance of coaching, a sizable portion of this chapter will focus squarely on how to conduct the best coaching possible to support an effort reduction strategy.

We know what you're thinking: *Now hold on just a minute . . . did they just say that training hurts performance?* Let's make sure we're crystal clear on this point. Organizations that focus on training (often at the expense of coaching) tend to have relatively lower-performing teams compared to organizations that prioritize coaching (often at the expense of training). This isn't to say that you should go fire all your trainers and move to a coaching-only model. There is a clear time and place for training, and there are some situations and development areas where

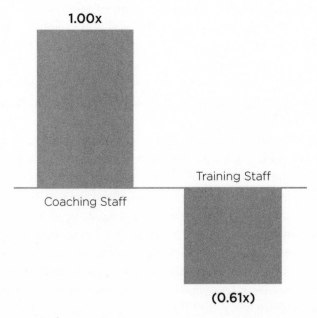

n = 3,134 frontline staff.

Figure 7.1 Relative Staff Performance Impact of Coaching versus Training in the Average Contact Center

training certainly yields performance improvement—like rote tasks, (e.g. learning how to use new systems and learning about new products). But for areas where the skills may seem more art than science—for example, using language to reduce the perception of customer effort (i.e., experience engineering)—overemphasis on training will actually *stunt* your team's performance.

Training is still acceptable for initially orienting teams to new ideas and new service approaches. But it fails to allow reps to truly explore the application of an idea, to gain proper applied learning with real-time feedback, or to discover how a new approach works best for them. Most training is a series of slides telling reps how to behave. If a good trainer is involved, there are perhaps some role-plays and, *maybe, just maybe,* a set of exercises to practice on the job the following day. Training is a medium for short-term comprehension, not sustained application. That's why organizations that rely on training as the primary means of introducing any type of new service standard see only short-lived success and very sudden reversion to old tendencies. Managers scratch their heads and blame the training. But the training itself could never have truly changed frontline behavior—it's not designed to do that. So as you kick off your effort reduction strategy, have a training session (share the change story from earlier in this chapter), but don't *just* have a training session. And don't let your teams rely on that training session to win the day. Because it won't.

One best practice for how to properly blend training and coaching comes from a UK-based financial services firm. This practice is grounded in onboarding new hires, but there are some immediately valuable takeaways that can be applied to your effort reduction strategy.

Traditionally, the onboarding of new hires at this company followed the standard "sheep dip" approach (where all the sheep are dipped into a big vat of training and then sent back into the pasture). The process took place over four weeks, with each week focusing on learning a new system or line of products. So in week one, for example, new hires received training on case management systems and telephony. In week two, they received training on this company's various financial products. In week three, they received process training on call flow, escalations, and other call management tactics. And so on. For most organizations, this is a fairly common approach to training new hires. Naturally, once reps completed training and were certified to handle calls, they'd quickly realize, once they started answering calls that they had no clue what they were doing or how to properly conduct themselves. In fact, it took an average of seven weeks for a frontline rep to reach a satisfactory level of performance. The heart of the issue is that treating processes, systems, and products as separate training instances leaves reps scrambling when they must call upon all three simultaneously (and while also serving a frustrated customer on the other end of the line).

So the company rethought their entire approach to new hire training and onboarding, instead teaching new hires how to handle only the ten most common issue types, beginning to end. So on day one, after introductions and morning coffee, the new hires dove straight into learning how to verify insurance policy information for customers, which was one of the most common types of calls they received. The systems, processes, and products were all rolled into a single session. Once the new hires had been trained on handling the ten most common issues, they were placed on the floor and started serving customers immediately—*but they were still "in training" for up to two more weeks.* Invariably an issue the new rep hadn't been trained on would arise. The company had a smart system for helping the reps in these moments. A certified call coach was dedicated to helping the new hire group. This call coach would join calls for these rarer issue types. In most instances, the coach would help guide the rep through the interaction, but in some instances the coach would just take over the call and tell the new hire to just listen in. But in all instances, the coach would immediately debrief with the rep to discuss what happened and what could or should have happened differently. This allowed for far quicker learning on how to handle tricky or extraordinary types of requests. If the call coach was unavailable, the new rep would simply ask the customer if he could call back once he found the answer to the question. The company found that most customers were fine with this option. This stripped-down training, with strong coaching, allowed the company not only to cut initial onboarding time down to three weeks on average, but their teams were also hitting the ground running well beyond just a "satisfactory" level.

Keying off of this company's approach, frontline teams can be trained on a handful of effort reduction techniques for your most common call types. One example is how to reduce effort for billing inquiries: learning when to use positive language to address billing inquiries, avoiding next likely issues related to billing inquiries, and so on. Reps are learning from beginning to end how to reduce effort for the most common issues. Once your teams have initially grasped effort reduction in the most common call types, provide a dedicated coach who can help reps work through the less common issue types and master effort reduction even in these scenarios.

As this financial services firm's example highlights, the importance of coaching in the contact center cannot be overemphasized. Unfortunately, in most organizations coaching is grossly misunderstood among supervisors. Ask any supervisor if they coach their team, and without fail you'll get a response like, "What do you think they pay me to do around here?" It's an assumed responsibility in the world of customer service. And since it's assumed, supervisors don't actively hold themselves to a terribly high bar for their coaching. Contrary to what many believe, coaching is *not* about assessing past performance, nor is it delivered once or twice a year. And it's not a lesson-of-the-month that all reps get from their supervisor (see figure 7.2). Coaching is focused on improving future performance, using past examples to illustrate the point. It's an ongoing dialogue between a rep and their supervisor, that's mutually owned by both parties. And it's tailored specifically to *who's* being coached and *what's* being coached.

Coaching is not...

Assessing past performance

Usually delivered biannually or annually

Manager-led with little input from the recipient

Generic content applied to all attendees

Coaching is...

Focusing on improving future performance

Ongoing

Equally driven by coach and coachee

Tailored to individual's development needs

Source: CEB, 2013.

Figure 7.2 Definition of Coaching

But as with so many things in life, it's not *that* coaching happens, but rather *how* coaching happens. Many service leaders falsely assume that good coaching is a product of the frequency with which coaching occurs. In fact, 80 percent of service leaders cite that a lack of time is the biggest barrier to coaching. However, our analysis shows that coaching frequency is not itself a major driver of its effectiveness (see figure 7.3). What matters more is the subject matter, the manner in which coaching is delivered, and that someone with close context and understanding of a rep's development needs actually delivers the coaching.

We've identified that two types of coaching tend to occur in contact centers. The first type, which forms the bulk of coaching, is scheduled coaching. This is quite literally scheduled time where a rep and a supervisor sit down, review calls, discuss performance, and take corrective action. Most service leaders wish even this happened with more regularity—but our research demonstrates that you might wish otherwise. In fact, supervisors that overemphasize this type of coaching

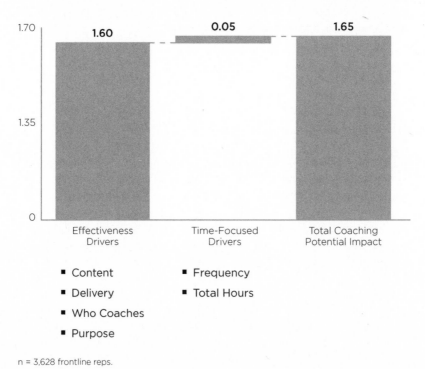

n = 3,628 frontline reps.

Source: CEB, 2013.

Figure 7.3 Coaching Drivers of Performance

actually have lower-performing teams (see figure 7.4). Scheduled coaching doesn't help nearly as much as most think. Here's why: Scheduled coaching is almost exclusively punitive, not developmental, in nature. Bad calls (which the rep often doesn't remember terribly well), are reviewed. They are often reviewed arbitrarily, since the supervisor needs to quickly come up with a development area, so the last poor QA-scored call typically serves as the subject matter. For reps, it's like running the gauntlet. It's a terrible experience, which contributes to disengagement and lower commitment to the work, clearly harming their productivity and overall effectiveness.

However, the other form of coaching—what we call *integrated coaching*—offers tremendous performance lift. Integrated coaching is on-the-job coaching, in close proximity to the specific customer situations the coaching is designed to improve. In fact, supervisors who overemphasize this type of coaching realize a lift of more than 12 percent in their team's performance.

The very best supervisors, it turns out, focus roughly 75 percent of their coaching on integrated coaching. The other 25 percent is spent

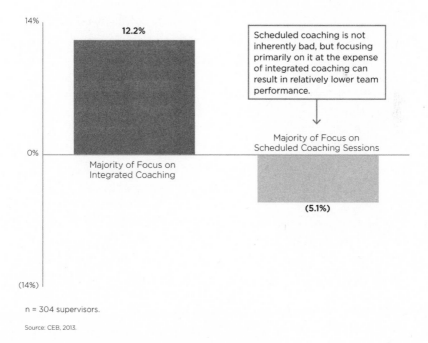

Scheduled coaching is not inherently bad, but focusing primarily on it at the expense of integrated coaching can result in relatively lower team performance.

Majority of Focus on
Scheduled Coaching Sessions

Majority of Focus on
Integrated Coaching

12.2%

(5.1%)

n = 304 supervisors.

Source: CEB, 2013.

Figure 7.4 Relative Effectiveness of Coaching Formats

doing scheduled coaching and using those instances to discuss rep development in an open and candid way, not nitpicking at past calls (see figure 7.5). In scheduled coaching time, supervisors and reps reach a "handshake" on what they'll jointly work on and how they'll plan to get there. The *real* coaching, however, happens on the floor during the regular course of business, not days later.

American Express's initial pilots around effort reduction were launched under a coaching-intensive model. Each week supervisors would review calls with the pilot team, assessing where effort reduction was well executed and areas for development. The calls that got reviewed were from *that* day so as to avoid any recall issues. While reps on the pilot teams received some initial training, they truly learned to reduce effort, primarily through coaching. We'll detail how they did this later in the chapter. But this coaching-intensive pilot approach closely resembles the integrated coaching approach discussed above. American Express noted how this approach allowed for more candid discussions and an opportunity for reps to explore this new service philosophy with their supervisor.

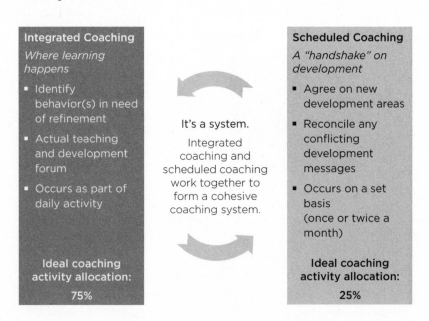

Source: CEB, 2013.

Figure 7.5 The Integrated/Scheduled Coaching System.

Effort reduction is an experientially learned skill with no clear-cut rules or scripts. Reps must be able to exercise proper discretion in the moment. As such, you should use training only to build awareness of this new service approach, not to drive behavior change. Behavior change can only be learned on the job, and supervisors must actively, and with laser-like focus, apply coaching to help reps develop and hone these new skills. If there's only one thing your organization prioritizes as you pilot and initially roll out effort reduction, it needs to be coaching. Of course, as with every big change, simply taking the very first steps on the effort reduction journey can seem overwhelming. Let's now turn our attention to tactical approaches to help initiate your organization's effort reduction journey.

Make It Real, Real Quick

Helping your front line make the mental and emotional connection to customer effort should be among the first exercises for your team. We've heard some really creative approaches from our member network to help teams quickly understand what qualifies as more or less effort for the customer.

1. **Sharing of personal customer experiences.** Have your frontline teams share bad customer service experiences from their personal lives. Pick an interaction that someone remembers in fairly vivid detail and write down the precise sequence of events across a whiteboard. Label this first row the "do" side of the interaction. Literally, what did your rep or supervisor have to do to get their personal issue resolved? Where did they start? web? Phone? Who did they first talk to? Did they repeat information? Were they transferred? Was the issue fully resolved? Did they have to call back? Below this sequence of events ask your rep or supervisor what they felt at each step. Label this row "feel" and capture the range of emotions they experienced. This might include questioning if the rep knew what they were doing, doubting the company, getting frustrated, perhaps raising their voice or even yelling. Lastly, make a row labeled "effort." As a group, talk about where customer effort occurred and what form it took. This exercise is extremely simple, but helps teams quickly grasp where

effort occurs and what causes it. It also, importantly, shows the strong linkage of effort to the rational and emotional side of the customer experience. This exercise is also a great one to run with senior executives and cross-functional partners.

2. Group quality assurance sessions. Another idea we've found several of our member companies using to build initial awareness of customer effort is group QA sessions. Prescreen some older customer calls, perhaps from reps who have since left the organization, and find a selection of instances that were undoubtedly high-effort, some that were arguably high-effort (or had a mix of high- and low-effort actions), and some that were clearly low-effort. Listen to the conversations and have the pilot team note where they believe the interaction was difficult for the customer, and where the rep did a good job of mitigating effort, or even making things easier for the customer. Again, encourage staff to consider both the customer actions and the emotional response. Discuss forms of customer effort that were controllable and could have been better influenced by the rep handling the call, versus those that were truly uncontrollable. Remember, even in instances where the rep had to tell the customer no, there are powerful ways language can mitigate a bad customer perception. Once this exercise is done, have the team break into smaller groups to create their own "customer effort QA form." If they were searching for customer effort, what dimensions would they look for in an interaction? This is a fun exercise that helps build awareness and socialize the idea of customer effort reduction across your team.

3. Customer effort diaries. This is an idea we've seen work very well. Reps on a pilot team are each given a notepad to capture the specific instances when they felt they did a great job of reducing effort. What was the customer issue? What happened in the interaction? How did they reduce effort? In a pre-shift meeting at the end of the week, each person shares two instances where they felt they did a good job of reducing effort. The lesson: Keep this exercise extremely simple and don't have lofty expectations—remember, this is simply a way to get staff to remember and publicly acknowledge great low-effort service. The flip side also works well: Have reps capture interactions when they could have done a better job *reducing* customer effort. Get together and encourage everyone to share their specific stories. Not only is this a cathartic exercise, but everybody gets better by learning from their colleagues' mistakes.

These are all highly tactical but effective ways to initially introduce the idea of effort reduction to pilot teams, and even to aid in the launch of effort reduction more broadly. But beyond building initial awareness, there are some key pitfalls to consider. For this, we'll turn our attention to the lessons learned from early adopters American Express and Reliant Energy, a Houston-based utility company.

Key Lessons from Early Adopters

Customer effort is a relatively new idea, and while dozens or organizations in our global membership have started to track the CES metric, the remainder of this chapter features two of the many organizations that have committed to effort reduction more broadly beyond the metric.

Don't Make Effort Reduction Another "Ask"

Early in American Express Consumer Travel Network's effort reduction journey, a significant hurdle became apparent. Years of adding metrics, quality assurance criteria, and new expectations for how frontline staff should conduct themselves meant that this new approach of reducing customer effort was naturally met with some skepticism. For the two teams that were picked to initially pilot this new approach, it felt like the flavor of the week and didn't evoke any sense of a new direction for the organization. There was *interest* in reducing effort—it made sense to frontline reps and their supervisors—but the idea itself didn't immediately take root with the team.

American Express realized that they had to streamline their expectations of the front line, removing many of the traditional requirements they placed on reps and supervisors, in order to allow staff to truly commit to the idea of reducing effort. Different organizations will find different expectations that pull staff attention away from effort reduction—there is almost always a natural gravity that governs how the front line focuses their energy. For some organizations this might take the form of being overly focused on customer delight and going above and beyond. Liberating staff from this expectation helps make effort reduction feel less like just another thing to do.

For other organizations, this can take the form of QA criteria—the checklist approach to managing the customer experience that we discussed in chapter 5. This was precisely where American Express focused their attention—reducing the number of things frontline staff were being asked to focus on so that they could make effort reduction more of a priority, not just another ask. In fact, they streamlined their quality assurance from twenty-six independently measured criteria down to seven technical behaviors and five loyalty competencies. In many ways, American Express had to kick off their effort reduction pilot with *what it wasn't*. It was fewer, not more, things the front line was being asked to do.

Reliant also found that reps' and supervisors' natural predisposition was to focus on those things that had always mattered in their organization—in their case, Reliant's long-standing handle time requirements. Asking reps to better manage customer effort, while simultaneously managing for a handle time metric, elicited the same response as American Express saw in its reps—it was just another thing to do. So Reliant vice president Bill Clayton called for a change in how average handle time (AHT) was evaluated. He decided that AHT would no longer be reported directly to reps, and only post-call wrap time and hold time would be clocked. In this way, reps could focus on serving customers during calls, but still maintain good productivity between calls. AHT was still tracked behind the scenes, and only the staff who were egregious violators of acceptable handle time thresholds received additional coaching or performance management. According to Clayton, this removed a chief obstacle to effectively serving customers and empowering frontline staff to do their job.

The point is that in order to get new behaviors to take hold, old behaviors have to be retired. Teams must be told what they're *no longer doing*. Service organizations are notorious for asking staff to take on new behaviors. Service leaders are quick to "add a prompt into the system" to remind staff to act on a new expectation. But there are limitations to the energy that reps and supervisors can apply to the job. Reducing customer effort has to displace something else. The commitment to reducing effort, and the permanence of that approach, needs to become a shift in expectations, not just a new expectation added to the top of the pile.

Baby Steps

Once staff feel liberated to focus on effort reduction, however, another obstacle emerges—specifically, frontline staff can quickly become paralyzed at the sheer number of ways they can personally reduce effort for customers. Ask nearly any rep how their company can serve customers better and you'll hear, "Where do you want me to start?" Reps know your organization's flaws all too well—they hear about them every day. Simply saying to a rep, "Okay, so we're lifting your AHT requirement so you can better reduce effort, now go make it easier for customers!" would surely be met with blank stares. The number of ways effort *could be* reduced is simply overwhelming for most reps, let alone management teams.

Narrowing your front line's attention to a small set of high-impact things they *should* focus on is critical for getting early wins and ultimately gaining broad frontline adoption.

Early adopters such as Reliant provide very prescriptive guidance for how frontline staff can take the initial steps to reducing customer effort. In fact, during their first series of pilots and initial launch, Reliant only expected their front line to reduce customer effort in two simple ways. They wisely chose to pursue two of the most impactful effort drivers—one emotional and one rational.

On the emotional side of customer effort, they chose to have reps take on the most basic form of experience engineering that we discussed in the Osram Sylvania case profile in chapter 4—positive language. The use of "can't" and "don't" was all too common on Reliant's contact center floors. So the Reliant pilot teams and, eventually, their broader teams, applied significant coaching attention to using positive language with customers. "I can't handle that issue, I'll need to transfer you to our sales department," became "Our sales team can easily help you with that issue, do you mind if I connect you?" The Reliant team identified the most common "no" scenarios, narrowing the list down to the most frequently occurring five instances.

Reducing effort through simple language tweaks is a great initial approach. It's simple. It demonstrates that effort reduction is *in the reps' control.* It helps orient reps to the more emotional side of the customer experience in a way that doesn't feel hokey or like some form of customer mind game. Reliant used these "no" scenarios to run interactive training workshops with the teams that were piloting this effort reduction approach. In these sessions, frontline staff engaged in group breakouts to come up with more positive language options, they conducted various role-plays, and they did one-on-one exercises around such scenarios. The power of language became apparent to the frontline teams in these interactive sessions. The most resonance came when staff played the role of a customer and experienced firsthand how it felt to be told no. As the Reliant team told us, having the reps place themselves in the customer's shoes was critical to driving this initial effort reduction approach. It's also worth noting that these interactive training sessions proved to be a really clever way to avoid the typical classroom-based training experience.

On the rational side of customer effort, Reliant armed reps to forward-resolve the likely implications that might cause a customer to call back, similar to the Canadian telecom's approach detailed in chapter 3. Instead of building a full issue tree, as that company did, Reliant instead chose to forward-resolve only one specific issue type: complaints related to abnormally high electricity usage. For customers calling to check account status, Reliant reps were trained to offer customers the opportunity to set personalized alerts about their power usage. For example, customers could elect to receive a text message or e-mail if their energy usage was trending above their typical monthly average. This proved to be a smart foray into next issue avoidance, because it (1) reduced customer effort and (2) also helped reduce the worst call Reliant reps fielded—the dreaded high bill complaint. Limiting how reps could initially reduce customer effort made the whole approach far more tangible and realistic to the first groups of reps that participated.

Starting with a small number of ways to reduce effort makes the shift to a low-effort organization more tangible. Reps know precisely what to do, and they develop a more refined sense for how effort reduction works. Plus, supervisors have a finite set of new behaviors to coach to. As your effort reduction pilot and initial rollout take hold, you'll want to ensure that any new effort reduction ideas don't just become a new checklist. The whole idea of effort reduction needs to be incorporated to the point where it isn't a set of discrete tasks, but rather an entirely new service expectation. The frontline teams will need to understand their role in effort reduction and manage to a new expectation of making it easier for customers to interact with your organization. So how do you avoid making effort reduction just a new checklist of tactics and instead a new expectation? American Express shared a terrific approach they developed throughout their pilots and initial launch.

Bake a Cake, Don't Just Focus on Individual Ingredients

As we've already discussed, American Express narrowed their set of service expectations down from twenty-six independent criteria to seven technical and five loyalty behaviors. But it wasn't so much that they cut this set by more than half; it was how they did it. They shifted their entire approach to call evaluation and coaching toward a more commonsense way of serving customers.

Their old model of evaluating calls was oriented almost exclusively toward checklist compliance, and their reps accordingly would optimize to the scorecard (see figure 7.6). The new model was instead optimized toward ensuring that customers had a low-effort experience. The analogy that American Express used was the difference between focusing on individual ingredients versus baking the cake. Reps were losing sight of the bigger picture of customer outcomes, and instead myopically focusing on the QA scorecard criteria.

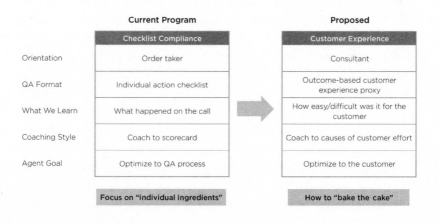

	Current Program	Proposed
	Checklist Compliance	**Customer Experience**
Orientation	Order taker	Consultant
QA Format	Individual action checklist	Outcome-based customer experience proxy
What We Learn	What happened on the call	How easy/difficult was it for the customer
Coaching Style	Coach to scorecard	Coach to causes of customer effort
Agent Goal	Optimize to QA process	Optimize to the customer
	Focus on "individual ingredients"	**How to "bake the cake"**

Source: American Express CTN; CEB, 2013.

Figure 7.6 American Express CTN's Old versus New Quality Assurance Process

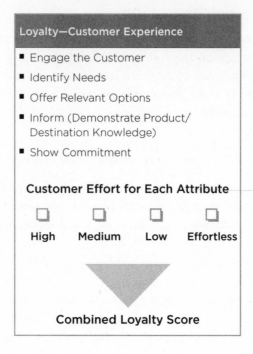

Source: American Express CTN; CEB, 2013.

Figure 7.7 American Express CTN's COREscore Program Overview

American Express coined the new approach "COREscore"—short for the core behaviors that any service experience should embody. No longer was the lengthy checklist the norm, but rather a more commonsense-oriented approach to serving customers in a low-effort fashion (see figure 7.7).

The seven technical behaviors, while more rote in nature, help ensure regulatory and critical business process compliance. These seven behaviors are evaluated as simple pass or fail. The loyalty behaviors, on the other hand, embody the biggest change in how reps are expected to serve customers. While these behaviors align to the typical call process, it doesn't matter *how* reps execute these behaviors—that's left to their individual discretion—all that matters is *that* they embody these core behaviors.

1. Engage the customer. Demonstrate a professional, confident, and engaging demeanor throughout the call. Match the customer's tone and pace. This isn't about being the customer's best friend, but allowing their personality to govern the tone of the call. (Note the similarities to the personality mapping techniques discussed in chapter 4 and how this appeals to the emotional side of customer effort.)

2. Identify needs. Actively listen and probe where required to understand what the customer needs. This includes both stated and unknown needs the customer may have. Reps are expected to take the time required to make sure everyone is clear. (Note the similarity to the Canadian telecom practice from chapter 3 and how this includes elements of unstated issue resolution, reducing the rational side of effort and specifically the need for downstream contacts.)

3. Offer relevant options. Explain to the customer, in a tailored way, how they can get their needs met. Help the customer assess the different options they have, and provide a consultative recommendation. (Note the similarity to the LoyaltyOne practice reviewed in chapter 4; American Express reps are encouraged to offer the customer choices, but ultimately provide a tailored recommendation— this reduces both rational and emotional effort.)

4. Inform the customer. Provide sufficient detail and share knowledge with the customer that they likely would not have exposure to otherwise. Play the role of expert, and help the customer make an informed decision. (Note that reps are encouraged to *teach* customers about travel tips, location details, or other useful pieces of information that the customer doesn't likely know, saving the customer time in advance of their travel.)

5. Show commitment. Communicate the actions taken and assure the customer that they are covered. Explain the next steps clearly to the customer, actively supporting their needs and demonstrating advocacy on the customer's behalf. (Note the use of smart experience engineering tactics; this step leaves the customer feeling confident in the resolution, and appeals to the emotional side of customer effort.)

Each of these COREscore criteria is assessed in quality assurance reviews against only one outcome—did the rep make it as easy as

Loyalty Reference Guide—Guideposts

	High Customer Effort	Low Customer Effort	Effortless
Engage the Customer	▪ Discourteous and/or unprofessional demeanor ▪ Lack of confidence in shared information ▪ One-way conversation ▪ Failure to connect/identify with Customer's perspective ▪ Failure to match Customer's pace, tone, manner, or style	▪ Professional and courteous demeanor ▪ Confidence in shared information ▪ Two-way conversation ▪ Matched the Customer's pace, tone, manner, or style ▪ Acknowledged the Customer's perspective/issue before attempting resolution	▪ Warm, engaged and interested, outgoing demeanor ▪ Conveyed information with authority and insight ▪ Very interactive conversation ▪ Demonstrated personal understanding of the Customer's perspective
Identify Needs	▪ Failed to recognize the Customer's spoken cues ▪ Failed to ask well timed and appropriate diagnostic questions to qualify the Customer's needs ▪ Did not ask sufficient questions to ensure all needs are identified	▪ Acknowledged the Customers spoken cues ▪ Asked well timed and appropriate diagnostic questions ▪ Confirmed needs have been met by asking close ended questions	▪ Identified unspoken needs not directly stated by the customer ▪ Effectively qualified the Customer's needs ▪ Asked probing, open-ended questions to confirm all needs
Offer Relevant Options	▪ Customer received irrelevant or insufficient recommendations to address their request ▪ Did not guide customer through options available ▪ Recommendations were unclear or not explained in sufficient detail ▪ Did not attempt to cross sell when appropriate ▪ Transition from needs to sale was awkward or abrupt	▪ Customer received relevant recommendations to address their request ▪ Guided customer through options available ▪ Cross-sell when appropriate ▪ Offered solutions to alleviate concerns ▪ Transitioned from options to closing the sale	▪ Relevant recommendations provided for both spoken and unspoken needs ▪ Provided clear explanations on how/why solutions would alleviate concerns
Demonstrate Product/ Destination Knowledge	▪ Did not clearly explain the features or benefits of the product/destination ▪ Did not offer additional research to be done on Customer's behalf, when necessary	▪ Clearly explained features, benefits, programs of the product and/or destination that were relevant to customer's needs ▪ Communicated to Customer more research needs to be done on their behalf, when questions could not be answered directly	▪ Provided a comprehensive, detailed explanation of the features or benefits of the product/destination ▪ Used value statements to explain why the program/benefit is of value/convenient to the customer's needs ▪ Attempted to educate Customer on something new
Customer Commitment	▪ Failed to provide a clear explanation on what will happen next ▪ Avoided taking responsibility for the customer's needs Internal Only: Did not efficiently book the Customer's request	▪ Provided a clear explanation on what will happen next ▪ Took responsibility for the customer's needs Internal Only: Efficiently booked the Customer's request	▪ Seized responsibility for the customer's needs by going above-and-beyond what was necessary to directly address the customer's request ▪ Took extra actions that were not directly requested to add convenience/ease for the customer

Source: American Express CTN; CEB, CEB Customer Contact Leadership Council, 2013.

Figure 7.8 American Express CTN's Loyalty Reference Guide

possible for the customer throughout the interaction? Supervisors assess up to ten calls per week for their team using a reference guide that helps diagnose just how effortful or effortless the rep made the call for the customer (see figure 7.8).

Each loyalty behavior has a set of direct and clear customer effort implications, and it's up the supervisor to help the rep understand where they did a great job reducing effort, and where they could still improve.

The pilot team supervisors were also involved in a weekly review session during the pilot phase where COREscore behaviors, the evaluation guidelines, and the pilot effectiveness were discussed. The model was tweaked several times based on supervisor input. In this way, American Express made sure that change was driven on the front line and in coaching conversations, not the classroom.

The entire focus of the COREscore is this: Chalk the field to establish broad service guidelines, but let reps do what they need to do to make the interaction as effortless as possible for the customer. That's it. No checklists, no requiring reps to use the customer's name three times, no scripts to establish a customer's need—all of that's gone. It's a very liberating approach, allowing reps to make their own judgment calls to ensure that each of the five loyalty behaviors are exhibited in a low-effort fashion.

Lay the Cultural Foundation

Effort reduction is not a quick-hit project. If it's treated as such, it will surely lose momentum and fail. It is a service philosophy. And like any change in philosophy or culture, it takes time, constant reinforcement, and removal of disincentives and obstacles that will sidetrack progress. In many ways, the big operational changes, like reducing AHT requirements or QA checklists, are more easily executed than the reinforcement of the little things, like thinking, *what can I do to make sure this customer won't need to call us back?*

These big changes take tremendous organizational commitment, with managers and supervisors diligently focused on building an organizational capability to think differently about service. It happens at the front line. The reality is that little of what senior management says or does matters in truly driving change—instead, frontline managers must be empowered to drive the cultural change and make the new behaviors stick at the individual level.

Beyond managers, the reps themselves have to coalesce around the idea of effort reduction. *Effort reduction lives or dies in the break room.* And while that may seem unfair, it's the reality of the customer service department. Frontline reps are almost entirely disconnected from the business decisions that you and your senior leadership team make day after day. You're corporate. They're not. They need to believe that effort reduction is better for the customer and how it's going to make their own jobs easier. For the frontline rep, effort reduction means fewer complaints. It means fewer four-letter words. It means they're making an impact, not running a script or ticking a checklist. It means you trust their judgment. *That* message needs to be abundantly clear and felt and practiced through this transformation. Your frontline reps have to sense this and share this sentiment with each other.

While it's difficult to offer you truly tactical advice for making this transformation happen, we can share one approach that Reliant shared with us that will prove helpful in getting your reps to appreciate this new approach. They call this the "Customer Effort Flight Simulator." Created by SimplySmart Solutions, which provide Reliant's customer care, the simulator is a safe place where reps can experiment and learn from peers how to use their own best judgment to serve customers. Beyond the development this approach affords, there's a bigger benefit: This is about reps helping reps. This isn't a supervisor telling a rep what to do or how to act. It's creating a social norm for a new behavior and trusting the reps to build that capability themselves. And that's pretty different.

Here's how it works: A team of three reps is armed with dummy accounts and their job is to work through a variety of service scenarios. One rep plays the role of rep, one plays the role of customer, and one plays the role of observer. There is no scripting, little guidance outside of how to start each scenario, and no "right" answer provided. In fact, there's no management presence at all. Through role-play, these teams use their own judgment to best resolve issues in the lowest-effort way possible. Each scenario is deconstructed at the end and discussed. The "customer" gives more perspective about what they had hoped the "rep" would say. The "rep" explains what they thought the customer wanted, or what they sensed the customer perceived. The observer offers more impartial feedback.

The whole system is simple, but hugely effective. In our research, we refer to this idea as *network judgment*—the idea of learning from your own personal network. The effectiveness of learning this way is incredible. But beyond the skills acquired, the social bonding and social understanding offer tremendous engagement and commitment benefits to the task at hand. While Reliant certainly doesn't point to this one approach as the reason they've had such a tremendous response to reducing effort, it is indicative of how they are approaching this significant change. And for those who say the proof is in the pudding, Reliant averages a full 26 percent better Customer Effort Score than their peers in the utilities industry.

Reducing effort is an ongoing challenge you will need to constantly support. Of course you need lots of top-down communication, good manager and supervisor support, and the right metrics. But most immediately, your priorities should be a great change story, significant coaching discipline, and clearly signaling the expectation that a low-effort experience should be the goal with every customer. Without creating a set of baby steps to help introduce your teams to effort reduction, initial rollouts will fail to engage reps, and effort reduction will lose steam. Not coincidentally, *making it easy* for your teams to take the first steps toward reducing effort will ensure your likelihood of success.

• • •

KEY TAKEAWAYS

♦ *Instead of training effort reduction, coach it.* The best companies understand that effort reduction can't be taught in the classroom. While training is helpful for building awareness, effort reduction involves frontline behavior change that can only be delivered (and sustained) through effective frontline supervisor coaching.

♦ *Draw a clear contrast between old and new behavior.* Explain how and why an effort reduction approach differs from the current service philosophy. Use a change story to continually reinforce why teams need to focus on effort reduction, what's at stake, and the nature of support they'll be provided.

♦ *Don't make effort reduction another "ask."* Simply tacking effort reduction on a long list of frontline requirements will signal a lack of organizational commitment and competing priorities. Remove requirements such as handle time or strict QA forms to allow pilot teams to truly focus on reducing customer effort, ultimately helping your organization determine the right—and wrong—ways to change behavior.

♦ *Make effort reduction easy.* Asking reps to "go out and reduce effort" without a clear sense of where and how will surely be met with failure and confusion. Narrowly scope initial pilot expectations for teams. This may include forward-resolving a specific type of service issue, or using positive language techniques for a small number of common issues. Provide heightened support and coaching as pilot teams get comfortable with these approaches.

8

EFFORT BEYOND
THE CONTACT CENTER

While our primary focus has been on customer contact interactions, the concept of reducing effort clearly extends beyond the four walls of the contact center. In this chapter, we'll explore other, non–contact center applications of the low-effort concept.

Customer Effort in Retail and
Live Service Environments

We love the Apple Store—but not for the reasons you might think. Sure, it's open and airy, sleek and cool, filled with enough technological wizardry to occupy even the most shopping-averse person for hours. But we'd argue that one of the keys to the Apple Store's success—why they've been able to bring in more revenue per square foot than any other retailer on earth—is because Apple has focused ruthlessly on making its in-store experience a *low-effort* experience.

Ron Johnson, former senior vice president of retail for Apple, admits that the Apple products themselves are one reason people visit the Apple Store, but the products themselves aren't the *main* reason. Customers flock to the store (despite the fact that there are other, often less expensive options for buying Apple products) primarily because it is "the anti-store"—a place that's all about helping the customer, not just selling them stuff: "People come to the Apple Store for the experience—and they're willing to pay a premium for that. There are lots of components to that experience, but maybe the most important—and this is something that can translate to any retailer—is that the staff isn't focused on selling stuff, it's focused on trying to make people's lives better. That may sound hokey, but it's true. The staff is exceptionally well trained, and they're not on commission, so it makes no difference to them whether you buy an expensive new computer or if they just help you make your old one run better so you're happy with it."[1]

Another big part of the Apple Store's success is that it has eliminated the single most glaring reminder of customer effort in retail environments: the line. While there are sometimes lines *outside* of the store in advance of new product releases, there are never any lines inside the store. We've all experienced the frustration of being in a store and waiting in line for something—the deli counter, the returns desk, the department store cashier. How does Apple manage to have no lines when its stores are packed with customers all the time?

First, Apple manages technical support traffic by allowing customers to schedule technical service appointments in advance. While most every other retailer requires customers to queue up (sometimes before the store opens) to get support from technical staff, Apple lets customers pick the time they want to come in for help. The incredibly user-friendly online scheduling system for the Genius Bar means that there's little to no waiting around when you arrive. And if they're running behind, there's still no waiting in line. You check in when you arrive and your name shows up on the big-screen monitor when it's your turn at the bar.

Second, there's no register or cashier's line at the Apple Store—another big source of the retail queue. Where most stores have dedicated checkout lines that create bottlenecks and lines between the store and the exit (ones that get particularly bad when there aren't enough registers open to quickly move customers through), Apple uses its own technology to turn every store employee into a cashier. Want to buy something? Just ask any Apple Store employee and they'll swipe your credit card on their iPod Touch using a special card-reader attachment. Oh yeah, and they even offer a low-effort receipt—they simply e-mail it to you while you're standing there.

We've seen other retailers employ similar ideas to enhance the ease factor of the shopping experience they provide. The clothing store Old Navy, for instance, has overhauled all of its locations to make the shopping experience easier for their target demographic: moms shopping with their kids.[2] Not only have they lowered the height of clothing racks (to enable moms to see where their kids are at all times), but the store has been reconfigured around an oval "track" with registers and changing rooms conveniently located in the middle. They've even turned the clothing hooks in the changing rooms into sorting aids—by labeling them "Love It," "Like It," and "Not For Me"—to help customers keep track of what they're trying on. And they've added "quick change" areas (simple booths with curtains) for trying on things like sweaters and jackets that don't require getting completely undressed. Lastly, they've added play areas and interactive displays for kids, to minimize the whining so that Mom can get her shopping done.

The role of low effort in the live retail environment is being explored in academic studies as well. Recently, we received a copy of a thesis written by a student at the University of Reading in England, entitled "The Role of Customer Effort on Customer Loyalty in Face-to-Face Retail Environments." The student had conducted his own survey research to understand what bearing, if any, effort had on the loyalty of customers to retailers. He surveyed customers in three different retail settings—grocery stores, department stores, and consumer electronics stores—and found that effort played a huge role in a customer's loyalty to the store in question:

> The results demonstrated that a significant relationship between customer effort and customer loyalty absolutely exists. . . . That is to say that if businesses intend to maintain their existing customers, they must ensure that customers put forth minimal amounts of effort to have their requests handled. . . . Customer Effort Score is a powerful metric that appears to have created the perfect link between customer experience and customer loyalty. . . . As this research demonstrates, CES can be seamlessly applied to face-to-face retail environments in addition of its early application to contact center environments. It is a dynamic metric in that sense and businesses are smart to adopt it and use its analysis widely.[3]

The student found that the two most critical factors when it comes to customer effort in the retail environment are "navigability" (how easy it is for customers to find what they're looking for) and "issue resolution" (how easy it is for customers to get help solving some problem). In the area of navigability, he highlighted tactics such as those of the UK retailer Tesco, which has created a smartphone app to help customers quickly locate an item in any Tesco store, as well as companies like Trader Joe's and Waitrose, whose floor staff actually walk customers to the items they're looking for rather than just telling them what aisle they are located on. Regarding issue resolution, he called attention to Macy's, which trains their floor staff not just to answer direct questions, but to proactively offer advice and opinions—including suggesting alternatives—to help customers make their purchase decisions.

Customer Effort in Product Design

We may never see tax code simplification in our lifetime, but at least software companies like Intuit (the makers of TurboTax) have made it simple to *do* your taxes. The secret to TurboTax is that it uses an intuitive, plain-English, question-based approach to helping taxpayers fill out their returns. When you're using the product, you're not doing some accounting exercise, you're just responding to a few questions asked in simple English. Instead of using the language on the IRS form that might say, "Enter your contributions to qualified tax-exempt retirement funds," TurboTax simply asks, "Look at box 11 on your W-2. If there is a number in that box, enter it here." And if you get stuck, there are easy help options right at your fingertips—not just jargon-free FAQs, but a link to an online support community where taxpayers and accountants offer free advice to one another. The taxpayer uptake for these types of programs has been nothing short of remarkable: In 2012, the IRS reported that fully *81 percent* of American taxpayers filled their returns using one of these online services. Their success is no secret at all—it's not marketing magic that makes such programs work; it's that they're incredibly easy to use. Other spaces have followed suit and begun to put technical and specialized tasks into the hands of ordinary people—for instance, LegalZoom, which helps consumers accomplish tasks one used to have to hire an attorney to accomplish, like writing a will or incorporating a company.

Simplicity of design and ease of use really make certain products stand out in a crowd. Perhaps nowhere is this more obvious than in consumer electronics. Apple's ease of use is legendary (many of its products come without instructions; they're that easy to set up and operate), but other, lesser known suppliers make seemingly difficult tasks incredibly easy to execute. For instance, the idea of setting up a streaming video service to take advantage of multiple video-on-demand offerings (from Netflix, Amazon, and cable channels like HBO) sounds like it would be complex or involve considerable effort, but Roku makes it a snap. The company's Roku Player, which is slightly larger than a hockey puck and has no buttons, sets up in an astounding two minutes, suddenly unlocking tens of thousands of video titles for the user.

Bose is another consumer electronics company that just plain "gets" the idea of low effort. Remember what it was like to get your speakers to work—futzing around with multiple wires and the frayed ends that all look the same and no idea which one plugs in where? Not with Bose equipment. The company puts simple color-coded tags on wires that match the color of the jacks they're supposed to plug into. Easy stuff.

Customer Effort in the Purchase Experience

In the spring of 2012, two CEB colleagues of ours, Patrick Spenner and Karen Freeman, published the results of a groundbreaking study of customer buying behavior in the *Harvard Business Review*. In their article, titled "To Keep Your Customers, Keep It Simple," Spenner and Freeman argued that marketers tend to overly complicate the purchase process for consumers, bombarding them with technical information that often deters customers from making purchases:

> Marketers see today's consumers as web-savvy, mobile-enabled data sifters who pounce on whichever brand or store offers the best deal. Brand loyalty, the thinking goes, is vanishing. In response, companies have ramped up their messaging, expecting that the more interaction and information they provide, the better the chances of holding on to these increasingly distracted and disloyal customers. But for many consumers, the rising volume of marketing messages isn't empowering—it's overwhelming. Rather than pulling customers into the fold, marketers are pushing them away with relentless and ill-conceived efforts to engage.[4]

Their study, which comprised multiple surveys with more than 7,000 consumers around the world, sought to identify exactly what makes a customer "sticky," or more likely to buy, buy more over time, and say good things about a product or supplier. Although there are so many variables that *could* drive stickiness, they found that "decision simplicity"—that is, "the ease with which consumers can gather trustworthy information about a product and confidently and efficiently weigh their purchase options"—is the single biggest driver.

Decision simplicity, it turns out, isn't rocket science. Spenner and Freeman found that simplifying a consumer's purchase decision comes down to three things: **making it easy for consumers to navigate information about the brand** (for example, the consumer electronics company that guides consumers to the content sources it knows inspire the greatest confidence and lowest likelihood of defection); **providing information that is trustworthy** (for instance, Disney's use of a "Moms Panel" to provide information to other families traveling to a Disney destination with children); and **making it simple for consumers to weigh their options** (such as De Beers's creation of the "Four C's" to help diamond buyers compare seemingly similar stones). "Brands that scored in the top quarter in our study," they explain, "were 86% more likely than those in the bottom quarter to be purchased by the consumers considering them. They were 9% more likely to be repurchased and 115% more likely to be recommended to others."

This phenomenon isn't strictly the provenance of B2C brands. CEB's Sales Leadership Council found that 53 percent of B2B customer loyalty

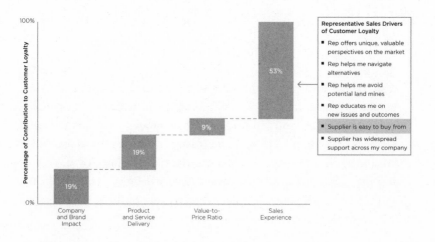

Source: CEB. CEB Sales Leadership Council, 2013.

Figure 8.1 Drivers of B2B Customer Loyalty

is a function of the purchase experience—surprisingly outweighing sup-plier brand, product and service quality, and price-to-value ratio (see figure 8.1). Peeling apart the most important elements of the purchase experience reveals something that, at this point in the book, should come as no surprise: The suppliers that gain customers' greatest loyalty are "easy to do business with."

Companies that overcomplicate the purchase are doomed to play catch-up to those suppliers who quickly and efficiently deliver new ideas (and, by definition, new solutions) to their customers.

Customer effort, it turns out, is more of an overarching business con-cept than it is a customer contact strategy. Companies that can build easy-to-use products, help customers execute a purchase in a simple way, and provide low-effort service on the back end will generate dispropor-tionate customer loyalty returns—especially in a world where the hassle factor tends to be more the rule than the exception.

KEY TAKEAWAYS

♦ *Effort should be reduced throughout the customer life cycle.* Our research demonstrates that reducing customer effort in pre- and post-sales customer touchpoints has measurable loyalty impact. The ease with which customers can learn about products or services, make a pur-chase, and obtain post-sales service and support provides a dramatic opportunity for brand differentiation.

♦ *The best companies live low-effort.* Top brands are adopting the princi-ples of a low-effort experience across multiple facets of their busi-ness, from product design to the sales experience. These companies ruthlessly question the accepted status quo: Should a customer have to wait in a line to buy something? Should a customer ever have to spend sixty minutes reading a product manual prior to using their new exciting product? These companies would argue that that's simply not acceptable.

ACKNOWLEDGMENTS

Principal Contributors

While this book has three authors on the cover, it is, like all CEB studies, the product of an enormous team undertaking. At the top of the list of contributors are several individuals who, along with the authors, formed the core of the research team behind this work:

LARA PONOMAREFF

Currently research director of our customer service program, the Customer Contact Leadership Council, Lara was the lead researcher on our work that uncovered the control quotient (CQ) as well as our work on customer service channel preferences—two studies discussed at length in this book. She was also a key lieutenant on several other critical studies that underpin this book—most notably our 2008 study that originally posited the notion of effort reduction. Through it all, Lara has been a phenomenal researcher, project manager, coach, and friend to all of those who have had the pleasure of working with her. A rare talent, Lara truly embodies all of the values we aspire to as a firm—Force of Ideas, Member Impact, Spirit of Generosity, and Stewardship of Exceptional Talent.

PETER SLEASE

Although he joined the team just as our initial discoveries about the power of the effortless experience were first uncovered, nobody has introduced this concept—and its implications—to more companies over the past several years than Pete. Working as our lead executive advisor, Pete has traveled the world many times over, conducting strategy-setting sessions and workshops covering every step of the low-effort journey. Pete possesses a truly rare combination of skills—he is both a former customer service leader as well as a former teacher—and this experience, as well as his incredible knowledge of our research, has made him invaluable to the thousands of CEB members he has worked with, as well as to the authors of this book. All three of us consider Pete to be truly extraordinary, both as a teammate and as a friend.

LAUREN PRAGOFF

Lauren was, as we say at CEB, "present at the creation"—not just of the customer effort concept, but of our customer service research program itself. Starting as a research associate with the program, Lauren is now a director of research, responsible for major deliverables and member engagements across the calendar year. Over her many years in our practice, she has played a role in nearly every research study and every finding referenced in this book. Topping it all off, Lauren is a truly gifted coach and developer of research talent. Nearly every researcher who has passed through the program in the past five years has Lauren to thank for their personal development and advancement in the firm.

KAREN FREEMAN

A founding member of our customer service research team, Karen served as research director of the group from 2007 to 2008 and was the driving force and principal thought leader behind the original customer effort research study. She also coauthored our 2010 *HBR* article on the research, "Stop Trying to Delight Your Customers." Karen currently serves as managing director of CEB University, our internal learning and development function, which is responsible for, among other things, providing the latest training and development experiences to new CEB researchers. Karen was a recipient of the "Force of Ideas" award, one of the highest honors bestowed to a CEB employee, in 2010. We are truly grateful for her phenomenal vision and research leadership.

With Sincere Thanks

Beyond the principal contributors to this research, there is also a long list of individuals and organizations without whose commitment and support this research and this book would never have seen the light of day.

First, we owe a tremendous debt of gratitude to the leadership of our firm, especially our chairman and CEO, Tom Monahan, and the general manager of the CEB Sales & Marketing Practice, Haniel Lynn, for their unwavering support of this research and this book itself.

Over the years, we've had the pleasure of working with many, many talented researchers and executive advisors in the customer service program, all of whom had a hand in producing and delivering the research that went into this book. We wish to thank current team members Brent Adamson, Chris Brown, Mark Dauigoy, Jonathan Dietrich, Tom Disantis, Brad Fager, Chris Herbert, Wasim Kabir, Jonathan Kilroy, Patrick Loftus, Lucyna Mackenzie, Yan Qu, Carol Shin, Gauri Subramani, and Judy Wang. We also want to thank former team members Rufino Chiong, Dan Clay, Shauna Ferguson, Rachel Greenblatt, Matt Hoffman, Michael Hubble, Jessica Klarfeld, Ben Koffel, Victoria Koval, Matt Lind, Peter LaMotte, Dave Liu, Liz Martin, Anastasia Milgramm, Dalia Naamani-Goldman, Melissa Schnyder, Coryell Stout, John Taddei, Louise Wiggins, Jacob Winkler, and Peter Yang.

Ours is a unique craft, and we rely heavily on the thought leadership and mentorship of those in our company who are best at what we do. Eric Braun is our head of research and has been intimately involved in the customer effort work from the earliest days. His fingerprints are all over this research, and the result is much better for it. Before Eric assumed this role, we had the privilege of studying under several research legends and masters of the "CEB Way," including Pope Ward, Tim Pollard, Derek van Bever, and Chris Miller. At different points over the past decade, these individuals taught us what it means to deliver research and insight worthy of our members' time and attention.

Last but not least, we are indebted to our own commercial team at CEB, who are ultimately responsible for helping our members derive value from and take action on our research. Among the many talented and dedicated professionals who have at one point or another represented the customer service program, we would like to thank Kristen Rachinsky, Kristie Shifflette, Lucy Bracewell, Erica Hayman, Cat Everson, Molly McGonegle, and Katherine Moore.

Outside of CEB, we of course owe tremendous thanks to Dan Heath for challenging our thinking with his own work as well as for writing the exceptional foreword to this book. We are honored to be associated with one of the most influential thought leaders and storytellers of our time.

All of our work at CEB is inspired by our members. They direct us to their most pressing issues, give generously of their time so that we can learn how these issues manifest for them and their organizations, and allow us to survey their reps, supervisors, and even customers and, when called upon, to profile their best practices and tactics so that other members might avoid reinventing the wheel.

Within a membership that now spans hundreds of companies and thousands of individual customer service leaders, we would like to specifically thank a few of our current and former members for their above-and-beyond contributions to this research:

- John Bowden and the team at Time Warner Cable
- Bill Clayton and the team at Reliant Energy
- John Connolly, and the team at Centrica/British Gas
- Derrick DeRavariere and the team at American Express TRS
- Sharmane Good, Fawzia Drakes, and the team at LoyaltyOne
- Mark Halmrast, of Blue Train Consulting LLP (formerly of Target)
- Elizabeth Orth, and the team at EarthLink
- Dan Rourke, of Homeaway.com (formerly of Cadence Design Systems)

We would be remiss for not acknowledging the support of the many talented and dedicated professionals who helped shepherd this book through each phase of the journey: our agent, Jill Marsal of Marsal-Lyon; the terrific team at Portfolio, including our very talented editor, Maria Gagliano; editorial assistant Julia Batavia; head of marketing Will Weisser and publisher Adrian Zackheim; our very patient graphic designer, Tim Brown; our own excellent marketing and PR team at CEB, including Rory Channer, Ian Walsh, Ayesha Kumar-Flaherty, Rosemary Masterson, Matt Stevens, Laura Merola, Leslie Tullio, and Shannon Eckhart; and last but not least, Gardiner Morse, senior editor at the *Harvard Business Review,* for his support in helping us to unveil this work to the broader business community.

The final thank-you is the most important one. This research and this book would never have been possible were it not for the support and encouragement of our families. Matt would like to thank his wife, best friend, and biggest supporter, Amy Dixon; as well as his four remarkable and beautiful children, Aidan, Ethan, Norah, and Clara. Delight in customer service might be overrated, but the delight provided by one's family is the greatest thing in the world.

Nick would like to thank his wife, Erika, for her encouragement and patience over the many years of research culminating in this book; his son Evan for providing love and comic relief in the way only an infant can; his brothers, Jeremy and Mikey (who still believe we create cartoons for executives); and his parents, Vern and Cathy, for their tremendous support.

And, finally, Rick would like to thank his wife, Jeannie (a gifted teacher with a master's in English who is a much better writer than her husband); his son Chris (a communications and marketing student at Dad's alma mater, Syracuse University—Go Orange!); and his parents, Don and Sue DeLisi of Spring Hill, Florida; his brother John and family of Fairfax, Virginia; and sister Donna and family of St. Joseph, Michigan (who deserve full credit for the QTIP story).

APPENDIXES

[APPENDIX A: Issue-to-Channel-Mapping Tool]

Directions:

Use this tool to map customer issues to the best-fit channel for resolution, taking into account both customer effort and cost to the organization.

1

Step 1: Determine Issue Type
Categorize the most common issue/request buckets for your organization. (For help, see the MasterCard issue filtering approach described on p. 41)

2

Step 2: Assess Channel Fit
Evaluate an individual issue/request bucket identified in Step 1 against the Yes/No questions provided for each channel.

3

Step 3: Calculate Channel Fit Score
Use your answers to the Yes/No questions in Step 2 to arrive at a numerical value that reflects the fit of the channel for resolving this issue type. Repeat steps 2 and 3 for each channel.

4

Step 4: Evaluate Results
Compare the individual Channel Fit Scores calculated in Step 3 to determine the best-fit channel for this issue type.

Repeat the above steps 2–4 for each issue bucket identified.

ISSUE-TO-CHANNEL MAPPING TOOL

Issue Type: _____

Use Screening Questions to Assess Channel Fit

Web Self-Service	
Prerequisite Questions	**YES/ NO**
1. Does the company offer the functionality to resolve this issue via web self-service? (for example, an online payment tool to pay bills online)	
2. Can the large majority of customers completely resolve this issue using web self-service?	
3. Can the service organization drive changes to the self-service portion of the website for this particular issue?	
■ If 'YES' to all of the above questions, proceed to questions 4-15. ■ If 'NO' to any of the above questions, web self-service is a poor fit for this issue. Skip to Step 3 and assign web self-service a Fit Score of '1'.	
Customer Effort to Resolve *Answering 'YES' to these questions indicates a low-effort experience in web self-service for this issue.*	**YES/ NO**
4. Can the resources for resolving this issue be accessed relatively easily via the website? (e.g., does the knowledge base or search functionality easily lead to these resources?)	
5. Can the request be resolved efficiently via self-service using a limited number of steps? (e.g. no more than three screens to click through to find an answer)	
6. Can the request be satisfied with a standard response and/or process that does not differ from customer to customer?	
7. Can the company easily and succinctly explain the information necessary to resolve the request? (as opposed to requests that require a more involved explanation)	
8. Does the issue rarely prompt related questions or problems from customers that need to be addressed by a live representative?	
9. Can the customer resolve the request via self-service without signing into an account or providing other specific information?	
Additional Effort-Related Questions *May not apply to all issues and/or organizations.*	**YES/ NO**
10. From a legal standpoint, can the request be resolved via the web self-service site?	
11. From a security standpoint, are customers comfortable sharing any personal information necessary to resolve the request via web self-service?	
12. Do a large majority of your customers have reliable access to the internet?	
Cost to Resolve *Answering 'YES' to these questions indicates that web self-service is a relatively low cost channel for resolving this type of issue.*	**YES/ NO**
13. Has the company invested in a proven tool to handle this request online?	
14. Is the web self-service capability robust enough to handle the request?	
15. Is this the lowest-cost channel by which the company can deliver quality service to customers on this issue?	
Calculate Channel Fit Score *Use your answers to the YES/NO questions in Step 2 to inform your Channel Fit scoring.* *If you answered 'YES' to most questions, assign higher numerical values to the Effort Impact and Cost Impact sections below.*	

Effort Impact 5 = Very Low Effort 1 = Very High Effort	Cost Impact 3 = Not Costly 1 = Very Costly	Web Self-Service Channel Fit Score *(Effort Impact x Cost Impact)* **Use this number in Step 4.**

X _____ = _____

IVR Self-Service		
Prerequisite Questions		YES/ NO
1.	**Does the company offer the functionality to resolve this issue via IVR?**	
2.	**Can the large majority of customers completely resolve this issue in the IVR?**	
■ If 'YES' to all of the above questions, proceed to questions 3-13. ■ If 'NO' to any of the above questions, IVR is a poor fit for this issue. Skip to Step 3 and assign IVR Self-Service a Fit Score of '1'.		
Customer Effort to Resolve *Answering 'YES' to these questions indicates a low-effort experience in the IVR for this issue.*		YES/ NO
3.	Is the request simple and straightforward enough to be accurately and efficiently resolved via IVR?	
4.	Can the request be resolved via IVR using a limited number of steps? (e.g. no more than three branches of menu options before resolution)	
5.	Can the request be satisfied with a standard response and/or process that does not differ from customer to customer?	
6.	Does the issue rarely prompt related questions or problems from customers that need to be addressed by a live representative?	
7.	Can the company easily and succinctly explain the information necessary to resolve the request? (as opposed to requests that require a more involved explanation)	
8.	Are customers comfortable using the IVR technology (in particular, speech or natural language IVR) to resolve the request?	
9.	For requests that require the customer to provide specific information, can he/she enter this information using only a telephone keypad?	
10.	Is this a request that cannot currently be resolved via web self-service?	
Cost to Resolve *Answering 'YES' to these questions indicates that IVR is a relatively low cost channel for resolving this type of issue.*		YES/ NO
11.	Has the company invested in a proven tool to handle this request via IVR?	
12.	Is the IVR capability robust enough to handle the request, including accurately capturing necessary information from the customer?	
13.	Is this the lowest-cost channel by which the company can deliver quality service to customers on this issue?	
Calculate Channel Fit Score *Use your answers to the YES/NO questions in Step 2 to inform your Channel Fit scoring.* *If you answered 'YES' to most questions, assign higher numerical values to the Effort Impact and Cost Impact sections below.*		

Effort Impact	Cost Impact	IVR Self-Service Channel Fit Score
5 = Very Low Effort *1 = Very High Effort*	*3 = Not Costly* *1 = Very Costly*	*(Effort Impact x Cost Impact)* **Use this number in Step 4.**
X	=	

[APPENDIX B: Toolkit for Issue Resolution]

A TOOLKIT FOR ISSUE RESOLUTION MEASUREMENT

The Council Model for Measuring Next Issue Avoidance

Understanding the Magnitude of Resolution Failure

 Use callback tracking to identify trends around next issue avoidance...

- Provides a broad-based perspective on resolution
- Captures individual performance and trends on under-/over-performance within a "healthy" variance range
- Serves as stimulus to focus QA monitoring and post-call customer-driven root cause analyses

Measurement Selection Decision Rules

Measurement Category	Measurement Method	Explicit[1] 1 = Does Not Capture 5 = Captures	Implicit (Adjacent)[2] 1 = Does Not Capture 5 = Captures	Implicit (Emotional)[3] 1 = Does Not Capture 5 = Captures	Sample Size 1 = Small 5 = Large	Fairness to Agent 1 = Unfair 5 = Fair	Inherent Bias 1 = Biased 5 = Unbiased	Derives Root Cause 1 = Ineffective 5 = Effective	Identifies Coaching Opportunities 1 = Unidentifiable 5 = Identifiable
Callback Tracking	Track Callbacks By Account Number	5	5	5	5	2	5	2	4
	Track Callbacks By Phone Number	4	4	4	4	2	5	2	3
	Agent Asks Customer At the Beginning of Call, "Is This the First Time You've Called Within the Last 30 Days?"	3	3	4	4	4	4	2	1
QA Reported	QA Monitors Calls and Assesses Issue Resolution	4	3	2	3	3	3	3	5
Customer Reported	Post-Call Survey (Delayed)	3	1	4	1	2	3	3	3
	Voice Analytics	1	1	4	5	1	4	2	3
	Post-Call Survey (Immediate)	2	1	3	2	3	2	2	2
	Agent Asks Customer At the End of Call, "Have I Resolved Your Issue Today?"	2	1	1	3	3	2	2	1
Agent Reported	Agent Marks the Issue As Resolved	2	2	1	4	5	1	2	2

[1] **Explicit Issue:** The original, customer-stated need, that is typically self-diagnosed by the customer and resolved by the company.

[2] **Implicit Issue:** Issues that transcend the customer-stated need, which typically go unnoticed by the customer until a later time. Such issues are not readily diagnosed by the customer. One type of implicit issue is an **Adjacent Issue:** A seemingly separate, but tangentially related, downstream issue.

[3] **Implicit Issue:** Issues that transcend the customer-stated need, which typically go unnoticed by the customer until a later time. Such issues are not readily diagnosed by the customer. One type of implicit issue is an **Emotional Issue:** Resolution experience triggers that prompt a customer to call a company back, typically to confirm resolution.

Understanding the Drivers of Resolution Failure

2 ...follow up with QA monitoring to surface root causes of explicit and adjacent problems...

- Improves accuracy of issue categorization (see Appendix for U.S. Cellular practice)
- Monitors agent performance to correctly identify coaching opportunities and process failures
- Offers opportunities to exclude "good" callbacks from resolution failure score

+

3 ...and combine with post-call customer surveys and feedback sessions to flag emotional sources of resolution failure

- Provides opportunity to understand differences between customer-defined and company-defined resolution
- Surfaces emotional reasons for callbacks
- Offers a method to collect and analyze Voice of the Customer to identify improvement opportunity areas (see National Australia Group practice)

True to Customer Perspective 1 = Untrue 5 = True	Infrastructure Requirement 1 = High 5 = Low	Average 1-5	Rank 1-9	🏛 CEB Council View	⚙ Implementation Tips and Tricks
3	1	3.7	1	■ Captures both explicit and implicit callbacks while mitigating against human coding error. ■ Is resource-intensive if systems are not currently in place to track issue resolution. ■ Under-reports resolution rates because it encompasses callbacks on any issue, but normalizes over time.	☑ Mitigate against agent perception of unfairness by applying the measure consistently and using it only for coaching opportunities (not for performance management). ☑ Track callbacks within a short period of time (5–14 days), as most customer callbacks occur shortly after the first call; this also allows for more effective coaching. ☑ Track callbacks within ranges because resolution has a natural variance. ☑ Allow agents to flag irrational or uncontrollable callbacks so these calls won't be counted against them. ☑ Asking "Is this the first time you called on this issue?" at the beginning of a call addresses only FCR, while asking "Is this the first time you've called (for any reason) within the last 30 days?" addresses next issue avoidance.
3	2	3.3	2		
4	3	3.2	3		
2	4	3.2	3	■ Often surfaces resolution failures around explicit issues, but almost never identifies implicit issues when used in isolation. ■ Offers opportunities to eliminate "good" callbacks from resolution failure score.	☑ Combine with other measurements, like callback tracking, to triangulate data and to analyze root causes of explicit and implicit problems.
5	2	2.7	5	■ Incorporates customers' perspective, which is valuable, as customers have the best insight into their own emotional resolution. However, customers rarely understand adjacent issues, and often do not know the status of explicit resolution until some time after the call. ■ Voice analytics is an emerging technology, and as such, is unproven in its ability to accurately assess resolution.	☑ Immediate post-call surveys capture only customer satisfaction with the call, while delayed post-call surveys more accurately capture resolution. ☑ Surveys have a small sample size, especially for delayed post-call, as many customers opt out of the process. ☑ Accurate surveys depend on clear and easy to interpret questions that consistently capture customer-perceived resolution. ☑ Utilize this method as a supplementary source by combining it with other methods, such as QA reported and callback tracking.
3	1	2.5	6		
3	2	2.2	8		
2	3	2.0	9		
1	3	2.3	7	■ Enables resolution failure rate tracking on most calls without the use of systems. ■ Is prone to subjective responses. ■ Allows agents to flag calls that are beyond their control.	☑ Utilize to mitigate against agent perception of unfairness with other measurements. ☑ Combine with QA and/or customer reported data if callback tracking systems are not available.

[APPENDIX C: Negative Language Toolkit for Trainers]

Toolkit for Trainers: Compiling Your Organization's List of Top Negative Language Scenarios

Creating a Negative Language Scenario Template

Thinking about what negative language scenarios occur most often in your company will help you train staff more effectively. Identifying the most problematic customer service situations that arise often in your industry can help you think of what kinds of conversations will elicit negative language.

Checklist: Steps to Take		People to Check in with	Target Completion Date
• Ask a few higher performing frontline staff members what their most difficult, commonly occurring calls tend to be. See if there are certain types of issues that lead to problematic calls, and if there are, focus your attention on identifying negative language that is used in those situations. Use any call categorization data you may have to help you.	☐		
• Do role play exercises with frontline staff with these most difficult calls, and listen for when they use negative language and what phrases they use.	☐		
• If possible, give your QA team a list of common negative language phrases and ask them to take note of call types in which they hear those phrases often. Listen to call recordings they identify to get a sense of how and when your staff uses negative language.	☐		
• Use this data to identify a list of the most common scenarios that elicit negative language. Create a separate list of the negative words and phrases that occur in those scenarios.	☐		
• Insert the list of negative words and phrases into the "Say This, Not That!" page of this workbook. Ask staff if they would change or add anything to the list. Brainstorm with staff and QA to come up with positive language to replace negative words.	☐		

[APPENDIX D: Customer Effort Score v2.0 Starter Kit]

CES v2.0 Starter Kit

How to measure customer effort at your organization

Use the implementation tips below to help integrate CES v2.0 into your existing customer voice.

- Use CES v2.0 to obtain a holistic picture of customer effort in the resolution process.

- Use a more detailed, effort-based survey to analyze discrete sources of effort throughout the resolution process.

- Consider changing the ending of the effort-based question to accommodate the type of reason for a customer request (e.g., "...to complete the sale?").

- To capture customers with unresolved issues or outstanding requests, add an "(n/a) Request Is Not Resolved" field to the response options (except if using an immediate post-contact survey).

- Use customer verbatim for a more comprehensive analysis of customer effort and to target proactive outreach.

Customer Effort Score v2.0—Standard Question

To what extent do you agree or disagree with the following statement:

	Strongly Disagree (1)	Disagree (2)	Somewhat Disagree (3)	Neither Agree Nor Disagree (4)	Somewhat Agree (5)	Agree (6)	Strongly Agree (7)
The company made it easy for me to handle my issue.	☐	☐	☐	☐	☐	☐	☐

Comparing Performance
Distribution of Company Scores on CES v2.0

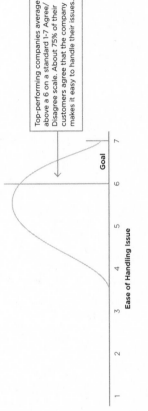

Top-performing companies average above a 6 on a standard 1–7 Agree/Disagree scale. About 75% of their customers agree that the company makes it easy to handle their issues.

Ease of Handling Issue

Source: CEB, 2013.

[APPENDIX E: Customer Effort Assessment—Sample Survey Questions]

  Customer Effort Assessment

Sample Survey Questions

Primary Loyalty Metrics

How likely is it that you would **recommend** <Company> to a friend or colleague?

- o   0 – Not at all likely
- o   1
- o   2
- o   3
- o   4
- o   5
- o   6
- o   7
- o   8
- o   9
- o   10 – Very likely

On a scale from 1 to 7, please indicate your level of agreement with the following statements:

	Strongly disagree	Disagree	Somewhat disagree	Neither agree nor disagree	Somewhat agree	Agree	Strongly agree
I intend to continue purchasing from <Company>	O	O	O	O	O	O	O
I am willing to consider new offerings from <Company>	O	O	O	O	O	O	O
I am satisfied with the value provided by <Company>	O	O	O	O	O	O	O

Customer Service Experience Outcomes

When was the last time you contacted <Company>'s customer service/support department?

- o   Within the last week
- o   Within the last month
- o   Within the last 2 months
- o   Within the last 6 months
- o   Within the last year
- o   Over 1 year ago
- o   Never

From the list below, please select the option that best matches your primary reason for contacting customer service.

- o   Resolve an issue with a product or service
- o   File a complaint
- o   Check or change status of an account
- o   Obtain account information
- o   Return a product or service
- o   Make a purchase
- o   General inquiry
- o   None of the above

Which of the following **customer service/support resources** did you use first to try to resolve the issue? (select all that apply)

- ☐   I **called** the company
- ☐   I looked for a solution on the company's **website**
- ☐   I used the company's **web chat** service
- ☐   I **e-mailed** the company
- ☐   Other

Please indicate the extent to which you agree or disagree with the following statements about your service experience, overall:

	Strongly disagree	Disagree	Somewhat disagree	Neither agree nor disagree	Somewhat agree	Agree	Strongly agree
The company made it **easy** for me to handle my issue	O	O	O	O	O	O	O
It took **less time** than I expected to handle this issue	O	O	O	O	O	O	O

Phone: *Automated Phone Experience (IVR)*

Please rate the extent to which you agree or disagree with the following aspects of your experience using <Company>'s automated phone system:

	Not applicable	Strongly disagree	Disagree	Somewhat disagree	Neither agree nor disagree	Somewhat agree	Agree	Strongly agree
The options available to me were very clear	O	O	O	O	O	O	O	O
I was easily able to navigate through the system	O	O	O	O	O	O	O	O

Phone: *Live Rep Phone Interactions*

The next set of questions asks about the **customer service representative(s)** you spoke with at <Company>.

	Not applicable	Strongly disagree	Disagree	Somewhat disagree	Neither agree nor disagree	Somewhat agree	Agree	Strongly agree
The session started quickly – I did not need to wait long to reach a representative	O	O	O	O	O	O	O	O
The representative responded quickly after each comment	O	O	O	O	O	O	O	O

E-mail

Please rate the extent to which you agree or disagree with the following aspects of your **experience with e-mailing the company**.

	Not applicable	Strongly disagree	Disagree	Somewhat disagree	Neither agree nor disagree	Somewhat agree	Agree	Strongly agree
I received a response back in a reasonable amount of time	O	O	O	O	O	O	O	O
The responses I received seemed scripted or generic	O	O	O	O	O	O	O	O

[APPENDIX E] cont'd.

General Feedback/Demographics

Is there any other information or feedback you would like to provide? If so, please do so here.

_____

_____

_____

_____

_____

_____

Approximately how long have you been a custome of <Company>?

_____

In what year were you born?

_____

❯ Customer Effort Audit Tool

Introduction

The Customer Effort Audit Tool enables you to identify the channel(s) where your customers are expending the greatest effort (e.g., Web, IVR, Phone) and directs you to resources that will help you reduce that effort. With this tool, you will answer these core questions:

1. **What can I do to reduce customer effort on a channel-by-channel basis?**
2. **Which channel offers the greatest opportunity area to reduce customer effort?**

Instructions

1. Answer the set of yes/no questions for channel selected. The "no's" are areas to consider changing.
2. Rate each channel's attribute categories on a scale of 1-5 on two criteria:

    a. How much effort is this area causing customers?

    b. How hard is this attribute to change?

[APPENDIX F] cont'd.

Web Site

Simply answer the "yes/no" diagnostic questions. Each question that receives a "no" response indicates a potential area of high customer effort.		
Attributes	**Effort Diagnosis Questions by Attribute**	**Response: Yes or No (Y/N)**
Navigability	Is information written in customer (versus company) language?	
	Is the site navigation designed for the customers you want to have use it?	
	Is the information accessible to customers in a variety of ways (event-based, product-based, *and* question-based)?	
	Is it easy to access the Web site (e.g., easy authentication or login)?	
	Have you ensured that your most-leveraged content is not buried in your Web site (users can find most content and access most functionality relatively quickly)?	
	Is it reasonably easy to contact customer service via the Web site?	
	Are customer service phone numbers intuitively organized?	
	Are there an appropriate number of phone numbers visible to customers?	
Information Quality	Do you make an appropriate amount of your knowledge base available on the Web site?	
	Is information prioritized intuitively for the customer?	
	Is the information of high quality?	
	Is the site language appropriately tailored to the customers you want to have use it?	
	Do you prioritize service information based on seasonal differences when appropriate?	
	Do you prioritize service information based on call volume drivers?	
Functionality	Can customers complete all reasonably simple service tasks on the site?	
	Is the site functionality appropriately tailored to the customers you want to have use it?	
	Once a customer completes a transaction, do you proactively offer related transactions or information?	
	Can customers track the status of an issue or purchase online?	
	Do you offer auto-fill or saved customer information whenever possible?	
	Do you have discussion boards?	
	If so, do you monitor them for quality?	
	If so, do you have employees participate in discussion boards?	
	Do you provide incentives to "power users" to participate in discussion boards?	
Metrics Do you track...	Number of clicks between pages	
	Number of searches	
	Length of time on the site	
	Number of pages visited	
	Ease of password reset	
	Number of failed login attempts	
	Age of knowledge base articles	
	Frequency of customers tracking status	
	Web issue resolution: number of live channel customers who first tried to resolve issue on the site	

Source: CEB, 2013.

IVR

	Simply answer the "yes/no" diagnostic questions. Each question that receives a "no" response indicates a potential area of high customer effort.	
Attributes	**Effort Diagnosis Questions by Attribute**	**Response: Yes or No (Y/N)**
Navigability	Do you communicate to customers what they can use the IVR for?	
	Do your reps help customers understand how to use the IVR?	
	Is it easy for customers to understand which options to select?	
	Are the options grouped intuitively for customers?	
	Does the IVR use customer (versus company) language?	
	Do you allow customers to skip listening to information that is not relevant to their inquiry?	
	Does the IVR inform customers of important information before they proceed through it (e.g., that the center is closed, etc.)?	
	If you have speech recognition, do you also give customers the option of using touchtone?	
	If customers must choose between a set of options, are they routed to specific rep queues?	
	Do you make your tree available online or via printed collateral?	
	Do you prioritize high call volume issues in the IVR (e.g., product recalls, alerts, etc.)?	
	Do you tell customers the number of options they will hear?	
	Have you tested how much time it takes to read your menus?	
	Have you solicited rep feedback about the IVR experience?	
Information Quality	Do you offer FAQs to customers through the IVR?	
	If so, is it clear to customers what FAQs they can expect to find?	
	Is the FAQ information in customer (versus company) language?	
	Do you update FAQs regularly to include the most important information?	
Functionality	Do you offer a zero-out option?	
	Do you allow opt-outs for frequently repeated information (e.g., bank account balance, menu options, etc.)?	
	Can customers save their IVR preferences or favorite transactions?	
	Do you relay information captured in the IVR to rep desktops via CTI?	
	Do you pull repeat callers out of the IVR or offer a "fast track"?	
Metrics Do you track...	Zero-out rate	
	Accuracy of routing (e.g., number of transfers)	
	Completion rate	
	How much time it takes the average customer to proceed through the IVR	
	Accuracy rate of voice recognition routing	
	Customer feedback about the IVR experience	

Source: CEB, 2013.

[APPENDIX F] cont'd.

Phone

Simply answer the "yes/no" diagnostic questions. Each question that receives a "no" response indicates a potential area of high customer effort.

Attributes	Effort Diagnosis Questions by Attribute	Response: Yes or No (Y/N)
Resolution	Do you provide incentives to reps around issue resolution?	
	Do you routinely reinforce the importance of issue resolution with reps?	
	Do you monitor reps for accurate issue diagnosis?	
	Do you treat customers preferentially on their second (or greater) call?	
	Do you root cause the sources of multiple contacts?	
	Do you allow reps to treat different customer personality types differently (i.e., provide emotional resolution)?	
	Do you require reps to own each issue to resolution (even when it requires involvement from other parties in the organization)?	
	Do you allow reps to call customers back?	
	Do you encourage reps to forward-resolve appropriate related issues?	
	Have you audited internal policies to ensure that they are not causing multiple calls to resolution?	
	Do reps have the ability to e-mail customers with follow-up information?	
	Do reps offer appropriate alternative solutions when they have to say no to a customer?	
	Do you inform customers when certain issues can and cannot be resolved?	
Transfers	Are customers routinely routed to the appropriate specialists when necessary?	
	Do you offer warm transfers when necessary?	
	If not, do you avoid making the customer repeat information?	
Call Processes	Do your escalation reps track when and why they say "no" or "I can't do that"?	
	Do you act to change resolution obstacles (when appropriate)?	
	Do you only ask customers for information that you immediately need?	
	Do you avoid asking customers for information that they have already provided through the IVR?	
	Do you avoid asking customers for information that you could get from internal sources (e.g., account information, filed information)?	
	Do you call other stakeholders on your customers' behalf to save your customers a step?	
	Do you require customers to fill out forms only when it is absolutely necessary?	
	Generally, are your forms written in customer (versus company) language?	
	Do you collect rep feedback on language used in forms?	
	Do you offer customers the option of returning forms in alternate channels (e.g., fax, e-mail, online)?	
	Do you confirm receipt of information?	
Wait and Hold Time	Do you inform customers of queue location and approximate time?	
	Do you offer callback functionality during peak periods?	
	Do you monitor for excessive hold time?	
	Do you set customer expectations around time to resolution?	
Metrics Do you track...	Issue resolution rate	
	Callback rate	
	Callback type analysis	
	Transfer rate	
	Warm versus cold transfer rate	
	Customer Effort Score—CEB's customer effort metric	
	Measures of customer time spend (e.g., hold time, time spent in IVR, wait time, etc.)	
	Quality assurance: accuracy of information	
	Quality assurance: issue diagnosis	

Source: CEB, 2013.

NOTES

FOREWORD

1. Alaina McConnell, "Zappos' Outrageous Record for the Longest Customer Service Phone Call Ever," *Business Insider,* December 20, 2012, http://www.businessinsider.com/zappos-longest-customer-service-call-2012-12.
2. Amy Martinez, "Tale of Lost Diamond Adds Glitter to Nordstrom's Customer Service," *Seattle Times,* May 11, 2011, http://seattletimes.com/html/businesstechnology/2015028167_nordstrom12.html.

CHAPTER ONE:
THE NEW BATTLEGROUND FOR CUSTOMER LOYALTY

1. Jessica Sebor, "CRM Gets Serious," *CRM Magazine,* February 2008, http://www.destinationcrm.com/Articles/Editorial/Magazine-Features/CRM-Gets-Serious-46971.aspx.
2. Mae Kowalke, "Customer Loyalty Is Achievable with Better Support," TMCnet.com, February 29, 2008, http://www.tmcnet.com/channels/virtual-call-center/articles/21858-customer-loyalty-achievable-with-better-support.htm.
3. Frederick F. Reichheld, *The Ultimate Question: Driving Good Profits and True Growth* (Cambridge, MA: Harvard Business School Press, 2006).

4. ANZMAC Conference 2005: Broadening the Boundaries (Fremantle, Western Australia, December 5–7, 2005), 331–37.

CHAPTER TWO:
WHY YOUR CUSTOMERS DON'T WANT TO TALK TO YOU

1. S. S. Iyengar and M. Lepper, "When Choice Is Demotivating: Can One Desire Too Much of a Good Thing?" *Journal of Personality and Social Psychology, 79 (2000): 995–1006.*
2. "Make It Simple: That's P&G's New Marketing Mantra—and It's Spreading," *BusinessWeek,* http://www.businessweek.com/1996/37/b34921.htm.

CHAPTER SIX:
THE DISLOYALTY DETECTOR—CUSTOMER EFFORT SCORE V2.0

1. Frederick F. Reichheld, "One Number You Need to Grow," *Harvard Business Review,* December 2003; http://hbr.org/2003/12/the-one-number-you-need-to-grow/ar/1.
2. M. Dixon, K. Freeman, and N. Toman, "Stop Trying to Delight Your Customers," *Harvard Business Review,* July 2010; http://hbr.org/2010/07/stop-trying-to-delight-your-customers.
3. A. Turner, "The New 'It' Metric: Practical Guidance About the Usefulness and Limitations of the Customer Effort Score (CES)," Market Strategies International, January 2011, http://www.marketstrategies.com/user_area/content_media/Customer%20Effort%20Score%20Ver%201.0.pdf.

CHAPTER EIGHT:
EFFORT BEYOND THE CONTACT CENTER

1. Ron Johnson, "What I Learned Building the Apple Store," *HBR Blog Network,* November 21, 2011, http://blogs.hbr.org/cs/2011/11/what_i_learned_building_the_ap.html.
2. George Anderson, "New Look Drives Comp Sales at Old Navy," *RetailWire,* July 13, 2011, http://www.retailwire.com/discussion/15374/new-look-drives-comp-sales-at-old-navy.

3. Ayad Mirjan, "An Examination of the Impact of Customer Effort on Customer Loyalty in Face-to-Face Retail Environments," Henley Business School, University of Reading (UK), March 30, 2012.

4. Patrick Spenner and Karen Freeman, "To Keep Your Customers, Keep It Simple," *Harvard Business Review,* May 2012.

INDEX